Old Chester Tales

Old Chester tales

By

Margaret Deland

with illustrations by

Howard Pyle

Ross & Perry, Inc.
Washington, D.C.

Ross & Perry, Inc. Publishers
216 G St., N.E.
Washington, D.C. 20002
Telephone (202) 675-8300
Facsimile (202) 675-8400
info@RossPerry.com

SAN 253-8555

Library of Congress Control Number: 2002106103
http://www.rossperry.com

ISBN 1-932080-28-7

Book Cover designed by Sapna. sapna@rossperry.com

♻ The paper used in this publication meets the requirements for permanence
established by the American National Standard for Information Sciences
"Permanence of Paper for Printed Library Materials" (ANSI Z39.48-1984).

CONTENTS

ILLUSTRATIONS

vii

THE PROMISES OF DOROTHEA

THE PROMISES OF DOROTHEA

I

Old Chester was always very well satisfied with itself. Not that that implies conceit; Old Chester merely felt that satisfaction with the conditions as well as the station into which it had pleased God to call it which is said to be a sign of grace. Such satisfaction is said also to be at variance with progress, but it cannot be denied that it is comfortable; as for progress, everybody knows it is accompanied by growing-pains. Besides, if people choose to burn lamps and candles instead of gas; if they prefer to jog along the turnpike in stage-coaches instead of whizzing past in a cloud of dust and cinders in a railroad car; if they like to hear the old parson who married them—or baptized some of them, for that matter—mumbling and droning through his old, old sermons; if they like to have him rejoice with them, and advise them, and weep with them beside their open graves—if people deliberately choose this sort of thing, the outside world may wonder, but it has no right to condemn. And if it had condemned, Old Chester would not have cared in the very least. It looked down upon the outside world. Not unkindly, indeed, but pityingly; and it pursued its contented way, without restlessness, and without aspirations.

In saying "Old Chester" one really means the Dales, the Wrights, the Lavendars — that includes Susan Carr, who married Joey Lavendar when she was old enough to have given up all ideas of that kind of thing; it means the Temple connection, though only Jane Temple lives in Old Chester now, and she is Mrs. Dove; at least that is her name, but hardly any one remembers it, and she is always spoken of as "Jane Temple"; the Dove is only an incident, so to speak, for one scarcely feels that her very respectable little husband is part of "Old Chester." The term includes the Jay girls, of course, and the Barkleys; though in my time only Mrs. Barkley was left; her sons had gone out into the world, and her husband — it must have been somewhere in the early sixties that Barkley senior, Old Chester's blackest sheep, took his departure for a Place (his orthodox relatives were inclined to believe) which, in these days, is even more old-fashioned than Old Chester itself. The Kings are of Old Chester, and the two Miss Ferrises; and the Steeles, and the John Smiths. The Norman Smiths, who own a great mill in the upper village, have no real connection with Old Chester, though the John Smiths are always very much afraid of being confounded with them; the two families are generally referred to as the "real Smiths" and the "rich Smiths." The real Smiths might with equal accuracy have been called the poor Smiths, except that Old Chester could not have been so impolite. The rich Smiths were one of several families who went to make up what the geographies call the "population" of the village, but they were never thought of when one said "Old Chester." The Macks were in this class, and the Hayeses, and a dozen others. Old Chester had nothing to say against these people ; they were rich, but it did not follow that they had not made their money honestly ; and their sons and daughters, having had time to get used to wealth, had reasonably good manners. But they were not "Old Chester." The very fact that they were not always satisfied with the existing order proved that. One by one these outsiders had bought or built in the village, because they had interests in the new rolling-mills in Upper Chester ; and they had hardly come before they began to make a stir, and try to "improve" things. Then it was that Old Chester arose in its might ; Heaven and the town vote were invoked for protection against a branch railroad to connect the two villages ; and the latter, at least, answered with decision. The proposition that gas should be brought from the mill town destroyed itself because of its cost ; even the rich Smiths felt that it would be too expensive.

So Old Chester pursued its own satisfied path ; it had a habit of alluding to any changes that the younger generation or the new people might advocate as "airs." Sam Wright said, gruffly, that what had been good enough for his father was good enough for him. This was when his eldest son suggested that a connection with Upper Chester's water supply would be a good thing. "Young man," said Sam, "I've pumped many a bucket of water in my day, and it won't hurt you to do the same." "It isn't a question of hurting," said young Sam, impatiently ; "it's a question of saving time." "Saving your grandmother!" interrupted his father; "since when has your time been so valuable, sir? Come, now, don't put on airs! I guess what was good enough for my father is good enough for you."

This satisfaction with the Past was especially marked in church matters. When Helen Smith—pretty, impulsive, and a dear good child, too, if she was "new"—told Dr. Lavendar that she thought it would be a good thing to have a girls' club at St. Michael's, the old minister said, his kind eyes twinkling at her, "The best club for girls is their mothers' firesides, my dear!"

At which Miss Smith pressed her lips together, and said, shortly: "Well, if you feel that way about a girls' club, I suppose you won't approve of a debating society for the boys?"

"Ho!" said Dr. Lavendar, "boys don't wait for their parson's approval to debate! There is too much debating already. If our boys here in Old Chester would talk less and do more, if they would stop discussing things they know nothing about, and listen to the opinions of their elders and betters, they might amount to something. No, we don't want any debating societies in Old Chester. They may have their place in big city parishes—but here! Why, there are only a dozen or two boys, anyhow, and I know their fathers, every one of them; they wouldn't thank me for making the boys bigger blatherskites than they are already—being boys."

"But, Dr. Lavendar," Helen protested, with heightened color, "you can't say the fathers' influence is always good. Look at Job Todd; his eldest boy is fourteen, and what a home to spend his evenings in! And there are the two Rice boys—no mother,

6

WENT PLODDING OUT TO SEE HIS PEOPLE WHO WERE SICK

and a half-crazy father; surely some harmless entertainment—"

"They come to Sunday-school; and the young fry have my collect class on Saturdays," said Dr. Lavendar; "and the boys in Maria Welwood's class, or Jane Temple's, get all the pleasant evenings they need."

"Well," Helen said, trying to keep the irritation out of her voice, "I suppose there is no use in saying anything more, only it does seem to me that we are behind the times."

"I hope so, I hope so," said Dr. Lavendar, cheerfully.

But in spite of snubs like this the new people had their opinions in matters ecclesiastical as well as civil. The Hayeses said that they thought a "more ornate ritual would bring in the lower classes;" and they added that they did wish Dr. Lavendar would have Weekly Celebration. The Macks, who, before they got their money, had been United Presbyterians, said that they could not understand why Dr. Lavendar wouldn't have an altar and a cross. He was very little of a churchman, they said, to just have the old wooden communion-table; which, indeed, never had any other decoration than the "fair white linen cloth" on the first Sunday of the month.

"I said so to poor, dear old Dr. Lavendar," said Mrs. Mack, "and he said, 'We have no dealing with the Scarlet Woman, ma'am, at St. Michael's!' Isn't he a queer old dear? So narrow-minded!"

And it must be admitted that the dear old man was a little short with ex-Presbyterian Mrs. Mack. The fact was, at that particular time, he happened to have enough to think of besides the whims of the

7

new people. It was that year that Old Chester—
the real Old Chester—had such deep disturbances:
There was Miss Maria Welwood's financial catastrophe; and the distressing behavior of young Robert Smith (he was one of the "real Smiths"); and
the elder Miss Ferris's illness, and the younger Miss
Ferris's recovery—both caused by Oscar King's extraordinary conduct; conduct in which, it must be
admitted, Dr. Lavendar was very much mixed up.

II

The Misses Ferris lived in a brick house a little
way out of the village, on the river road. The house,
which was very tall and narrow, was on the low
meadow-land, just below the bend, where the river
widened out into a motionless sheet of water, choked
along the shore with flags and rushes. A Lombardy
poplar stood at the gate, flinging its long, thin shadow back and forth across the bleak front of the
house, which looked like a pale face, its shuttered
windows the closed eyelids, weighted down in decent death. It was a big, gaunt house, lying in
the autumn sunshine, silent and without sign of life,
except the shadow of the poplar swaying back and
forth like some gray finger laid upon dead lips. In-
doors one knew how still it was because of the rustle of a newspaper slipping to the floor, or the scratch,
scratch of a pen. Sometimes from the long, holland-
clad parlor there would come through the silent
house some faint burst of music from the jingling
old piano; and Miss Clara Ferris — the well Miss
Ferris—would look up, frowning a little, and saying

8

to herself that she hoped Dorothea's practising would not disturb dear Mary ; and there was generally a sigh of relief when the music faltered and ceased and the silence closed in again. Sometimes it did disturb dear Mary, who was the sick Miss Ferris, and she would call out from her dimly lighted room beyond the sitting-room that she was so sorry to interfere with Dorothea, but really— And then Miss Clara would rise hastily, and go and tell Dorothea that dear Aunt Mary was very low to-day, and so would she mind not practising?

If Dorothea minded, she did not say so. Everything in that house revolved upon Aunt Mary—the "sick Miss Ferris," as Old Chester called her; who, thirty years before, upon being deserted by her lover, had taken to her bed, where she had remained ever since. It was her illness, not the Ferris money, which made the two ladies so important in Old Chester. For, of course, a lady whose sensibilities are so delicate as to keep her in bed for thirty years is an important figure in this unromantic world.

When Dorothea came to live with the aunts this family scandal and grief had been told her by Miss Clara in a proud, hushed voice. "Your dear aunt Mary has never risen (except on Saturdays, when the sheets are changed) from her bed since that fateful day ; and she never will, until she is carried hence."

"But what is the matter, Aunt Clara?" Dorothea said, her voice hushed, too, from its pretty girlish note. "Is she sick?"

"Sick? No, certainly not. Why should she be sick? I am sure nobody ever had more constant care. But she was forsaken at the altar, and her

9

heart was broken. It has remained so. Your aunt
Mary is so delicate and refined that she could not
recover from such a blow. Refinement is a characteristic of the females of our family, Dorothea. Your
aunt Mary would not move even on Saturdays but
that it is a necessity; and then she is assisted, as
you know, to a couch." This Saturday moving was,
to tell the truth, a thorn in Miss Ferris's side; she
would have preferred entire helplessness. " But she
has never recovered," Miss Clara repeated; " she is
entirely crushed."

Thirty years! Thirty years of remembering! It
was dreadful to Dorothea even to think of; the
pride which her aunt had in it never touched her;
it was a horror—the old, pallid, waxen face there on
the pillow in the great four-poster in the best bedroom; the almost helpless limbs lying like sticks under the covers; the thin hands that were cool, like
the petals of a faded flower. To Dorothea it was
all ghastly and repulsive; and to her young mind
the silent house, and the broken heart, and the
shadow of the poplar coming and going across the
high ceilings of the empty rooms, came to be all a
strange, dreamlike consciousness of something dead
near her.

It was into this life that Oscar King came to make
love to Dorothea—came like a torch among dead
leaves. Oscar had gone away from Old Chester about
the time that the younger Miss Ferris took to her
bed with a broken heart — some five years before
Dorothea was born; he came back now, fifty years
old, a handsome, determined, gentle-hearted man,
and fell in love with Dorothea the very first Sunday
that he saw her at church. Old Chester, regarding

the back of Oscar's head as he sat in the rectory pew that first Sunday, speculated a good deal as to his future. He had come home with money, it was said, and he probably would not want to live with his brother, Dr. William King, whose house was as small as his income. Old Chester chuckled when it said this, for poor Willy King labored under the disadvantage of having been known in his youth—in his babyhood, indeed — by most of his patients. And, really, you can't blame Old Chester; for, when you come to think of it, it is hard to receive your castor oil or opodeldoc from one to whom you have administered them—perhaps with spankings. Nor was it likely that Oscar would want to settle down and live with his elderly sister, Rachel, and her little adopted child, who would doubtless be a nuisance to a bachelor like Oscar—"who has seen a great deal of the world, it is to be feared," Old Chester said, with a sigh. No; the proper thing for Oscar to do was to marry, and have a home of his own. Old Chester was prepared to give him much good advice on this subject : There was Rose Knight, a nice intelligent girl, not too pretty, and a good, economical house-keeper. Or Annie Shields. On the whole, Annie Shields was perhaps more desirable ; Annie was nearly forty, and suitable in every respect. " She has such admirable common-sense !" Old Chester said, warmly. " How comfortable she would make a middle-aged man like Oscar ! Very likely he has rheumatism, you know, or something the matter with his liver—he has been knocking about the world so long. Dear, dear, it's to be hoped he has no undesirable habits !" Old Chester said, sighing ; " but certainly Annie is just the wife for him." And, really, Old Chester's advice was based on reason; therein was its weakness. Men don't fall in love with women from considerations of reason. The ability to sew on buttons, and nurse husbands through attacks of indigestion, and give good whole-some advice, does not attract the male mind; these evidences of good sense are respected, but when it comes to a question of adoration—that is different: a man prefers a fool every time. Well—well; one of these days we may understand it : meantime we are all ready to sew on buttons, and keep house, and give advice—while Oscar Kings look over at little, vague, mindless girls, and fall in love with them.

"Who is that girl who sat in the second pew from the front, and looked like a Botticelli Madonna ?" Mr. King said to Dr. Lavendar, when he went home to dinner with the old clergyman.

"I suppose you mean Dorothea," Dr. Lavendar said. " She doesn't look like any of your popish idols she is a good child, and she lives with the Ferris girls. They are sucking the life out of her. She has no more will of her own than a wet string. I wish some-body would run off with her !"

"I will," said Oscar King, promptly.

III

So that was how the train was started which was to cause such violent disturbance in the silent house on the river road.

Oscar King lost no time in calling on the Misses Ferris. That very Sunday afternoon he walked out into the country, through the warm October haze, and pushed open the clanging iron gate at the foot of the Ferris garden. Then he stopped, for his Botticelli Madonna was standing waist-deep among the golden coreopsis in the garden border. Oscar King stood still and looked at her, and said to himself that he had found his wife. If any one had asked him the reason of this conviction he could not have told them; but convictions do not imply reasons. Look at women's belief in their husbands!

He went forward, abrupt and commonplace:

"I am Oscar King; and I'm sure you are Miss Dorothea Ferris. I saw you at church this morning, and I have come to call upon your aunts. I wonder if this is the orthodox hour for calling in Old Chester?"

She looked at him with eyes that brightened slowly through some vague abstraction, before she saw him; then she seemed a little frightened, and the color came into her cheek.

"Oh yes," she said, in a fluttered voice. "Aunt Clara is in the parlor, and—and please come in." She moved through the yellow cloud of coreopsis and came out into the path beside him, her head bending like a lily on its stalk. She was not a pretty girl: she had the high forehead, the soft, pale hair, parted and smooth on each side of her brow, the delicate lips, and, most of all, the mild, timid eyes, that make a type too colorless for prettiness. But Oscar King, as he walked beside her to the house was stirred through and through. Why? Who can say! If Beauty and the Beast is unexplainable, the Beast and Beauty is just as remarkable.

Not that Oscar was in the least a beast; but he was a big, active, masculine creature, and this passionless girl was like an icicle in the sunshine. But, for all that, he wanted her; he wanted, then and there, to lift her in his arms and kiss her pale mouth.

"I am going to marry you," he said to himself, watching her while she opened the door and led him into the dark hall; "I'm going to marry you, you saint!"

"It is Mr. Oscar King, Aunt Clara," Dorothea said, in her little, retreating voice. And then she went and sat down in a corner. Oscar did not see her look at him again that whole hour of his call, though he prolonged it from moment to moment hoping that she would just once lift those vague soft eyes to his.

Miss Ferris had received her caller with a frigid bend of her body from the waist; then she sat down on a straight chair, her hands locked upon her lap, her lips pressed together, and waited for him to begin the conversation.

"How is Miss Mary?" he asked, cordially; "I hope I may see her."

"I thank you. My sister is as usual. Entirely crushed."

"Crushed?" Oscar said, puzzled.

"You have forgotten," Miss Clara said, icily, "that my sister was deserted at the altar. She has never recovered."

Oscar King was sympathetic, and murmured his hope that Miss Mary might soon "get about. A man who would do that is not worth regretting!" he said, warmly.

"Men do very strange things," Miss Clara Ferris said, with precise and cold significance. Oscar King look puzzled. Miss Clara grew colder and more

" SHE SEEMED ' A TALL WHITE LILY,' HE SAID "

monosyllabic. But it was not until she responded
to the proposal that he should some day bring some
photographs to show Miss Mary, by saying, " I thank
you ; my sister does not care for photographs," that
he felt departure was no longer a matter of choice.

"Well, I am afraid I must go," he said, rising, the
frank regret of his voice and eyes all directed to
Dorothea, who sat by the window, never once looking towards him. "Won't you come out and give
me a bunch of those yellow daisy flowers ?" he asked
her. This was a burst of inspiration, for Oscar King
did not know one flower from another. Miss Clara
opened her lips, but Dorothea replied before her :

"Oh yes, if you would like some."

"Good - bye, Miss Ferris," said Oscar, blithely.
" Next time I come I hope I can see Miss Mary."

" I thank you. My sister is—" began Miss Clara,
but the unwelcome caller was already in the hall,
saying something eagerly to Dorothea.

In the garden he prolonged the flower - picking
process by minute and critical choice, and he talked
every moment, plunging at once into personalities.
He told her how pleasant it was to be back in Old
Chester again, to see all his old friends—"and make
a new one, perhaps," he said. He asked her about
herself : was she lonely ? had she many interests ?
might he come and see her ? was she willing to have
a new friend ? Then he told her that she had seemed, as she stood among the coreopsis when he came
in, like a flower—"a tall white lily," he said.

It was a quick, almost rough beginning of his
wooing, these personalities. Dorothea, hardly answering, hardly daring to look at him, her color rising and paling, felt as though she had been caught

in a great wind that was whirling her along, astonished and helpless.

"Yes;" "No;" "I think so"—she faltered to this
or that tempestuous assertion; her thoughts were
all confused. Suddenly into the monotonous drift
of her silent life had come, in a day, in an hour—
"since dinner-time," she said to herself, this—what?
Dorothea had no terms; but she was a woman, and
something in her knew that this torrent of words,
these kind, warm looks, this big pressure of his hand
when he went away, meant—something. The girl
was really breathless when she went back, alone, to
the house.

"Dorothea!" Miss Clara called, from her aunt
Mary's room.

"Yes, Aunt Clara," she said, obediently.

The two aunts were evidently agitated. Miss Mary's
face was flushed; Miss Clara was pale.

"Dorothea," said Miss Clara, "do you know who
that person was who has just been here?"

"Mr. King?" the girl said, hesitating.

"Yes. My dear Dorothea, he is an improper per·
son."

"Oh, Clara—" the invalid remonstrated.

"My dear, allow me to speak. Mr. King has lived
away from Old Chester for thirty years, in foreign
parts; *and no one knows what has gone on!*"

"I don't think you ought to say that before Dorothea," sighed Miss Mary.

"Dorothea doesn't know what I mean," Miss Ferris replied; "but you and I know. A man who has
lived away from home for thirty years is a suspicious
person. I consider that it was a great liberty on
his part to call. He had forgotten your unhappy

affair. He said he hoped you would 'soon get about.'"

"I wish I might," Miss Mary said, faintly.

Miss Ferris snorted with contempt. "It showed a coarse mind. He has no understanding of the delicacy of a lady's feelings."

Miss Mary sighed.

"Of course you will never 'get about'; but he had forgotten the whole matter. It just shows what sort of a man he is! You must be polite to every one, Dorothea. But you must always disapprove of improper persons."

"Oh yes, Aunt Clara," said Dorothea.

IV

Oscar King may have lived in foreign parts, and "*no one have known what went on*," but he was still sufficiently of Old Chester to realize that he must inform himself upon Miss Mary Ferris's condition, if he would make himself pleasing to the family. Hence he made it his business to see Dr. Lavendar, and be refreshed as to facts. The old minister was very communicative; he remembered perfectly that June day, thirty years ago, when he in his surplice waited in the vestry, and Mary Ferris in bridal white waited in the vestibule — waited, and waited, and heard through the open windows the buzz of the bees in the locust-tree, and by-and-by the murmur of wonder from the wedding-guests in the church. Then had come the word that the man had fled. "And I had to tell that poor girl! That's what ministers and doctors are for, I suppose — to do other men's dirty work. It was like putting a knife into some helpless dumb creature's throat to tell her. Well, we took her home. She was sick for weeks. Then she began to revive, poor soul; but the affair had taken hold of Clara's imagination, and she kept saying that Mary was crushed. As soon as she saw any tendency to rise, she sat on her, so to speak. It has been the one interest of Clara Ferris's life. It has been something for her to talk about, you know —Mary's delicacy and refinement. Then the brother died—you remember Algernon Ferris?—and his little girl came to them. Dorothea was twelve then; she's twenty-five now, though you wouldn't think it. She's 'crushed,' just as poor Mary is. I wish I knew how to save the child; it's an unnatural life."

"I'm going to marry her," Oscar said, thoughtfully; "I hope that will save her."

Dr. Lavendar clapped him on the shoulder. "My boy, you'll be a Perseus to Andromeda! Couldn't you manage to take Mary too?"

"I'll leave her for you, sir," Oscar informed him, gravely.

When Mr. King next presented himself at the Ferris house, it was with diplomatic commiseration for the lady whose heart had been so irreparably broken. Miss Clara became slightly less icy at this interest, though her doubts concerning his European exile never faded.

It was not until he had made several calls that she began to have certain dark suspicions: Could it be that Mr. King meant to include Dorothea in his visits? The day that this possibility changed into probability, Miss Clara was standing at her sister's window, looking down at Oscar King saying good-bye to Dorothea on the front steps. His fare-wells took a long time, it must be admitted. He stood on the door-steps talking and talking; then, suddenly, he reached out (this was what Miss Clara saw) and took Dorothea's hand and held it, saying something which made the girl turn away a little, and put her other hand up to her eyes.

"Good heavens !" said Miss Clara, and sat down as though faint.

"What is it?" cried the younger sister from the bed. "What is the matter? Oh, if I had my legs !"

"You haven't, and you never will have," Miss Ferris replied, faintly; "and the reason of it is the same as—as what's going on now !"

"What do you mean?"

"He has taken a liberty with Dorothea ; that's what I mean ! I saw him saying good-bye. 'Good-bye!'—he didn't say good-bye to *me* that way ; he held her hand—"

"They do that," murmured the other.

"It is terrible ! There—he's gone. I heard the gate close. Well, it is time," said Miss Ferris, in an awful voice—"*it is time*. I shall speak to Dorothea at once."

"Oh, sister," protested the other, "I wouldn't. Perhaps he didn't mean anything. And suppose he did ? It's nothing wrong—"

"Nothing wrong ! Well, Mary, I don't know what you call its effect on you—"

"But it isn't always so," said Miss Mary, beginning to cry ; "and if she loves him—"

"She doesn't. She is too young—he has been abroad—no one knows—" Miss Clara was so agitated that she was incoherent. "I must compose

19

myself before speaking to her," she said. "I will go to my chamber for a little while, and then she may come to me."

She passed Dorothea in the large sitting-room, into which Miss Mary Ferris's bedroom opened, but she was too disturbed to look at the girl. Perhaps it was as well. Dorothea's face was burning; her eyes shone, but they were dazed, and there was a glitter of tears in them. She took up some work and went over to her little window-seat, but she walked as one in a dream.

"Dorothea!" Miss Mary called, in her weak, flute-like voice.

The girl started, and answered, tremulously.

"Come in here, my child," the old aunt said. Dorothea came, still blushing, and with dazzled eyes.

Old Miss Mary Ferris lay back on her pillows, frail and faintly pretty, like some little winter-blossoming rose; all these years of having been shut out from the sun and wind of daily living had not made her ill; they had only "preserved" her, as it were.

She looked up at Dorothea with strange curiosity, as perhaps the dead look upon the living.

"Dorothea, your aunt Clara says—she thinks she saw—tell me, is it so? Did he—speak?" Her eager, shivering voice was like the touch of something cold.

"I don't know what you mean, Aunt Mary," Dorothea faltered.

"Did he speak of—*love ?*" She took the girl's limp little hand in her own cool, satin-smooth fingers, and pulled her, with a vampirelike strength, until she sat down on the edge of the bed.

"I think so," Dorothea stammered.

20

Miss Mary dropped her hand and covered her own face.

"Oh, Dorothea! it is so long ago! Do you love him? Tell me."

"I—I don't know, Aunt Mary."

"Did it make you happy to have him speak to you?"

"I—think so," Dorothea said, crying.

"Then," Miss Mary said, "you love him"; and stared at her with vague eyes that seemed to look beyond her; "you—love him."

She drew a long breath, and turned over on her side; she seemed to forget Dorothea.

It was a pity Miss Clara should have sent for the child just then; she was like some little weak chicken being helped, perhaps a little roughly, out of its shell; and now the assistance ceased.

Miss Clara was quite composed when Dorothea came into her bedroom to stand before her and answer her searching questions. There was a moment of awful silence before the questions began. Miss Clara sat in a big chintz-covered arm-chair, which had side pieces like ears, against which she leaned her head, overcome by emotion and fatigue. Dorothea stood at the foot of the bed, following with nervous fingers the carving of a pineapple on the tester-post; she was twenty-five years old, but she looked eighteen.

"Dorothea," Miss Clara said, "I saw the gentleman who called this morning upon your aunt and me, speaking to you in the porch. I observed him take your hand. Why did he do this, Dorothea?"

"I don't know, Aunt Clara," the girl said, panting.

"You are young, and, very properly, inexperienced,

my dear, therefore you do not know why such things are done, nor what they portend. But, my dear, I would not be doing my duty to my dead brother's child if I did not tell you that it was a liberty on Mr. King's part; and warn you that that was the way your dear aunt Mary began. And see the result! I do not, of course, mean to imply that gentlemen's attentions invariably end in this way. But the person who called here this morning has lived abroad for many years, and we do not know *what* has gone on. Therefore I do not wish you to permit him to take such liberties, or say good-bye to you again in this manner. I trust no words were uttered that I should have objected to?"

Dorothea turned red, and white, and red again.

"Dorothea! Did he say anything to lead you to suppose that he entertained sentiments of affection for you?"

"I think so," Dorothea confessed, beginning to cry.

"I am shocked! I hope, I *trust*, you answered as your poor aunt Mary's niece should? What did you say?"

"I said—I didn't know."

"Didn't know what? You don't know anything, of course. But what was it that you 'didn't know'?"

"He asked me if I—cared. And I said I didn't—know." Miss Clara gave a sigh of relief.

"Very proper, my dear. Of course you don't know. But I know, and I will tell you: you do *not* care, Dorothea. I have read all the best books on the subject of love, besides having observed your dear aunt, and I am able to judge, as you are not, whether a young woman cares. I rejoice that you do not, for I should feel it necessary to say that you must at once desist. But as you do not, all is well."

Dorothea did not look as though all were well; Miss Clara's voice took a note of anxiety.

"There are many ways of judging of the state of a young lady's affections; many tests; for instance, do you, or do you not, feel that if this person went away, you would be heart-broken, like your dear aunt Mary, and would lie, as she has done, for thirty years, crushed by grief, upon your bed?"

"Oh no, Aunt Clara," the girl said, shrinking; "no, I couldn't."

"Well, you see!" said Miss Clara, triumphantly. "Now, my dear, that settles it; so think no more of the matter. It is very indelicate for a young lady to dwell on such subjects. I will communicate with Mr. King, and then we will say no more about it; but promise me to remember what I have told you."

"Oh yes, Aunt Clara," said Dorothea, wretchedly, "I promise."

And then Miss Ferris kissed her, and tapped her cheek playfully, and all was pleasant again.

V

Miss Ferris lost no time in communicating with Mr. King. Her letter, couched in majestic but most genteel phrase, reached him Friday evening; and Oscar, in his room at the tavern, read it, standing by the lamp, his shadow falling, wavering and gigantic, on the wall behind him. Then he sat down in one of the rickety chairs, put his hands in his pockets, thrust his feet out straight in front of him, and thought hard for ten minutes. Then he rose with a spring that made the lamp flare, and went whistling about the room.

"I won't waste time at my age," he said to himself. "First I'll see the aunt; then I'll see Dr. Lavendar; then I'll see—*her !*"

He saw the aunt that night, and received her assurances that Dorothea was indifferent to him; but that if she were not, her aunts would not permit her to regard him with sentiments of esteem.

"You are not suited to my niece," said Miss Clara, "and I cannot but regard it as a liberty on your part to address her. You are much older than she, and *you have lived abroad very many years.*"

"I don't see what that's got to do with it," Dorothea's lover insisted.

Miss Clara pursed up her lips and looked modest.

"Well, Miss Ferris, I suppose there is no use arguing such a question; and, after all, Dorothea must be her own judge."

"My niece's judgment always coincides with mine," said Miss Clara, rising.

Oscar King rose too, smiling. "Well, I will abide by her judgment."

"I hardly see how you can do otherwise," Miss Clara commented, dryly.

"*That's* over," Mr. King said to himself as he strode along in the dusk to the rectory. But the second part of the programme was not so quickly carried out; it was midnight before he came out into the moonlight again and went back to his room in the tavern.

"Sunday morning—Dorothea !" he said to himself.

"But if the aunt comes to church with her, I'll have to wait another twenty-four hours. Confound the old lady!"

But Miss Clara had no thought of going to church. A small cold rain began to fall at dawn, and she would have been horrified at the idea of taking the horses out, and of course at her time of life she could not go trudging along the country road under an umbrella, as Dorothea might; but, besides that, Miss Ferris was quite prostrated by her interview of Friday night.

"I am suffering because I have defended you, Dorothea," she said, faintly, to her niece; "but I am sure you are grateful, my dear, and that is all I want."

But when did youth know gratitude? Dorothea only murmured, "Yes, Aunt Clara," in a wretched voice.

In these days, when young people not only have opinions, but express them, unasked, Dorothea's unresisting plasticity seems scarcely natural. But that only means that Old Chester is not of these days. The girl who makes one think of a violet still exists there. Dorothea was silenced, trembling like a little bird in some strong hand, just because her aunt did not happen to approve of the man who made love to her, and whom she—would one say "loved"? The fact is, the man who falls in love with one of these negative young creatures hardly takes the trouble to ask whether she loves him; he loves her. And he wants to have her for his wife—to do as he wishes, to think as he thinks, to echo his opinions, and to admire his conduct; gentle, silent, yielding—such a combination is almost the same as adoring. At all events, it answers just as well, in the domestic circle. And it wears better, conjugally.

Anyhow, Oscar King had made up his mind. Poor little Dorothea had no mind to make up; so she walked along to church in the fine chill rain, feeling a lump in her throat, and her eyes blurring so that once or twice a hot tear overflowed, and ran down her cold, rain - wet cheek. Dorothea's little heart was beating and swelling with misery and wonder and joy; but if one had said the word "love" to her, she would not have recognized it. She was very wretched when she reached the church; she knelt down and hid her face, and swallowed hard to get rid of the tears; then she took her prayer-book and read the marriage service, and thought that it was not for her. If Dorothea had not been so entirely behind the times, she would have decided to enter a sisterhood, or go and nurse lepers. As it was, she only saw before her long, pale years of obedience, and silence, and thin, cold autumnal rains. Yet all the time that her inward eye was fixed on Melancholy she was giving swift, low glances about the dark church. And when she saw Oscar in the rectory pew, a wave of lovely color rose and spread up to her smooth forehead, and down to the nape of her neck, and her hands trembled, and she could not see whether the psalter for the day was for morning or evening prayer.

After all, there is nothing like that first wonderful beginning of love. But, nevertheless, when the girl is just that sort of girl that a man like Oscar King wants, she does not know that it is love; she only knows it is pain.

Oscar waited for her at the porch door, and

26

opened her umbrella in the most matter-of-fact way.

"I am going to walk home with you."

"Oh—I don't think Aunt Clara would like it," she protested, faintly.

"But I'm not going to walk home with Aunt Clara. Dorothea, won't you look at me?"

"Oh, I think I'd—rather not," poor Dorothea said, trembling.

"Dear, your aunt Clara won't let you be engaged," he said, guiding her steps along the church-yard path to the street—"(look out! there is a puddle; come over here). She won't let us be engaged, and so we are going to be married."

"Oh, Mr. King!"

"Yes, you little love. To-morrow morning."

"Oh, Mr. King, Aunt Clara—"

"Never mind Aunt Clara. I only wish Miss Mary could come to the wedding—"

"She can't," poor Dorothea said, panting, seeing a possible means of escape; "she has never been out of bed, you know, since the time she was going to be married—"

"Well, you see, dear, how dangerous it is not to be married. To-morrow morning you are to meet me, and we'll go to Dr. Lavendar."

"Oh, Mr. King, I can't, I *can't!*" Her anguished tone of fright went to his heart.

"You little sweetheart! I hate to have you worry about it for twenty-four hours longer; I wish it could be to-day; but the license is made out for to-morrow. Dearest, you are to walk along the river road about nine o'clock."

"Oh, Aunt Clara won't allow me to, I'm *sure*," she said.

"Well, then, dear, we will have to go right back to Dr. Lavendar now," he told her, with his kind, determined smile. "Promise to meet me, darling, or I'll have to get married at once." He stood still, looking down at her, amused and threatening.

"Oh, I'll promise just to meet you," she said, faintly.

"Ah, you little love, you little angel!" he murmured; and did nothing but talk this masculine baby-talk all the way to the Misses Ferris's gate, Dorothea blushing, and murmuring little soft, frightened "Ohs."

"You will meet me at nine to-morrow morning at the bend in the road," he said when he left her, "and then we'll talk things over."

"I don't mind just talking," she said, "but—that other thing—"

"Oh, that doesn't need to be talked about," he reassured her; "now promise, dearest, to meet me, or I'll have to come into the house with you now. I won't leave you until you promise."

"Oh, *please!*" poor Dorothea said. "Oh yes, Mr. King, I'll promise. But I don't know how—but yes, yes. Oh, please, go away. I promise."

VI

Dorothea slipped into the house, noiselessly, but as she closed the front door softly behind her she heard an awful voice:

"*Dorothea!*"

There was a pause, and then two other words dropped from the upper landing:

28

THE PROMISES OF DOROTHEA

"Come here."

The girl felt her heart really and literally sink in her breast. Her lips grew dry, and her breath fluttered in her throat so that she could not speak. She came into Miss Clara's room and stood, her eyes downcast, guilt in every line of her face.

Miss Ferris was sitting very erect in her big chair.

"Dorothea, I observed you from my chamber window."

The girl looked at a little hole in her glove; her hands trembled.

"Dorothea, what do you mean? I ask you, what do you mean by such conduct?"

"What conduct, Aunt Clara?" asked Dorothea, in a very little voice.

"I tell you, I observed you! Do not seek to deceive me and add the sin of a lie to that of impropriety!"

The girl swallowed, took off her glove, and pulled the fingers smooth and straight.

"Do you hear me, Dorothea?"

"Yes, Aunt Clara."

"Then see that you heed me. I am pained and humiliated to find that it is necessary to instruct a niece of mine, a niece of your aunt Mary's — your aunt Mary, so refined that her disappointment at the altar laid her upon her couch, from which she has never risen—(except on Saturdays). I am pained, Dorothea, to have to tell *her* niece that when a young woman refuses a gentleman, it is not becoming to walk home from church with him afterwards. It is indelicate. It is immodest. He takes a liberty when he offers to accompany her. Need I say more?"

"Oh *no*, Aunt Clara."

But Miss Clara said more :

"I had not thought it necessary to forbid your seeing this person. I had not, for that matter, thought it necessary to forbid your stealing, or murdering ; all the females of our family have been perfectly modest and delicate, so I did not suppose such a command necessary. But it appears that I was mistaken. It is necessary. I forbid your seeing this—person. Do you hear me, Dorothea?"

There was no answer. Dorothea, deadly pale, lifted her terror - stricken eyes to her aunt's face, and then looked down again, speechless.

"I regret," said Miss Clara, with dreadful politeness, "that I must ask you to promise this. It appears, if you will pardon me for saying so, that otherwise I cannot trust you."

Still silence.

"Come, Dorothea, let us have no further delay. Promise."

Dorothea's face suddenly quivered ; her voice broke, steadied, and broke again.

"I think—I won't, Aunt Clara."

"Won't what ? Won't see him ?"

"Won't promise, Aunt Clara."

Miss Ferris, her lips parted to speak, stared at this turning worm.

"You—won't ?"

"I think I'd rather not, please, Aunt Clara."

"Why not ?"

"Because I—promised I would."

There are no exclamation points which can tell Miss Clara Ferris's astonishment.

"You promised him ?"

THE PROMISES OF DOROTHEA

" Yes, Aunt Clara."

" You had no right to make such a promise; therefore you must break it. Do you hear me?"

" Yes, Aunt Clara."

" Very well; then promise."

" I think—I won't."

There was a moment of stunned silence. Miss Ferris opened and closed her lips in a breathless sort of way. And certainly the situation was trying. The sensation of finding a command of no avail is to the mind what sitting down upon a suddenly withdrawn chair is to the body. Miss Ferris said, faintly,

" Dorothea, do you mean to defy me?"

" Oh *no*, Aunt Clara!"

" Then you will promise me not to see or speak to this bad man again. He is a bad man, to have produced in a hitherto obedient girl such awful, such wicked, such—such indelicate conduct!"

She waited; she dared not risk another command, but she waited. There was no reply.

The silence grew embarrassing. And with the embarrassment there was the bewilderment of discovering that there is nothing in the world which can be quite so obstinate as a yielding, mild, opinionless girl.

" Is this all you have to say?" Miss Ferris demanded. She paused; still silence. Then she amended her question, to save her dignity.

" *If* this is all you have to say, you may retire to your chamber. I hope reflection and prayer—you need not come down to dinner—will bring you to a better frame of mind."

She waved a trembling hand in the direction of the door, and Dorothea fled.

It was well that no clairvoyance made it possible for Oscar King to see his sweetheart lying, crying and shivering, upon her bed that long, dreary, rainy Sunday afternoon. He might have relented, and repented having wrung a promise from her; or he might have stormed the cold, silent house, and carried her off, then and there.

VII

Probably Miss Ferris trusted for obedience to the traditions of the past; at all events, she did not lock Dorothea's door. What prayer and reflection might have accomplished, in connection with a key, who can tell? As it was, the next morning, Dorothea, white and trembling, came down-stairs, and went quietly out of the house. The child was not clandestine; she proposed returning in the same open way. She also proposed telling Mr. King that she would make no more promises.

It was a dull, dark day; the mud on the river road was ankle-deep; in the woods shreds of mist had caught on the bare branches, and the clouds hung low and bleak behind the hills.

Oscar King sat in a buggy drawn up at the side of the road, just out of sight of the Ferris house. He flecked with his whip at the dripping branches of a chestnut, or neatly cut off the withered top of a stalk of golden-rod, and all the while he looked intently down the road. When he saw her coming his face lighted; he jumped out, backed his horse a little, and turned the wheel.

"You darling! Come, get in."

32

"Get in?" faltered Dorothea ; but already he had lifted her like a feather and put her on the seat.

"Sweet, everything is arranged. Here, let me tuck this rubber apron around your little feet. I suppose it didn't occur to you to bring any things ? It doesn't matter in the least. We can buy all you need in Mercer."

"But, Mr. King, I'm going back in a minute. I only came to tell you— Oh, Aunt Clara frightened me so !"

He was in a hurry, and alert for the sound of pursuing wheels, but he stopped his horse, and put his arm round her and kissed her, his face darkening.

"Dearest, never think of her again. You are mine now. We are going to be married, my sweet. Do you hear ?"

"Oh," said Dorothea, pushing away from him and sitting up very straight, "you don't mean *now ?*"

"Yes, now. I wish it had been three weeks ago ; it's just so much time wasted !"

She began to say she couldn't, she mustn't, Aunt Clara would be, oh, so dreadfully angry !

But Oscar King interrupted cheerfully : "Now, Dorothea, listen : when I take you to Dr. Lavendar you won't back down if he asks you whether you want to get married?"

"Oh, if Dr. Lavendar disapproves, I *must* go home," cried poor Dorothea, in anguish.

"He'll disapprove if you break my heart, Dolly," he told her, gravely ; then he went over all his plans. He did not entreat or plead ; he announced. They were in Old Chester by this time, and it must be admitted that Mr. King had some anxieties as to the outcome of this high-handed wooing, for Dorothea, when he stopped for breath, still protested, faintly. If Dr. Lavendar thought that she was not as deter-mined as her lover, he would certainly induce her to go back and ask Miss Ferris's consent; which would mean—Oscar King was ready to believe it would mean a dungeon and bread and water ! He checked his horse a little, slapping the wet rein on the bay's steaming back, and meditated.

"Dolly, dear, Dr. Lavendar wanted to marry us, instead of letting the justice of the peace do it in Upper Chester. He made me promise to bring you to him. He said it was proper. Of course you don't want to do anything that isn't proper ?"

"Oh no," Dorothea answered, with agitation.

"So I promised; and you see I can't break my word."

Dorothea looked frightened.

"So you must tell him you want to marry me. You do, don't you, Dolly ?"

"Oh yes, Mr. King," she answered, tremulously, "but not just—"

"Never mind about that. Just tell him you do want to, Dolly. Never mind about the time. Prom-ise me you will tell him you want to be married ? After to-day you shall never make a promise again as long as you live. If Dr. Lavendar asks you if you are doing this of your own free will, you say 'yes.' Because you are, you know. I will stop the buggy right here, if you want to get out."

He drew up in a hollow of the road, where the water stood in a puddle from one side to the other. "You can get out, dear." Dorothea looked over the dripping wheel tired in mud. "Promise just to say 'yes' if he asks you."

34

"Oh!" said Dorothea. They were almost at the rectory gate. Oscar King had a worried line between his eyes.

"Dolly, I'll tell you what: when Dr. Lavendar asks you anything I'll repeat it, and you answer me; will you? Come, now, I'm not asking very much! Promise."

"I promise," faltered Dorothea.

When Oscar King, leading Dorothea, pushed open the door and came in, it was like a gust of west wind and a gleam of pale sunshine. Dr. Lavendar looked up from his lathe, a little irritated at being interrupted; but seeing who it was, he smiled and frowned together. He had on his queer old dressing-gown, and his dog was tucked into his chair behind him.

"What!" he said. "You've got her, have you?" And then he looked very grave. "Dorothea, my child, I need hardly tell you that this is a serious thing you are thinking of doing."

"You know it's serious, Dolly, don't you?" Mr. King said, gently.

"Oh *yes*, Mr. King," Dorothea answered, almost with passion.

"My dear," proceeded Dr. Lavendar, "I don't approve of runaway marriages, as a rule. I made Oscar promise to bring you here, because I couldn't have one of my children married by anybody else. You are of age, and you have a right to be married, and I believe Oscar to be a good man, or else I wouldn't let you do it, if I had to lock you up in that closet; but I must be sure first, my dear, that you realize what you are doing, and that you love Oscar with all your heart, and that is why you want to

35

marry him. Not merely to get away from conditions which are, I know, hard and unnatural."

"Do you love me, Dolly?"

The room was very silent for a moment; a coal fell out of the grate upon the hearth; Dorothea drew a long breath and looked up at him, a sudden reality dawning in her face.

"Why—I do!" she said, vague astonishment thrilling in her voice.

"You are not going to marry me on your aunt Clara's account, are you, Dolly?" he asked her, persuasively.

"Why, no, Mr. King," she said, in a bewildered way.

"You are not being overpersuaded?" Dr. Lavendar insisted, anxiously.

She looked at her lover, who, smiling, shook his head. "No," she repeated, faintly.

"Now, sir," Oscar broke in, cheerfully, "I don't want to hurry you, but we haven't any time to waste—"

"Well," the old man said—"well, I suppose there is nothing more for me to say, but—"

"But 'Amen!'" Oscar assured him, with a glance out into the rainy mist. Suppose Miss Ferris should appear! "Never mind a surplice. Come, Dolly, give me your hand, my dear—"

"Of course I shall mind a surplice, sir!" said Dr. Lavendar. "Any child of mine shall be married decently and in order. Here, show me your license."

Then he went away, and came back in his surplice, with his prayer-book, and in ten minutes the Amen was said.

36

THE PROMISES OF DOROTHEA

VIII

"Why," said Miss Clara Ferris afterwards—"why I did not swoon when I discovered Dorothea's deceit, and That Person's baseness, and Dr. Lavendar's improper conduct, I shall never know! Providence, I suppose, sustained me."

Miss Ferris had breakfasted in bed that morning, for the prospect of meeting Dorothea at the breakfast-table was not attractive ; so it happened that the girl's absence was not discovered until Oscar King's letter announced it, and her marriage also. There was, of course, an instant and agitated departure for Old Chester.

"I will save her," Miss Clara told Miss Mary, weeping ; "she shall desert him—if it were on the steps of the altar !"

"But it's all done," protested the invalid, also weeping ; "they've left the altar."

"Well, I'll tell James Lavendar what I think of him ; I'll tell him he has taken a great liberty in interfering in my family affairs !" Miss Ferris declared, shrilly, and went whirling into Old Chester as fast as the two fat horses which never went out in the rain could take her.

Miss Mary, lying in her bed, heard the whir of wheels beneath her window ; for a moment she thought, passionately, how it would seem to be driving into this blowing fog of rain, feeling the wet wind against her face, and smelling the dead, dank leaves underfoot. Then her mind went back to this amazing news and her sister's anger : Clara would kill the child ! Oh, if she could only walk ! If she

37

could only go and save her! Where was she?
Clara would drag her home, and another Ferris
heart would be broken! Miss Mary moaned aloud
in her grief and helplessness.

"Oh, if I had my legs!" she said to herself; and
then suddenly she stopped crying, only whimpering
a little below her breath, poor old soul! and slid
along towards the edge of her bed—slid along until
her feet touched the floor, and she stood, shaking,
quavering, holding on to the foot of the bed and
looking about her.

"But I haven't any clothes," she said, plaintively;
"Clara has taken my clothes."

Somehow, on her tottering, long-unused feet, she
crept across the room to her sister's wardrobe. She
moaned under her breath; her heart beat horribly.
Yet somehow she began to put on some of Miss
Clara's clothing. She had almost forgotten how to
do it; the feeling of stockings and shoes upon her
feet was as strange as would be any harsh contact
with one's face; but she put them on, flushing and
breathing hard, and half sobbing. Then she looked
about for a cloak, and went out into the hall, creeping and thrilling with this strange sensation of being
fastened into something. Miss Mary had not seen
that upper hall since the day she had come up the
stairs dazed and bewildered and deserted; she looked
about her with a sudden horror of all the dead and
stifled years since that vital day. How she got down
the stairs no one ever knew; she clung to the hand-
rail, sliding, slipping, half falling, and reached the
lower hall. It seemed to her that the shoes she had
put on were like leaden cases; she felt the shoestrings cutting into her instep; she felt the weight

of her skirts about her ankles. She sat down on the bottom step, panting with exhaustion and overcome with memory, but determined to save Dorothea. And then she fainted.

Miss Ferris found her there when she came back from the journey, which had revealed Oscar King's wickedness and Dorothea's undutifulness, and Dr. Lavendar's complicity—found her, and realized that the illusion and the interest of her life had been destroyed : Miss Mary was no longer crushed !

Miss Clara fell ill, poor lady, through excitement and chagrin ; and Miss Mary, acquiring her legs and some clothing, nursed her tenderly. But life was never the same for the two sisters afterwards. To poor old Mary there came a dreadful suspicion of herself ; perhaps, after all, her heart had not been broken? perhaps her fine delicacy had not existed? perhaps—perhaps ! There was no end to her moral and physical distrust of herself—a distrust that made her shamefaced and silent, afraid to say she had a headache or a twinge of rheumatism, lest Clara should turn and look at her—and doubt !

Miss Clara, for her part, had no pangs of conscience, but she suffered agonies of mortification. If she had a consolation, it was that Oscar King's conduct in marrying Dorothea justified her opinion of persons who had lived abroad very many years.

As for Oscar, he told his wife once that it was hard on poor old Clara to have Miss Mary get well ; and Dorothea opened her mild eyes, and said :

" Why, Oscar, what *do* you mean ?"

Which goes to show that she still retained the mental characteristics which endeared her to her lover.

GOOD FOR THE SOUL

GOOD FOR THE SOUL

I

It was about twelve or thirteen years before Dr. Lavendar startled Old Chester by helping Oscar King elope with that little foolish Dorothea Ferris that, one night, in the rectory study, with Mary and his brother, Joey Lavendar, as witnesses, he married Peter Day. Peter, with a pretty girl on his arm, drifted in out of the windy and rainy darkness, with a license from the Mayor's office in Upper Chester, and a demand that Dr. Lavendar perform the marriage service. Both the man and the woman were strangers to him, and the old minister looked at them sharply for a minute or two — he had misgivings, somehow. But the girl was old enough, and looked perfectly satisfied and intelligent, and the man's face was simple and honest—besides, the license was all right. So he asked one or two grave and kindly questions: "You've thought this well over? You know what a solemn thing marriage is, my friends? You are well assured that you are acting soberly, discreetly, and in the fear of God?"

"Yes, sir," said Peter Day; and the girl, a pretty, sick-looking creature, opened her big brown eyes with a glimmer of interest in them, and said, also:

"Yes, sir." So Dr. Lavendar did his duty, and found a surprisingly large fee in his hand, and went back to smoke his pipe and write at least a page on his great work, *The History of Precious Stones.*

That was the last he saw of the unknown bride and groom for many a long year. Once he heard of a new threshing-machine that was being tried at the Day farm, in the next county, and was interesting two or three farmers in his own parish; but he did not connect the rich and successful farmer of Grafton, a village near Upper Chester, with the man he had married that stormy July night. So, though his neighbors had found them interesting enough, Peter Day's affairs had never come to Dr. Lavendar's ears.

Peter had been commiserated for forty years: His farm was prosperous; it kept pace with all the new machinery, fertilizers were not despised, and there was no waste; the Day heifers had a name all through the State; and a thousand acres of haying-land meant a capital as reliable as government bonds. "I guess he's worth seventy-five thousand dollars if he's worth a cent," his neighbors said; "but the old lady, she won't let on but what they're as poor as poverty." Certainly there was no doubt that Peter Day was prosperous; but, nevertheless, he was commiserated—*he had a mother.*

"The farm is the best farm in Westmoreland County," his neighbors said, "but whether Peter can keep it up when the old lady goes, that's another question."

"He may not keep the farm up, but he can let himself down," Henry Davis, who was the black-

smith, declared; "and I'll be glad of it! Before
Peter Day goes to heaven — I guess there's no
doubt of Peter's going there in due time?—he ought
to know something about the earth. He's acquainted with the Other Place, dear knows, with the old
woman!—not that I'd say anything against her now
she's on her death-bed." Henry put a hand on the
bellows, and a roar of blue flame burst through the
heap of black fuel on the forge. "Don't you let on
to anybody, but I doubt if Peter 'll ever be more 'an
three years old. His mother's bossed him every
breath he breathed since he was born, and he'll be
just real miserable learning to walk alone at forty."

It must be admitted that here was cause for commiseration: All his forty years Mrs. Day had dom-
inated her son's life; she had managed his farm, and
he had fetched and carried and improved according
to her very excellent judgment. She had formed
his opinions — or, rather, she had given him her
opinions; she had directed his actions, she had
bought his clothes, she had doled out every dollar
he spent, and taken scrupulous account of the spend-
ing; she had crushed, long ago, any vague thought
of marriage he may have had; and she had assured
him over and over that he was a fool. A hard,
shrewish, hideously plain, marvellously capable old
woman, with a temper which in her later years drew
very near the line of insanity. Then she died.

The August afternoon that the little train of silent
people carried her out of her own door up to the
family burying-ground in the pasture (the Days
were of New England stock, and had the feeling of
race permanence in their blood, which shows itself
in this idea of a burying-ground on their own land)

—that August afternoon was sunny and still, except for the sudden song of a locust in the stubble, stabbing the silence and melting into it again. Some sumacs were reddening on the opposite hill-side; and the blossoming buckwheat in the next field was full of the murmur of bees; its hot fragrance lifted and drifted on any wandering breath of wind. Peter Day walked behind the coffin in his new black clothes, with his hat in his hand; then came the friends and neighbors, two by two. A path had been mowed through the thin second crop of grass; but the women's skirts brushed the early golden-rod and the tangling briers in the angles of the snake-fence. Up in the pasture, where the burial-lot, enclosed by a prim white paling, lay under a great oak, a bird, balancing on a leaning slate headstone, burst into a gurgling laugh of song. The oak dropped moving shadows back and forth on the group of men and women who stood watching silently that solemn merging of living into Life—of consciousness and knowledge and bitterness and spite, of human nature, into Nature. This ending of the mean and pitiful tumult which is so often all that individuality seems to be, this sinking of the unit into the universe, is like the subsidence of a little whirling gust of wind which for an instant has caught up straws and dust and then drops into dead calm. There is a sense of peace about it that is not exactly human; it is organic, perhaps; it only comes where there is no grief. They felt it, these people who stood watching, silently, unbelieving in their hearts that they too would some time go back into sun and shade and rolling world. There was no grief, only curiosity and interest and the sense of peace. When it was

46

over, they walked slowly back again, pausing for some low-voiced talk at the Day doorway, and then leaving Peter, and drawing a longer breath perhaps, and raising their voices to chatter together of the dead woman's temper and meanness and the money she had left.

The little whirl of shrewish wind had fallen into calm ; it was " all over," as the saying is—and so much greater is Life than living that it was as though it never had been. Except to Peter Day. The house had the stillness of that grave he had left up in the pasture. He heard some one moving about out in the kitchen, and the clock ticking in the hall. But there was no strident old voice to bid him do this or that ; no orders to obey, no fierce and insane fault - finding. The silence was deafening. He sat down in the parlor—the occasion seemed to demand the dignity of the parlor. The chairs had been put back in their places, but the open space in front of the fireplace struck him like a blow ; and the lingering scent of the flowers made him feel sick.

He was a short, sturdy-looking man, with a soft black beard, and kind, quiet, near-sighted eyes, which his round spectacles magnified into lambent moons. There was no weakness in his face ; but there was patience in every line ; just now there was bewilderment.

" Dead ?" He was trying, dumbly, to adjust himself to the fact ; to understand it, or at least to believe it. He felt something swell in his throat, and very likely he thought it was grief. Habit does much for us in this way ; a carping, uncomfortable companionship of forty years is yet a companionship.

Life runs in rough grooves, but they are grooves; and when it leaves them there is a wrench and jolt, and perhaps even a crash—and very often it is all mistaken for grief. Peter, in his simple way, called it grief. As he sat there in his black clothes, looking at that open space where the coffin had stood, he was vaguely conscious that he wished he had his dog Jim beside him ; but after forty years of being told that he "could not bring dogs and cattle into the house," and that "he was a fool to want to," he would have found the effort of freedom absolute pain. So he sat still until it grew dusk, trying to believe that she was dead, thinking about heaven—for he was a religious man—and saying to himself that she was "far better off." But never saying that he was "far better off," too.

Of course, as the weeks passed, he adjusted himself to the difference in his condition ; he grew accustomed to certain reliefs. Yet he did not realize that he was free. He was like a horse who slips his halter in a tread-mill, but goes on and on and on. He was not harassed by the goad of the strident voice, but he did the same work, in the same way, in the same harsh and unlovely surroundings — and he did not bring Jim into the house for company ! He spent his money on meagre essentials of food and fuel, and on the necessary improvements of the farm ; but he missed his mother's judgment and shrewd foresight in such matters. He went to church, and slept heavily during the service ; but he never went to the church sociables. His mother had despised them, and he was too old to acquire social habits. He made no effort to be intimate with his neighbors. Mrs. Day had quarrelled with them all, and would not have their names spoken in her presence if she could help it ; so, if Peter had a capacity for friendship, these speechless years had made it dumb. Hence he was singularly isolated, untouched by the interest or the gossip or the knowledge of the life about him. He spent his days as he had always spent them, following the lines his mother had laid down for him. He went through the usual round of daily work. In the evenings he read his agricultural paper or an old book of sermons. There was no one to tell him to go to bed ; and once he fell asleep, his arms stretched on the table in front of him, and wakened in the cold early light, stiff and bewildered, and heavy with fatigue. But there was one point on which Peter Day was perfectly clear : he might, through stupidity or dulness, go on in the treadmill now that the halter was slipped, but—he was glad to miss the goad !

The final awakening to a knowledge that he was free came some ten months later. It was in June ; a hot, sparkling day, when every hand on the farm had twice as much as he could do. Something had gone wrong about the mower ; and Peter, with Jim at his heels, went into the village to get the blacksmith to weld a broken rod together. It was a loss of time, this hanging about the blacksmith's shop waiting for the work to be done, and the old habit of uneasiness, because of his mother's rage at any delay, made him tramp about, frowning, and looking up the road as though expecting some messenger sent to bid him hasten.

The shop was dark, except for the red flicker when the smith thrust his pincers into the heap of ashes with one hand and started the bellows with the

D   49

other. Then a shower of sparks flew up the great black cone of the chimney, and Peter could see his piece of broken iron whiten in the flames. He looked at his watch and walked to the door and back.

"Ain't you 'most done?"

"I ain't. And I won't be for a half-hour," Henry Davis said. "What's the matter with you, Peter, anyway? What's your hurry? It wouldn't kill anybody if you didn't get back till to-morrow. Your other machine's going. There ain't no dyin' need of this here one, anyhow."

"Well, I ain't one to waste time," Peter said. Jim yawned, and stretched himself on the bare black earth of the floor. He, at least, was in no hurry.

"Well, whose time are you wastin'?" the smith insisted, good-naturedly. "It's your own, ain't it? I guess you got a right to loaf. There's no one to say you nay," he ended.

"That's so," said Peter. But he still tramped back and forth, until the smith, turning the bar about on his anvil, cried:

"For the Lord's sake, Peter Day, get out! Go up the street and get a shave. Get out o' here, anyway."

Peter laughed, and went, saying that he would be back in ten minutes. "And mind you have that rod done!"

He loitered along, looking at his watch more than once, and coming to a standstill before the window of a grocery-store. He did not go in. All these years the curb of his mother's will had held him away from the shiftless and friendly gatherings about the stove or around the back counter, and it held him yet. So he only looked into the dusty window. There were wooden rakes stacked up at one side, and boxes of cotton lace, and two jars of red and white sticks of candy, and some fly-specked cups and saucers in thick earthen-ware ; there were two advertisements of poultry food pasted against the glass, and a print of a new mower. He took these in absently, wondering if the rod was nearly done. And then his eye caught a colored lithograph propped up against a pile of dusty tin-ware : a row of girls, smiling, coquettish, marching, each with slippered foot well advanced, holding out a gay skirt with the thumb and forefinger of one hand, and flirting with the other a huge feather fan across arch and laughing eyes. The flutter of the pink and blue and white skirts, the slender ankles, the invitation and challenge and impertinence of the upward kick, seemed to Peter Day perfectly beautiful. He gazed at the picture, absorbed and entranced. The owner of the shop, standing in the doorway, watched him, grinning.

" You better go see 'em, Mr. Day. They're to be here to-night. The parson's mad, I tell you."

Peter came to himself with a start, and read the announcement of the production in the town-hall, on such a date and at such an hour, of " Sweet Rosy." The notice below the picture set forth :

The Four Montague Sisters will Perform their Charming, Refined, and Side-splitting Farce, with all Accessories of Magnificent Scenery, Exquisite Music, and Elaborate Costumes. The Ballet is pronounced to be the most Beautiful, in Loveliness of Form and Perfection of Grace, ever seen in America.

YOUTH. GRACE. BEAUTY.

ADMISSION, 35 CENTS.

" We've never had one of these here shows up here," said the storekeeper ; "but of course I've seen 'em. I always go when I'm in the city, because my example can't injure nobody there. Here it's different. Why don't you go and see 'em, Mr. Day ?"

Why didn't he ? Peter Day went back to the black-smith's shop for his rod, and walked home "study-ing." Why shouldn't he go to see the show ? He did not ask himself whether there was anything wrong in such shows—he never had asked such questions. There was nothing abstract about Peter. He had simply ducked and winced under his mother's tongue, and accepted her decisions of what was right or wrong, avoiding, by a sort of instinct, the things that roused the furious temper which lay always ready to flash and roar and shake the house down at the most trivial excuse. In ten months he had gotten more or less used to peace, even if he had not taken advantage of it. But why shouldn't he take advantage of it ?

He looked through his round spectacles with absent intentness at Jim, jogging along in the dust in front of him. "I'm going to see them," he said to himself; "why not ?"

II

The town-hall in Grafton stood in the square ; winter rains had washed and washed against its narrow, faded old bricks until the plaster between them had crumbled and their angles and edges had worn down. The white paint on the facings and on the great beam that made the base of the pediment, had flaked and blistered ; a crack ran from a second-story window down towards the front door, which sagged a little in its battered white frame. Inside, the wooden steps were so worn that the knots stood out on them : —innumerable town meetings, fairs, lectures, and all such entertainments as this of the Montague Sisters, made much travel over the wide, shallow staircase. The walls were bare, the plaster stained and cracked, even broken in two or three places, and studded with nails for all the different decorations of pine or flags or crape or flowers which had gone up and come down in more than fifty years. There were lanterns in brackets along the walls, and eight lamps in a dusty chandelier cast flickering shadows down on the bare floor and the rows of wooden settees, which, when Mr. Day arrived, were quite empty—such was his anxiety to get a good seat. The audience came stamping and scuffling in, with a good deal of laughter, and much loud, good-natured raillery, and some cat-cries. Very likely the parson had reason for "being mad." "Sweet Rosy ; or, The Other Man" was the play, and there was a suggestiveness in the names of the acts which would have forewarned any-body but Peter. He had no experience in indecencies.

He was tingling with excitement ; the sudden and unusual concentration of thought and feeling was not without pain—it was, mentally, like the awaking of a hand or foot which has been asleep.

The curtain rolled up, caught—and displayed a pair of slender ankles, and opposite them two Wellington boots, fiercely spurred—rolled on, and showed a man decorated with stars and sashes and sword, which informed the audience that he was a soldier ; and a girl, in fluffy pink skirts, high-heeled pink slippers, low pink satin skin-tight bodice, pink lips, pink cheeks, pink hat and feathers. Her neck and bosom were as white as swan's-down, and glittered with "diamonds," that did not seem any more sparkling than her arch brown eyes, which laughed over her pink fan—laughed and winked, and looked right down at Peter Day in the front seat. Peter's mouth fell open; he looked at his programme, the flimsy sheet rustling in his big hands until his neighbors frowned at him with impatience.

"Bessie Montague." That was her name—Bessie! The soldier, it appeared, was Bessie's brother, who was instructing her about the "Other Man," Mr. Wilson, who was shortly to appear—hampered, indeed, by a Mrs. Wilson; but if Bessie and her sisters, Minnie, Nellie, Mamie, would play their cards properly, the mere incident of the wife would make no difference. They would go to a picnic with the Other Man, and then, and *then*, and THEN!—came a rollicking chorus, with Minnie and Mamie and Nellie dancing round and round, Bessie the gayest of them all, and the Other Man and the Incident coming on to be hoodwinked, in sober and decent clothes and sanctimonious air. The audience roared at each innuendo; and Peter, smiling and palpitating like a girl, took it all to mean that the four girls wanted the fun of the picnic, and were going to get the old dodger with the hay seed in his hair to give it to them. At least, when he thought about the play at all, that was his construction of it; but he hardly thought of it—the dancing enthralled him. It seemed to him that Mamie and Minnie said things that weren't just modest sometimes, but a girl doesn't understand half the time what words mean; very likely they didn't know why the masculine part of the audience roared so.

Nellie had almost nothing to say, and Bessie was the première danseuse, and only joined in the choruses. To Peter, from the first moment, she was the most fascinating figure on the stage. Her dancing and coquetting and pirouetting, her glances and gurgling laughter and gestures, went to his head. He saw nothing else; the tawdry scenery, the soiled cotton velvet and flimsy crumpled satin, the reek of vulgarity, never touched his innocent mind. He looked at her open-mouthed, breathless. The play was about half over, when it seemed to him that this angel, or fairy, or whatever she was, flagged and began to look tired. Once the soldier frowned, and made a gesture to show that she had done something wrong, and he saw a frightened wince under the smiles and paint on the girl's face. Peter Day ground his teeth. How dared the brute look that way at his sister? That was no way for a brother to act! From that point he only looked at Bessie; he saw her growing white and whiter, though he noticed that the color in her cheek was as bright as ever—which seemed to him a very unhealthy sign.

"It's that way in consumption," he thought. He felt impelled to leap up on the stage and tell her brother he ought to take better care of her; and then her dancing fascinated him so that he forgot her pallor for a while—then noticed it, with sharp compunction.

The last whirl and pigeon-wing, the last kick and flurry of gauze skirts, the last leer—then, standing on one leg, each sister kissed her hand, bit her lip, looked down into the audience and winked, and—it was over!

Peter Day sat like a man in a dream. Somebody

cuffed him on the shoulder and said, " Did they put you to sleep?" and there was a guffaw of laughter.

He shook his head silently and got up; he looked about in a dazed way for a minute, and then went stumbling out into the cool night.

As for "Bessie," she sat down on an overturned soap-box behind the scenes and panted.

"You've got a mash, Liz!" one of the girls called out, beginning to wash off the paint.

"Oh, I'm so tired!" she said, faintly. "Oh, this is a dog's life!"

"Guess he's waiting at the side door," Mamie suggested; "he looks good for a supper, anyway. Make him stand up to us all, Liz, will you?"

"Shut up!" the girl said. "I'm nearly dead."

"You'll hear that from Dickinson, I bet," one of the "sisters" informed her; and then, with rough kindliness, brought her a dash of whiskey in a dirty tumbler. "There, brace up! I don't believe he'll say anything. My God, I thought you were going to drop there once! Did you see Johnny Mack glare at you when you crossed behind? If he'll keep his mouth shut and not complain, I guess you won't hear from it. I wish you didn't have to move on to-morrow, though."

III

However, they did move on; that is what it means to be "on the road" and have one-night stands. The "Montague Sisters" moved on, and Peter Day moved with them.

The first step into liberty had been taken when he went to the play; then some door seemed to shut behind him; the automatic life stopped short; he felt, for the first time since he was twenty (when his mother had nipped in the bud certain tendencies towards love-making), the consciousness that he had a life of his own. And he began to live it. He announced that he was going away for a week or two.

"What! *now?*" ejaculated one of the hands. "Why, we're that busy—"

"I'm going," his employer said, and set his lips in a dogged way that he had learned under his mother's scoldings; it meant that he had no explanation to give, and no retort; but it meant, too, in this instance, will. So he packed a valise made of Brussels carpet—crimson roses on a cream-colored ground —and said good-bye to Jim, and started.

The Montague Sisters went to Mercer, and on to two or three smaller places, and then back again on the circuit towards Old Chester. It took nearly three weeks, and Peter Day never missed a performance. The company grew hysterical with laughter over him; the "sisters" played to him, and winked at him, and kicked their high-heeled slippered feet in his direction, and threw kisses to him over their white shoulders that were so dangerously above their bodices; but it was more than a week before he made the acquaintance of the manager and was introduced to them.

"It's a dead mash for Liz," the manager announced. "Say, Liz, can't you get him to give you a theatre? Come, now, don't forget the company when you strike it rich." Liz laughed, and groaned, and dropped down on the broken springs of the horse-hair couch in the parlor of the little hotel.

"Somebody'd better give me a grave," she said.

"Say, Dickinson, I'm played out." She began to cry, and the manager told her, good-naturedly, not to be a fool.

"I'll send you up something that'll make you feel better," he said. But the cocktail and the kindness only made her cry the more.

"I don't know what's going to become of me," she told the "sisters." "I can't keep this up; there's no use talking!"

Mamie sat down on the table, swinging her legs back and forth, and looking concerned. "Well, now, can't you go home awhile?" she said.

Bessie looked up impatiently. "I haven't any home. I haven't had for six years. I came into this to support mother, and when she—died, I didn't have any home. As for relations, I've got some relations somewhere, but they're too good for the likes of me! No, no!" She got up, the tears dried and her dark eyes sparkling wickedly; the cocktail had brought a little color into her cheeks, and she was as pretty as when she stood before the foot-lights in vivid rouge and snow-white powder. She took two dancing steps. "No—no !—

"I care for nobody,
And nobody cares for me!"

"Except Hayseed," Mamie reminded her, with a thoughtful frown. "He cares, it appears. I say, Liz, I suppose you *could* lay off, and—"

The girl turned on her savagely. "Now look here; shut up! *He's good.*"

Mamie shrieked with laughter. "Oh, he doesn't bite, doesn't he?"

"He doesn't try to make me bite," the other said, sharply; then suddenly broke down again, and flung up her arms, and said she wished she was dead. "Talk about a home! If I could stop, if I could have a little house of my own, and maybe a garden —well, there! I'm a fool. You needn't tell me; I know it. But I tell you what, Mame, it's hell; that's what it is, this road business—putting yourself up to be insulted by every man that pays fifty cents to see you dance. I'm dead tired of it. Oh, my God, I wish I was dead!" But even as she said it she burst into a laugh, her brown eyes crinkling up with fun. "Mamie, what do you suppose? He asked me to-day what my sisters thought of my working so hard. 'Sisters?' I said—I was so tired, I was just dead stupid. 'Sisters?' I says. 'I haven't any sisters.' He looked dumb-struck. Then I caught on."

"He *is* an innocent!" Mamie said.

"He's good," the other answered, with a sob.

She was as inconsequent and unmoral, this little, flashing, suffering, pretty creature, as the sparkle of sunshine on a rippling wave. And she was, just now, almost at the limit of her strength. The simple-hearted man who, through his big steel-rimmed spectacles, looked at her every night from the first row, and came to see her every morning, as silent and as faithful as a dog, saw in her all the beauty and grace and good-nature of which his harmless life had been starved. He thought to himself, over and over, how pleasant she was. He had had little enough pleasantness in his forty arid years, dear knows! so it was easy to recognize it when he saw it.

He was bewildered, and dazzled, and happy, and tumultuously in love. He felt as if he wanted to play with her; to romp, and run, and laugh, as though they were boy and girl. He was getting young, this sober, elderly man, and the warm-hearted, quick-witted little actress, with her peals of laughter, her funny winks, and grimaces, and good-natured raillery, was the cause of it. He never knew how hotly she defended him from the suspicions of the rest of the company; she was so quick to recognize his "goodness" that she turned white with anger when his motives were assailed. When he told her once, blushing, that he was glad she just only danced, because some of the things the other young ladies said weren't just according to his notions, she winced and set her white teeth. "I don't like those jokes," she said; "truly I don't, Mr. Day."

He laughed at that, in his soft, big voice, his eyes beaming at her through his spectacles.

"You! Well, you needn't tell me that, Miss Montague. You don't understand, even. Well, now, a girl seems to me just like one of those white butterflies that's always round milkweed. You know 'em? 'Brides,' the young ones call them. Their wings— you can't hardly breathe on 'em but what they're spoiled! Well, it's like touching their wings to have girls sing trashy songs; and I'm right sorry the other ladies feel obliged to do it."

"Oh, if I ever had time to go to walk in the country and see the 'brides'!" she said, her eyes suddenly wet. "I'm pretty tired of this kind of life."

He made an impulsive gesture, and opened his lips; but he dared not speak. As for her, she went into the hotel parlor, and sat on the horse-hair sofa under the steel engraving of the "Landing of the Pilgrims," and told Mamie she wished she was dead.

GOOD FOR THE SOUL

Peter Day knew no better than to make his protest to Dickinson, who winked at the barkeeper to call his attention to the joke. "I'm thinking of getting up a Sunday-school play for 'em next season," he said.

Peter was no fool; he did not pursue the subject; but he had his own views. In his cramped, unlovely life, the single exponent of the everlasting feminine had been his mother. Yet he had his ideals: he believed in goodness and in purity in a way that even a man who had known them in their human limitations might not have done. In his grave and simple way, he knew the world was wicked. But he would not have those white-winged creatures whom he revered have even so much knowledge as that.

At the end of the third week the Montague Sisters came to Old Chester; they had two nights here, and it was on the second night that Bessie broke down absolutely, and fainted dead away. They were all very kind to her—the manager and the other "sisters." They were in and out of her room all that night, and Dickinson would have given her all the whiskey the tavern afforded if it would have done any good. But business is business; the troupe was advertised to appear in the next town, and they had to move on. So, with protestations, and most honest anxiety, and the real, practical kindness of leaving some money for her board with the tavern-keeper, they moved on. But Peter Day stayed behind.

He saw her every day for a week; he went up to her room, and washed her little hot face and hands, and fed her with cracked ice, and told her about Jim; and his eyes, behind his magnifying spectacles, beamed like two kindly moons.

"I'm going to marry her," he told the tavern-keeper, "just as soon as she can get out."

It was a week before she could sit up; when she did, in a big wooden rocking-chair, with roses painted on the back, and slippery linen covers tied on the arms, he came and sat beside her and put his hand on hers.

"Miss Montague," he said, his voice trembling, "I am going to ask a—a favor."

"My name isn't Montague," she told him, her eyes crinkling with a laugh; "that's only my stage name."

"Oh!" he said, blankly; "I thought it was. Still, it doesn't matter; because—because, Miss Montague—"

"Donald," she interrupted, smiling.

"Because, Miss Donald, I was going to ask you to —to change it."

"Change it? My name?" she said. "You don't mean—"

"I want you to marry me," he said, his hand suddenly closing hard on hers. She drew back with a cry; looked at him with wide eyes; then she put her hands over her face and began to cry, poor child, in a wailing, heart-broken way. To cry—and cry—and cry, while he just put his arms about her and drew her head down on his breast, and stroked her soft, dark, curling hair, soothing her and cuddling her, and saying: "There—there! I frightened you. Never mind; it's only me. It's only Peter. There, there, there!"

She tried to say: "No; oh *no!* he must not think of it. He—he didn't know her. On no—*no!* She was not good enough. No, she couldn't, she couldn't!"

But he gathered her up in his arms, and put his

cheek down against her hair, and said, " There, there; it's all right, and I'll get the license."

She was so weak that suddenly she fainted, and Peter was like a madman until young Dr. King had been rushed in, and had said it was all right, and she would be none the worse the next morning. Which, indeed, she was not. Something had braced her; perhaps it was the human kindness that went to her heart like wine.

" I'll be good to him; I'll make it up to him," she said, crying peacefully to herself. " Oh, I will be good to him; and I'm so tired—tired—*tired*. And I'll do everything for him. And I can rest; for all my life, I can just rest."

So that was how it came about that, the evening of the first day she was able to go out, Peter took her, carried her almost, to Dr. Lavendar's study, where they were reminded that marriage was not to be entered into lightly or unadvisedly—but soberly, discreetly, and in the fear of God.

IV

Of course it is perfectly obvious how a " sober and discreet " marriage of this nature must end. The elderly, simple-minded, plain countryman, and the little actress whose past had never been laid under her neighbor's eyes—what could happen, says the wise world, but disaster and pain?

And yet neither befell.

He took her home, this gentle, passionate, pitying husband, and nursed her, and petted her, and played with her. All the checked and stunted youth in him blossomed out. He told her his thoughts—for in his slow way he had thoughts. He let her see his simple adoration of the ideals which she embodied—gentleness, and prettiness, and purity. He was jealous to shield her from every rough wind, from every cruel knowledge; all the love of all his bleak unlovely life was poured into her lap. And she was very "pleasant" with him. She felt towards Peter that warm-hearted admiration which begins in appreciation and ends in love. He was so good to her—that was the first thing the wife felt; and then, he was so good!

She laughed at him and sung to him, and even put on her pink dress and danced for him sometimes. And she brought Jim into the very parlor itself! At first, very likely, it was all part of the play of life to her. She could appreciate, if Peter could not, the stage setting, so to speak—the bare, ugly parlor, with its landscape-papered walls and faded photographs of dead relatives hanging in oval black frames very near the ceiling; the lustres on the high wooden mantel-piece; the big Bible on the crocheted mat of the centre-table; the uncomfortable horse-hair sofa, and the rosewood chairs standing at exact angles in the windows; and Peter, with Jim's head on his knee, sitting, gaping at her—gaping at the incongruous, joyous, dancing figure, with the pink skirt twirling over pink gauze petticoats! At first the fun of the contrast was a keen enjoyment; but after a while—

However, that came later.

Meantime she *rested*. Sometimes on his knee, with her head on his shoulder, while he tried to read his agricultural paper, but had to stop because she teased him into laughter; sometimes on a little couch out

64

under the trees, on the sunny side of the house, where she could see Peter working in the garden. She found not only rest but intense interest in this garden, which, to be sure, was rather commonplace. There were clumps of perennials in the borders, upon which each year the grass encroached more and more; and there were shrubs, and some seedlings sown as the wind listed, and there were a dozen ragged old rose-bushes. But Bessie Day threw herself into taking care of all the friendly, old-fashioned fragrance, heart and soul, and body too, which made her tired and strong and happy all together. She used to lie awake those summer nights and plan the garden she was going to have next year; and she pored over seedmen's catalogues with a passionate happiness that made her bright face brighter and brought a look of keen and joyous interest into her eyes.

That was the first year; the second, the ballet dress was put away, for there was a baby; and by-and-by there were two babies—a young Peter and a young Donald. And then a little girl that the father said must be named Pleasant. It was then that Bessie got dissatisfied with her own name, and insisted that she be called Elizabeth. So the old name, like the old pink satin dress and fan and high-heeled slippers, was put away in the past. Sometimes Peter talked about them, but Elizabeth would scold him and say she was tired of them, and she wouldn't allow them to be mentioned. "I'll steal your spectacles, Peter, if you tease me," she would threaten, gayly; "I go to church, nowadays, and the minister says it isn't right to dance—though I don't know that I just agree with him," she would add, a little gravely.

"Anything you ever did was right—right enough

for a minister to do himself!" Peter would declare, stoutly.

"I wouldn't like to see the parson in pink petticoats," Elizabeth would retort, her eyes twinkling with fun.

She always went to church with Peter, and he kept awake to look at her pretty face in her Sunday bonnet; and later, when the children were old enough to come, too, he had his hands full to keep the boys in order, and not let them read their library books during the sermon. Elizabeth, in her best lavender silk, which had little sprigs over it, and an embroidered white crêpe shawl, and a bonnet with soft white strings, sat at the top of the pew, with Pleasant's sleepy head against her shoulder, looking so cheerful and pretty that it was no wonder Peter looked oftener at her than at the parson.

As for the neighbors, social life came slowly, because of Peter's long indifference to it; but it came, and people said they liked Mrs. Day because she was so different from other folks—"always real pleasant," her neighbors said. " I never heard Peter's wife say a hard word about anybody," Henry Davis said once; "and when a woman's got a smart tongue, like she has, they most always say funny things about other folks that make you laugh, but would hurt the folks' feelings if they heard 'em. But Mrs. Day she's just pleasant all the time."

So the placid years came and went, and by-and-by Peter's wife was no longer slight; but she was as light on her feet as a girl, and her face was as bright and pretty as ever, and her laugh was like the sunny chuckle of a brook; her children and her garden and her husband filled her life, and she made theirs.

GOOD FOR THE SOUL

It was nearly ten years before that shadow, of whose coming the world would have had no doubt, fell, little by little, into the dark bright eyes and across the smiling lips.   Fell, and deepened and deepened.

"You're not well, wife ?" Peter said, anxiously.

"Nonsense !" she said, smiling at him.

But when he left her, her face settled into heavy lines.

"If you don't look better to - morrow," Peter threatened, " I'll have the doctor."

"The doctor !" his wife cried, laughing.   "Why, I am perfectly well."

And, indeed, the doctor could not discover that she was ill in any way.   "Then why does she look so badly ?" Peter urged, blinking at him with anxious eyes.

"Oh, she's a little overtired," the doctor assured him, easily.   "I think she works too hard in that garden of hers.   I think I'd put a stop to that, Mr. Day."

And having done his worst, this worthy meddler with the body departed, to prescribe physical exercise for a brain-worker at the point of exhaustion. But Peter was grateful for some positive instructions.

"The children and I will take care of the garden, and you can just look on.   What you need is rest."

So, to please him, she tried to rest ; but the shadow deepened in her eyes, and the fret of thought wore lines in her smooth forehead.   She shook her head over Peter's offer to take care of the garden.

"What ! trust my precious flowers to a mere man ?" she cried, with the old gayety, and burlesque anger.   "Indeed I won't !"

67

The garden Peter had made for her was a great two-hundred-foot square, sunk between four green terraces ; it was packed with all sorts of flowers, and overflowing with fragrance ; all the beds were bordered with sweet-alyssum and mignonette, and within them the flowers stood, pressing their glowing faces together in masses of riotous color—the glittering satin yellow of California poppies, the heavenly blue of nemophila ; crimson mallow, snow-white shining phlox ; sweet - pease and carnations, gilly-flowers and bachelor's-buttons, and everywhere the golden sparks of coreopsis ; there were blots of burning scarlet, sheets of orange and lilac and dazzling white. Elizabeth used to sit down by some border to weed, smiling at her flowers, putting her fingers under some shy sweet face, to raise it, and look down into it, rejoicing in the texture and color and perfume—and then, suddenly, her pleasant eyes would cloud and her energy flag, and she would sit there, absent and heavy, the pain wearing deep into her forehead.

By the time another year had come her whole face had changed ; her eyes so rarely crinkled up with fun that one had a chance to see how big and sad and terror-stricken they had grown, and her mouth took certain pitiful lines, and seemed always about to open into sad and wailing words. Another year —they had been married twelve years now—had certainly brought this husband and wife nearer to that dreadful verge of disaster, which the sober looker-on must surely have prophesied on that night when the man and woman stood up to be married in Dr. Lavendar's study.

It was in June that Elizabeth Day said to her husband, gayly, that she had a plan. "Now don't scold, Peter, but listen. I suppose you will say I'm crazy ; but I have a notion I want to go off and take a drive, all by myself, for a whole day."

"I'll drive you," he said, "anywhere you want."

"No," she said, coming and sitting on his knee ; "no ; let me go by myself. I'll tell you : I think I'm a little nervous, and I've a notion to take a drive by myself. I think maybe I'll feel better for it."

"Well," he said, wistfully, "if you want to ; but I'd like to go with you."

But she would not listen to that ; and she was so cheerful at the very prospect of her drive—"just real senseless glad!" her husband called it, anxiously—that he began to think that perhaps she was right, and it would do her good.

"Like giving a sick person what they've got a longing for," he told himself. "I know mother told me how she knew of a child that was getting over scarlet-fever, and wanted a pickle, and teased and teased for it ; and they gave it to her and she got well. Very likely Elizabeth just has a kind of craving to ride round for a day. Well, she shall. Mercy ! she shall have just anything in the Lord's world, if I can get it for her ! I wish the buggy wasn't so shabby. I must be getting a new one for her."

Still, when the moment came for her to start, he was anxious again.

"Suppose you take one of the children along for company ?" he said, as he helped her into the buggy. (Oh, how light she was ! What a thrill and tremor he felt in her hand when his big fingers closed over it !) "Take Pleasant," he entreated. And she agreed, with a sigh.

" I don't mind, if you want me to, Peter."

So Pleasant, uttering shrieks of joy, ran for her hat, and began to climb up to join her mother, too excited to wait for her father's helping hand.

Elizabeth Day gathered up the reins and gave a little flickering look up at the front of the house—at the two boys sitting on the porch steps—at her husband standing beside the buggy, stretching over the wheels to tuck the duster around her feet. It was early—she had stipulated for an early start—the dew stretched like a cobweb over the grass, and in the border a cloud of scarlet poppies were beaded with drops like silver ; the honeysuckle at the end of the porch was pouring its fragrance from curved and polished horns. She had planted that honeysuckle twelve years ago. How happy she had been then ! Now, faithful wife, tender mother, modest, careful housewife—*good*, too, she thought to herself, humbly —she was not happy. Oh, most miserable, most miserable !

How strange it is that the tree whose fruit is suffering and pain, is the knowledge of good as well as of evil ! Perhaps the single knowledge of either would not mean anything ; or perhaps there cannot be knowledge of one without knowledge of the other. Here is a great mystery : we poor little creatures cannot understand that He both makes peace and creates evil for his own purposes—for sin is the prerogative of God. This poor girl, in her pure and placid life here on the farm, had eaten of this tree, and the anguish of the knowledge of goodness had fallen on her. She groaned under her breath, looking at the dear house and at the dear love. . . .

Elizabeth shook the reins and nodded, smiling : "Good-bye, boys, don't bother father ; be good children. Good-bye, Peter."

"When will you be back ?" her husband said, his hand on the bridle—the horse backed and fretted, and his wife scolded good-naturedly.

"I'll never get off ! Come ! go on, Captain. Oh, well, then—to-night, maybe."

"To - night !" Peter echoed, blankly. "Well, I should say so ! Pleasant, take care of mother ;" and he let her start, but stood looking down the road, watching the hood of the buggy jogging up and down, until the light dust hid it.

Elizabeth leaned back in her seat and drew a great breath of relief. Pleasant, smiling all over her little round face, looked up at her.

"Mother, may I hold the reins ?" she said.

"Take the ends of them," Elizabeth said ; "mother will keep her hands in front of yours, for fear Captain should take a notion to run."

Pleasant, beaming, and crinkling her eyes up as her mother had done before her, shook and jerked at the ends of the reins, saying, " Get up, there !" and clucked as she had heard her father do ; then, squaring her elbows, she braced her feet against the dashboard. "If Captain was to run, mother, this is the way I'd stop him," she said, proudly.

"Yes, dear child," the mother answered, mechanically. She drove without any uncertainty or hesitation as to her route, and carefully sparing her horse as one who has a long journey before her. It was growing warmer ; the dew had burned off, and the misty look of early morning had brightened into clear soft blue without a cloud. There was a shallow run beside the road, which chattered and chuckled over its pebbly bed, or plunged down in little waterfalls a foot high, running over stones smooth with moss, or stopping in the shadows under leaning trees, and spreading into little pools, as clear and shining and brown as Pleasant's eyes.

"It would be nice to wade, wouldn't it, mother?" the child said; and the mother said again, mechanically,

"Yes, dear."

But she did not look at the run, which by-and-by widened into a creek as it and the road went on together; and when Captain began to climb a long, sunny slope, she only knew the difference because the sweating horse fell into an easy walk. Pleasant chattered without ceasing.

"It's nice to come with you, mother. Where are we going? Mother, I think I must have been unusually good, don't you, for God to let me have this ride, and hold Captain's reins? I wonder if Captain knows I've got the ends of the reins? He doesn't *try* to run, you see; I guess he knows he couldn't, with me to help you hold him. Oh, look at the bird sitting on the fence! Well, I'm glad I've been good lately—or else, probably, I wouldn't have come with you. Donald was bad yesterday; he pulled the kitty's tail very hard; so I notice God didn't let him come. I never pull the kitty's tail," Pleasant ended, virtuously. Then she said, "Get up, Captain!" and jerked the reins so hard that her mother came out of her thoughts with a start.

"Don't, Pleasant! Don't pull so, dear."

"Mother, when you were a little girl, did you ever go and drive with your mother, like me?"

"Yes, Pleasant."

"Was she nice—was she as nice as you?"

"A great deal nicer, Pleasant."

"My!" said Pleasant. "I suppose she let you drive altogether—not just with the ends of the reins?"

Elizabeth did not answer. Pleasant slipped off the seat and leaned over the dash-board to pat Captain; then tried sitting sidewise with her legs under her.

"This is the way the cat sits; I never understood before what she did with her back legs. The tail is easy; she just lays it over her front legs." Then she slid down again to sit on the floor of the buggy and hang her head over the wheel to see the tracks in the dust. Elizabeth came out of her dream at this, and bade the child get up on the seat.

"Where are we going?" Pleasant said, climbing up joyfully; but she had to repeat her question before her mother heard it.

"To Old Chester, dear child."

"Oh, that's miles and miles away!" Pleasant said, excitedly; and turned and knelt down on the seat so that she could clasp her mother's neck with both little warm, loving arms. "Oh, I am glad we're going so far away; it's so interesting to take a long journey. I was afraid you would be turning round pretty soon. Who are you going to see, mother?"

"I'm going to see a minister who lives there, Pleasant."

Pleasant looked serious, as befitted the mention of a minister.

"Why are you going to see a minister?"

"Pleasant, you must not ask so many questions! I never knew a little girl talk so much."

Pleasant looked troubled, and drew a long breath. "Well, mother, it's my thoughts. If I didn't have so many thoughts, I wouldn't talk. Do you have thoughts, mother?"

Elizabeth laughed. "Well, yes, Pleasant, I do."

"Well, you see!" cried Pleasant, triumphantly. "Tell me a few of your thoughts, please, mother."

"Oh, my dear child, do be quiet!" the mother entreated. "Oh, my *God!*" she said, under her breath. There was something in her face that did silence the child, for a time at least. Elizabeth drew up at a spring under the trees by the road-side, and brought out a lunch-basket and gave the little girl something to eat. She did not eat herself, but sat absently flecking at a weed with her whip, and watching Captain plunging his nose down into the trough. Pleasant climbed out to get a drink, putting her lips against the mossy wooden pipe from which a single sparkling thread of water fell into the great hollowed log. They could hear some one whetting a scythe in a field higher up on the hill, above the woods. The sunshine sifted down through the thick foliage, and the yellow flower of the jewel - weed, just on the edge of the trough, caught it, and glittered like a topaz. Captain stamped a little among the wet stones and mud, and pulled at the reins; and Elizabeth said, "Well, go 'long, Captain."

The horse started in a steady jogging trot, keeping carefully on the shady side of the road. A fresh wind had sprung up, and along the horizon a few white clouds had heaped themselves into shining domes, but the sky was exquisitely and serenely blue. The creek had widened into a little narrow river, deep and brown, and fringed with sycamores;

"ALONG THE HORIZON A FEW WHITE CLOUDS WERE HEAPED IN SHINING DOMES"

men were haying in the meadows and in the orchards on the hill-sides, and the hot smell of newly cut grass was in the air.

Elizabeth Day drew up beside a mile-post, and leaned out of the buggy, trying to read the nearly effaced figures. "It's only three miles more, Pleasant," she said, breathlessly.

"Shall we get some dinner in Old Chester?" Pleasant asked, with anxiety.

"Why, my dear child, you've just had some dinner. Still, there is more in the basket, if you want it. You can eat it while I get out and visit with the minister. You must be a good girl, Pleasant, and wait outside in the buggy. I'll hitch Captain."

"I'll hold the reins," Pleasant declared; "he won't try and run if you hitch him and I hold the reins. Captain is a good old horse — good Captain! good boy!" she continued, hanging over the dash-board to stroke his black tail. Captain switched it, with mild impatience, and Pleasant drew back, offended; then tried sliding off the seat: "But the dash-board gets in the way of my knees," she complained. Her mother did not notice her. The little warm body pressing against her, the sudden embraces, the bubbling words, the overflowing activity and restlessness, were like the touch of foam against a rock.

"Mother," Pleasant began, "one of my thoughts was, whose little girl would I be if you hadn't married father? Would I live with him, or would I live with you? It's very interesting to have thoughts like that," said Pleasant.

"It's very foolish," Elizabeth said, sharply; and again the child was silenced, looking sidewise at her mother, not knowing whether she had been naughty or not.

It was nearly twelve when they reached Old Chester. Pleasant was quite cheerful again, and bubbling over with questions.

Mrs. Day was pale, and her whole body tingled and trembled. How familiar it all was: The stone tavern with the wide porch—that had been her window, the one in the corner. She had sat there, in the painted rocking-chair, when Peter told her he wanted to marry her. And that was the church; right beyond it was the minister's house. She remembered that they had walked across the green in front of the church to go to the rectory. It suddenly came over her, in a wave of terror, that he might be dead, that old man! She took out the whip, and struck Captain sharply; he leaped forward, and the jerk fairly knocked the breath out of Pleasant, who was in the middle of a question. Elizabeth felt, poor woman, that she could not bear one instant's more anxiety: if he were *dead*—oh, what should she do? He had been an old man, she remembered.

Captain went briskly down the street, and Elizabeth was so weak with misery and apprehension she could scarcely stop him at the parsonage gate.

V

"Will you be quiet, Pleasant, and not get out?" Elizabeth said. She got the oat-bag from the back of the buggy, and then pulled the weight from under the seat and fastened the catch into Captain's bit. He put his soft nose against her wrist, and she stopped, trembling, to pat him.

Then she went up the path between the garden borders : she and Peter had walked along that path. Oh dear, she was beginning to cry ! She could not speak to the minister if she was going to cry. She had to wait and wipe her eyes and let the tremor and swelling of her throat subside before she rang and asked if she might see Dr. Lavendar.

"He's goin' to have his dinner in about fifteen minutes," Mary said, sourly. She did not mean to have the rectory meals delayed by inconsiderate people arriving at twelve o'clock. "And she'll worry the life out of him, anyhow," Mary reflected : Mary had seen too many tragic faces come to that door not to recognize this one.

"Who's there ?" demanded Dr. Lavendar from the study ; and then came peering out into the hall, which was dusky, because the vines hung low over the lintel, letting the light filter in green and soft across the threshold. When he saw the strange face he came forward to welcome her. He had on a flowered dressing‑gown, and his spectacles had been pushed back and rested on his white hair, which stood up very stiff and straight. "Come in," he said, abruptly ; and Mary, feeling herself worsted, retired, muttering, to the kitchen.

Mrs. Day followed the minister into the study, but when he closed the door behind her and pointed to a chair, and said, cheerfully, "And what can I do for you, ma'am ?" she could hardly find her voice to answer him.

She was conscious of a sense of relief that the room did not look as it did the night that she and Peter had stood up to be married. The furniture had been moved about, and there was sunshine instead of lamp-light, and through the open window she could see Pleasant hanging over the dash-board stroking Captain, who was tossing his feed-bag up to get at his oats.

"I suppose you don't remember me; sir?" she said.

"I'm afraid I don't," he confessed, smiling. "An old man's memory isn't good for much, you know."

She tried to smile too, but her face felt stiff.

"You married us, sir; my name is Day. Peter Day is my husband."

Dr. Lavendar reflected. "Day? The name is familiar, but I don't recall— Let me see; when was it?"

"It's twelve years ago next month, sir," Elizabeth said, and added that she had come from Grafton, and, with a little pride in her voice, that her husband was well known in Upper Chester. "Why you must have heard of Peter Day!" she said.

But Dr. Lavendar did not commit himself. He hoped Mr. Day was well? And was that little girl in the buggy hers? Had she other children? And all the while he looked at her with his kind, shrewd old eyes, that were always beaming with his good opinion of his fellow-men—an opinion that grew out of his belief that the children of his Father could not be so very bad, after all!

"I came to see you," Elizabeth began, in a wavering voice, "because—because I thought you would give me some advice."

"I find it's easier for me to give advice than for people to take it," he answered, good-humoredly; but now she did not even try to smile.

"I'm in great trouble, sir; I—I thought you were the only person who could help me. I've thought of coming to see you for the last year."

"Have you had any dinner?" demanded Dr. Lavendar, looking at her over his spectacles.

"No; I don't want any, sir. I only want—"

"You want food," he declared, nodding his head; and called Mary, and bade her bring in dinner. "Yes, you must have some food; the advice of one empty stomach to another isn't to be trusted. Come! you'll feel better for a cup of tea." Then he stopped, and put his veined old hand on her arm: "You haven't the worst trouble in the world," he said; "be sure of that."

Afterwards she wondered what he meant. What trouble could be worse than hers? But he said no more about trouble. He called Pleasant, and he made his two visitors sit down with him; he talked about his bee-hives, and promised to show Pleasant his precious stones, and let her give his shaggy little dog Danny a crust of bread. Then he asked her whom she was named after.

"Why, after mother!" said Pleasant, astonished that he did not know. "Mother's front name is Elizabeth, but father says he named me Pleasant because mother's eyes were pleasant, and her voice was, and her face was, and her—"

"Pleasant, you must not talk so much," Elizabeth protested, much mortified. "My husband is such a kind man, sir, he says things like that," she explained.

But Pleasant, excited by the strangeness of the occasion, could not be restrained; she was bubbling over with information—Captain, and her two broth-

79

ers, and mother's garden, and father's dog Jim, that had a grave in the orchard, and a really marble tombstone that said, "Jim—a good friend." "He died before I was born, so I don't remember him very well," she said; but father had given mother a new dog, named Fanny; and he had given her, Pleasant, a duck, for her own, which hatched chickens. "And their own mother can't make 'em swim!" Pleasant informed her hearer, excitedly. "Father said I mustn't try and teach 'em (though I would just as leave), because it would worry mother. Would it worry you, mother?"

"Pleasant, dear, I think you had better run out and sit in the buggy now—"

"For fear Captain will run away?" suggested Pleasant, eagerly.

"She talks a great deal, sir," Elizabeth apologized. "She's our only little girl, and I'm afraid we spoil her."

Perhaps Dr. Lavendar had gained what he wanted from the child; he made no protest at her dismissal, and she went frolicking out to climb up into the buggy and sit in the sun, chattering to Captain, and weaving three long larch twigs together to make a wreath.

Mrs. Day and the minister went back into the study. Her heart was beginning to beat heavily. She sat down where she could look through the open window and see Pleasant, and the light fell on her pretty, worn face. She was rolling up the corner of her pocket-handkerchief, and then spreading it out on her knee and smoothing it with shaking fingers. She did not once raise her eyes to his face.

"It's this way, sir : I wanted to ask you—I thought

I'd come and ask you, because you married us, and you are a stranger to us (and you are a minister)—oh, I thought I'd ask you what—I must do."

Dr. Lavendar was silent.

"There's something I've got on my mind. It's just killing me. It's something my husband don't know. If he wasn't just the best husband in the world, it wouldn't kill me the way it does. But there never was anybody as good as Peter—no, not even a minister is any better than him. We've been married twelve years, and I ought to know. Well, it ain't only that he's just the kindest man in the world—it's his being so good. He isn't like other men. He don't have the kind of thoughts they do. He don't understand some things—not any more than Pleasant does. Oh, Peter is so good—if he only wasn't so good !"

She was red and then white ; she held her shaking lip between her teeth, and looked out at Pleasant.

" It seemed as if you could help me if I told you ; and yet now it seems as if there wasn't any help anywhere."

" There is help, my friend."

She seemed to grasp at his words.

"Oh, sir, if you'll tell me what to do— Well, it's this : you see, you married Peter and me suddenly ; he didn't really know anything about me ; he fell in love with me, seeing me in a play. Well, before I met Peter—that's what I want to tell you—"

" Do not tell me."

" Don't tell you ?" She looked at him in a bewildering way.

"Is there any reparation to make ? Is there anything to be set right ?"

F   81

"No," she said, with a sob; "oh *no!* nothing can make it right."

"Then it is not necessary for me to know, to advise you. Let us say, for the sake of argument, that it's the worst thing that could be. Now, my dear Mrs. Day, the worst thing that could be differs for every one of us. It might be murder for one person; it might be a lie for another person; it might be the preaching of the gospel for somebody else. But say it's your worst. Do you doubt your husband's forgiveness?"

"I don't think he'd even call it forgiveness," she said, after a pause, twisting and untwisting the corner of her handkerchief with trembling fingers. "Peter just—loves me; that's all. But it would—oh, it would *hurt* Peter so!"

"You have a good husband, I am sure of that," he said, quietly. "And your question, as I understand it, is, shall you tell him some grievous fault, committed before you knew him? I can say at once"—Elizabeth looked ghastly—"that you ought to have told him before you married him."

"So I ought to tell him now?" she said, in a whisper.

"Do you want to tell him?"

"Oh, sometimes it seems as if I would die if I didn't," she said. "It would be such a relief. I think, if he knew it, I could forget it. I lie awake nights, thinking and thinking and thinking how I can tell him, till my mind's sore, it seems to me. I think to myself that I'll tell him as soon as he wakes up." She stopped, and swallowed once or twice, and pressed her lips together as though to force back tears. "And then, again, I feel as though I would die if I told him. Why, Peter thinks I am about perfect, I believe. It sounds foolish to say that, but it's true, sir. It would be like—like I don't know what—like stabbing him. I don't mean he'd be unkind to me, or anything like that. It isn't that that scares me. But it would be like putting a knife into him. But perhaps that's part of my punishment," she ended, wretchedly.

"Mother," Pleasant called from the garden path, "may I go and see the minister's bees?"

Dr. Lavendar went to the window and told her cheerfully that she might. "But you must not touch the hives, remember," he cautioned her.

Then he came and sat down again at his table. He took off his spectacles and put them into a little shabby leather case; then he passed his hand over his eyes once or twice.

"'Part of your punishment.' You would not wish to escape any part of it, of course? There is a great satisfaction in punishment."

A quick understanding came into her face. "I know what you mean. I've thought sometimes I'd like to be a Catholic and have penances; I could beat myself to death, and call it happiness!" she ended, passionately.

"Yes; you must not shirk your punishment," he said, slowly. "But there's one thing we must find out: does your husband deserve any punishment?"

"Peter!" she cried. "Why, he never did anything wrong in his life!"

"Then have you any right to make him share your punishment? You say that if he knew this old sin of yours, you could forget it; but would he forget it? You would pay a great price for forgetfulness, my dear friend, if you brought him into the shadow in which you walk. Have you ever thought you might be selfish in not being willing to bear this weight alone?"

"*What?*" she said, breathlessly—"not tell him?"

"Listen," he said, with a sudden stern dignity; he was the priest, instead of the kindly old man: "you have sinned long ago. I don't know how—I don't want to know. But it is passed, and there is no reparation to make. You have sinned, and suffered for your sin; you have asked your Heavenly Father to forgive you, and He has forgiven you. But still you suffer. Woman, be thankful that you can suffer; the worst trouble in the world is the trouble that does not know God, and so does not suffer. Without such knowledge there is no suffering. The sense of sin in the human soul is the apprehension of Almighty God. Your salvation has drawn nigh unto you! Now take your suffering; bear it, sanctify it, lift it up; let it bring you nearer to your Saviour. But do not, do not, put it on shoulders where it does not belong. Do not stab your husband's heart by weakly, selfishly—*selfishly*, mind you!—telling him of a past with which it is too late now for him to concern himself."

She drew a long breath. "But you don't know what it was. If you knew—"

"It does not matter what the sin was. All that matters is, what your love is."

"But I am afraid—oh, I am afraid that in my heart I don't want to tell him. Oh, I may be deceiving myself if I call it a duty not to tell him!"

"No, you are not deceiving yourself. You don't want to tell him because it is your instinct to spare

him. Perhaps, too, you have the instinct to spare
yourself, in his eyes. But silence does not really
spare you — don't you know that? It only spares
him! Silence is agony to you sometimes. Well,
then, bear the agony for his sake. Don't you love
him enough for that? You talk about penance—my
friend, such silence will be worse than any penance
of the Romish Church!"

She clung to his hands, crying now unrestrainedly.
"And I am not to keep thinking, 'Shall I tell Peter?'
I'm not to keep thinking I'm deceiving him?"

"My child, you are not deceiving him. He thinks
you are a good woman: *you are.* Look back over
these years and see what wonderful things the Lord
hath wrought in you. Go down on your knees and
thank Him for it. Don't deny it; don't be afraid to
own it to yourself—that would be ingratitude to
your Father in heaven. Instead, thank Him that you
are *good!* And now listen: I charge you bear the
burden of silence, because you love your husband,
and he is good."

Elizabeth looked at him, rapt, absorbed. "I am
not to be afraid that it is for my own wicked fear
that I am not telling him? No, it isn't that, it isn't
that! I know it isn't. For his sake—for his sake—"

"Yes, for his sake."

But he looked at her pityingly. Would this comfort of deliberately chosen pain be temporary?
"Try," he said, "and think that you stand between
him and pain; take all the misery yourself; be glad
to take it. Don't let it reach him."

"If I think of it that way," she said, breathlessly,
"I—I can *love* it!"

"Think of it that way always."

He made her sit down again, and went out to find Pleasant, leaving her with the peace of one solemnly elate at the recognition of the cross on which she must agonize for the happiness of some other soul.

" Suppose," said Dr. Lavendar, watching the buggy pulling up the hill—" suppose I hadn't found her a good woman, and a good wife, and a good mother— should I have told her to hold her tongue? Well, I'm thankful it wasn't that kind of a question! Lord, I'm glad Thou hast all us puzzled people in Thy wise keeping. Come, Danny, let's go and see the bees."

MISS MARIA

MISS MARIA

I

MISS MARIA WELWOOD'S house was on Locust Street—the street that climbs the hill, and melts into a country road, and then joins the turnpike over which the stage used to come every day from Mercer. It was such a house as one sees so often in Pennsylvania and Maryland — stone and brick— mostly stone, so that the bricks seemed to be built in in patches, to help out. It stood back from the street, behind a low brick wall that was crumbling here and there where the plaster had fallen out; but the vines heaped on the coping and trailing down almost to the flag-stones of the foot-path outside hid the marks of years and weather, so it never seemed worth while to repair it. In the spring these flag-stones were white with falling blossoms of the plum-trees just inside, and petals from the *Pirus japonica* drifted over and lay among them like little crimson shells ; later in the season Persian lilacs waved their delicate purple plumes over the head of the passer-by, who could see, for the wall was low, a pleasant old garden at one side of the house. To be sure, it held nothing more choice than old-fashioned perennials, that showed their friendly faces year after year — peonies, and yellow iris, and the powdery pink of queen-of-the-meadow — and between them what annuals might sow themselves, with here and there a low bush of old-man, or musk, or clove-pink. The house itself was low and rambling, and much bigger than Miss Welwood needed —her family being herself and a cousin, Rose Knight. A nephew, Charles Welwood, lived with her until he was twenty-four, and, for that matter, considering the number of his visits, continued to live with her, now that he was thirty. But the nominal household was herself and Rose; a "good girl," Old Chester called Rose, sensible, and modest, as a girl should be, and not too pretty, for that inclines to vanity. As for Miss Welwood, she had certainly been pretty when she was young; and now that she was fifty she was like some little ruddy winter apple; there was the touch of frost on her brown hair, but her cheek had a fresh color, and her eyes were bright and smiling. She was little, and had a pretty figure, which she held very erect. "Because," she used to explain, "when I went to Miss Brace's academy, my dear, I was obliged to carry atlases on my head to make me stand straight." Miss Maria would have liked to put atlases on Rose's head; but, alas! Rose did not agree with her; and there it ended, for Miss Maria was one of those people who always want other people to do what they want to do. This characteristic does not belong to the reformer, but it is agreeable to live with. "*Dear* Maria Welwood," Old Chester called her—except Mrs. Barkley, who called her, generally, "a perfect fool." Now Mrs. Barkley loved Miss Welwood, that was why she called her a fool; and, besides, she limited this opinion to Miss

MISS MARIA

Maria's way of allowing herself to be imposed upon. When you come to think of it, there is nothing which makes us so angry at the people we love as their way of letting themselves be imposed upon.

Charles Welwood and his little income of about $300 a year had come to Miss Maria as the legacy of a dying brother, and for twenty-three years she had devoted herself and her pocket-book to him. When Charles was nearly sixteen, Rose, the orphan daughter of a far-away cousin, was also left, as it were, on her door-step—probably on the principle of to him that hath shall be given. "And if you don't call that an imposition!" Mrs. Barkley said. "She's got those two children on her hands, and it will interfere with her chances of marrying—you see if it doesn't!"

Perhaps it did; certainly Miss Maria had not married. There had been a time, when she was about twenty-eight, and Mr. Ezra Barkley, Mrs. Barkley's brother-in-law, came to live in Old Chester, that she may have had hopes; but nothing came of them. Miss Maria began by admiring Mr. Ezra because of his learning; and then his kindness to everything and everybody went to her own kind heart. But, to tell the truth, except for that kindness, which made him excessively polite to her as well as to everybody else, Mr. Ezra did not notice Miss Maria very much. She used to look at the back of his head in church, and listen, awe-struck, to his conversation when she came to tea with Mrs. Barkley; and she was apt to take her afternoon walk—Charles clinging to her hand—down the street by which Mr. Ezra returned from his office. But though Mr. Barkley offered her a hymn-book once or twice, and bowed with great friendliness whenever they met, and politely saw her home, with a lantern, when she spent the evening with his sister-in-law, she could not feel that there was anything significant in his attentions. He offered the same civilities, with the same gentility of manner, to every lady in Old Chester. So Miss Maria hid her little fluttering tenderness in her own heart, where it lay, like a fly in amber, while the placid years came and went. But the memory of the buried hope was like some faint soft fragrance in her life. She never forgot it.

As for her two young people, when they arrived at those years of indiscretion of which matrimony is often the outward and visible sign, propinquity suggested that they might marry; but for once it would appear youth was prudent. Neither displayed any tender symptoms.

Charles was absorbed in making water-color sketches, in the hope that he might one day be an artist, and had no time, he had been heard to say, contemptuously, for sentimentality. As for Rose, she had never "taken to Charles," as Miss Maria used to express it, sadly; besides, all such possibilities ended when Charles, at twenty-four, still dependent on his aunt, save for his $300, married, suddenly, a nice, inefficient sickly girl, without a cent, who promptly presented him with twins.

"And who's going to support 'em?" demanded Mrs. Barkley. "I declare—*twins!*"

"But you can't blame dear Charles for that," Miss Maria protested.

"Not blame Charles? Well, I'd like to know who—" Mrs. Barkley began; but ended by telling

" ' AND WHO'S GOING TO SUPPORT 'EM?' DEMANDED MRS. BARKLEY "

Miss Maria again that she was a perfect fool about
that boy. "You've always spoiled him, and you
always will!"

Miss Welwood had spoiled Charles, according to
Old Chester rules; and yet, he really was the one
child to whom the "spare-the-rod" precept did not
apply—he was naturally good. Unnaturally good
might be a better term. If he had died young (as
Miss Maria always feared he would) he might have
had a memoir written about him, which would have
been in all the Sunday-school libraries; for in those
days the anæmic child was a great part of spiritual
literature. He had a sort of angelic beauty when
he was five or six, with his pink cheeks, his large
blue eyes, and his yellow hair that every afternoon
was curled up into a long, sleek roll called a "roach,"
and tied with a blue ribbon; he looked "good," and
he was fond of hymns, and used to say things about
heaven that brought tears to your eyes. Dr. Lavendar once compared him to little Samuel, and said
he was a "godly child." Afterwards, Dr. Lavendar
may have apologized to Samuel; though Charles
never was a naughty boy. He never robbed birds'
nests, or smoked behind the barn, or played marbles
on Sunday. Perhaps that was why Dr. Lavendar was
apologetic. But be that as it may, he kept on being
good in spite of prophecies that a child who had
never been tied to a bedpost, or sent supperless to
bed, must turn out badly. He was a "good young
man," too; and by-and-by he was a good husband,
and a better—or at least a more extensive—father
every year; for when he was thirty, he and his poor
foolish wife had themselves and five children to
look after. The way in which Charles looked after

93

them was to bring them, whenever things were going badly with him, to visit Miss Maria. But never
mind that : he certainly did do everything a mortal
husband could do for his sickly Edith, and he loved
each of the five babies dearly, and was ready and
willing to love five more, if the Lord sent them to
him—for Charles was a religious man, and believed
that the Lord was responsible for bringing into the
world all these delicate little children, whose father
could not support them. He had also a sincere
affection for his aunt, and meant it in all simplicity
when he told her that it was very sweet to him to
take favors from her hands.

"Why don't you tell him," demanded Mrs. Barkley, when Miss Maria, touched and beaming, repeated
this to her—"why don't you tell Charles Welwood
that it would be very sweet to you to take favors
from his hands?"

The color came into Miss Welwood's face, but she
only said, mildly, "You never did appreciate Charles."

"Oh, I appreciate him," Mrs. Barkley said, grimly.
Mrs. Barkley sat straight up in her chair darning
stockings; she was a little woman, with a thin, mel-
ancholy face, and a very high crown to her head.
Her hair, which was still brown, was parted in the
middle, or a little to one side of the middle, and
brought down over her cheeks in loops and then
twisted up behind her ears. She had very bushy
eyebrows, which twitched when she talked in a way
that, being coupled with a deep and masculine voice,
inspired her listener with a sort of alarmed respect.
"Now, Maria," she went on, "this is the sixth time
he has come to stay with you since he was married;
and those children—"

94

"Bless their little hearts," said Miss Maria, "they are such pretty children!"

"They're well enough. I only hope you won't spoil them as you did their father."

"Well, he is very unselfish, Matty, anyhow," Miss Maria defended him, "and amiable; never a word of complaint! There are not many men who would not rebel at having a sick wife on their hands."

"Maybe their aunts might rebel," Mrs. Barkley said.

"I think it was noble in Charles to marry Edith to take care of her," cried Miss Welwood.

"Then why doesn't he take care of her? And look at all those children; he is perfectly delighted with this last one!"

"Well, I should hope so!" said Miss Maria, with spirit. "Matty, how can you pretend to be so heartless? Would you have a parent indifferent to his offspring?"

"Indifferent?" cried Mrs. Barkley, with a snort. "What do you call bringing five children into the world, just to starve 'em? I call it something worse than indifference."

Miss Welwood held up her hands, horrified.

"My dear Matty, I can't think that is quite delicate."

"If they were kittens, he could drown 'em. As it is, he just gives them to you."

"My *dear* Matty!" said poor Miss Welwood again. She said to herself that some time she would certainly lose her temper with Matilda Barkley.

"There's no use getting into a passion, Maria. I'm only speaking the truth. You know I am always perfectly open with you. You seem to like being imposed upon ; I suppose that's why you are supporting Charles's family—though my opinion is that a man hasn't any business to have a family if he can't support it. He is worse than an infidel—"

" Matty—"

"That's the Bible. I suppose I may quote the Scriptures ?"

Miss Welwood sighed. Mrs. Barkley pushed her spectacles up on the bridge of her nose, and said, "How's Rose ?"

"Why," said Miss Maria, "she's very well, the dear child !"

After that there was peace, for Mrs. Barkley liked Rose as much as she disliked Charles, and she listened with a grim chuckle when Miss Maria told her that Rose had done this or that—put up ten quarts of strawberries, or made over her best dress so that it would do for another season. "She won't let me buy her a new one," said Miss Maria, beaming ; "such an obstinate child !"

"Pity Charles hasn't a little of her obstinacy," Mrs. Barkley retorted. At which the color came into Miss Maria's face; but she only said it was time for her to go home.

Afterwards she felt she had been severe with Matty ; and when she said her prayers that night, she asked for grace to control her temper.

II

Mr. Ezra Barkley was a fat, placid man, rather bald, with that look of aged youth which is so confusing. He might have been fifty or thirty with equal probability; in point of fact, he was nearly fifty. He was a good deal of a dandy; and though not exactly wordly, was supposed to have rationalistic tendencies—believing, it was said, that the world had been created in six periods of time instead of six days. Thus the awful interest of the freethinker was attached to him, and it was known that Mrs. Barkley made his conversion a subject of special prayer.

Perhaps Miss Welwood prayed for him too; but she never said so.

Mr. Barkley's deplorable rationalism was the outcome, his sister-in-law thought, of his learning, and she was apt to remind him, in a sad bass, that the wisdom of men was foolishness with their Creator. His wisdom, it must be admitted, was almost entirely confined to statistics; but that did not shake Old Chester's belief that he was a learned man. Beside his knowledge, he was further distinguished by his genius for listening. Now there are few things that are more endearing than the grace of listening with attention; indeed, it is more than endearing, it is impressive—for no one knows what wisdom lies concealed in silence!

As for Ezra Barkley, he listened to everybody, and never interrupted; when he did speak, it was generally to give some small, quite irrelevant piece of information of a statistical nature; but he expressed no opinions of his own. This had led his sister-in-law, in the course of years, to the conclusion that he had no opinions. But that was her mistake.

"What do you suppose," Mrs. Barkley demanded, the evening of the day that she had been so candid with Miss Maria — "what do you suppose, Ezra?

That boy Charles has put every cent of his money into some patent oil-can ! I only hope he won't induce Maria to put hers into it. I know she's giving him money to live on now—he hasn't anything to do. How different he is from Rose ! She is so sensible and industrious."

Mr. Ezra Barkley crossed his legs, as one who would assent, comfortably.

"Well, Maria said that Charles said it troubled him dreadfully to be dependent on her even for a little while ; and then, if you please, she said that nobody was 'more sensitive in such things than Charles was.' I told her I was glad to hear it—very glad indeed to hear it !" said Mrs. Barkley, in a dreadful bass.

Ezra rose and went over to a large wicker cage which held some of his pets ; he opened the door and took out two little green paroquets, and balancing one on each forefinger, he came back to his armchair. He expressed no opinion concerning Charles's dependence upon his aunt ; he seemed absorbed in scratching the head of one of the little parrots, which uttered small, shrill cries of approval. But he was listening.

"And then what do you suppose she said ? She said that it was very difficult for the artistic temperament to consider earning money. I just said, 'Maria Welwood, the artistic temperament is another name for dishonesty !' (You know, Ezra, I make a point of being perfectly open with Maria.) 'There is too much of this "genius" that doesn't pay its debts, or lets its female relations support it,' I said. And just think of all those children, Ezra !"

Ezra shook his head in melancholy assent. "Are

you aware," he said, "that the word lullaby—your reference to Charles's family suggests the fact—the word *lullaby* is thought to be derived from the name of Adam's first wife—Lili Abi? She was said to be queen of the succubæ — devils who had taken the female form."

"I told her," Mrs. Barkley continued, as though Mr. Ezra had not spoken, "I just wished Charles had half the spirit Rose has!"

Ezra watched the paroquets climbing up his leg, heels over head, so to speak, for the little creatures, grasping at his trousers with beak and claw, lifted themselves up and up until they gained his welcoming hand and were fed with small crumbs of sugar.

"Rose is a superior girl, Ezra," Mrs. Barkley announced, in the tone of one who dares a contradiction. Mr. Barkley scratched one of the little green heads too hard, and the bird bit at him angrily. "But she is an expense to Maria," Mrs. Barkley went on, "and I wish—I wish she had a home of her own, Ezra."

"She converses somewhat rapidly," observed Mr. Ezra ; "at times I find it difficult to—"

"To follow her? Oh, well, one would get used to that."

"—to apprehend her. Nevertheless, she is a very pleasing young lady." With this Mr. Ezra Barkley put the parrots back in their cage. Now Mr. Barkley could put two and two together as well as anybody else : *Rose was a superior girl ; he was an unmarried man.* He had listened to Mrs. Barkley too many years to doubt either of these propositions—or the obvious deduction ; but he still continued to listen, and stroke his parrots' heads, and look blind.

On this particular evening, however, he was really interested in what his sister-in-law said of Miss Welwood and Charles. The fact was, Ezra Barkley knew that Miss Maria believed in that oil-can to such an extent that she wanted to put every bit of her money into her nephew's hands, that he might invest it for her and they might both grow rich together. She had met him only the day before, and had told him of Charles's project. She was to contribute the money to start the enterprise, she said, and Charles was to contribute time, and they were to divide the profits. That she was getting the best of the bargain she never doubted.

"Charles says he is going to divide all the profit with me," she said; "but of course I sha'n't allow that! At least I'll leave it all back again to those precious children."

"But suppose he does not acquire this, as you might say, fortune?" Mr. Barkley inquired. "If you will permit me to say so, Miss Maria, I cannot but feel—ah—anxious."

But Miss Welwood's confidence could not be shaken. "If there was any doubt about it, my darling boy wouldn't want me to invest my money in it, you know."

Mr. Ezra said nothing, and Miss Maria felt she had silenced him by her logic, but she hoped she had not hurt his feelings. He certainly did not look wounded; he bowed politely, and asked her if she had any idea how many eggs there were in a shad roe. She said, with immediate interest, she supposed quite a number—over two hundred, perhaps; and when Mr. Barkley gave what he called the "approximate number," she threw up her hands in the greatest astonishment, and said : " Dear me ! You don't say so ! You have so much information, Mr. Ezra."

Later in the evening Miss Maria repeated what she had learned concerning shad roe to Rose, and added that it was very improving to talk with Mr. Barkley.

" I'm sure it must be," Rose said, gravely, " but it's very serious to think of eating so many little fish at a time."

Miss Welwood looked at her young cousin side- wise ; it seemed to her Rose was making fun of Mr. Barkley.

" Well, there is nobody so kind as Mr. Ezra, any- how," she said, with spirit ; " and I only wish I knew half as much as he does !" And then Miss Maria be- gan to talk about the oil-can and her future wealth —(" for I won't have Ezra laughed at," she said to herself).

As for the oil-can, Miss Welwood had made up her mind to put almost half of her little capital into Charles's hands. The fact was, her nephew's enthu- siasm about the oil-can was as sincerely hopeful as though he had been the inventor, instead of merely the promoter.

" Why," he said, his big visionary blue eyes shining with excitement, " there is absolutely no doubt. It can't fail. It simply *can't*. Why, just see : the country population of the United States is, well, say so much : now supposing there are nine souls to a family — well, say ten — it's easier to divide by ten, and it's better to be on the safe side ; though, of course, there are a great many families where there are only five — or even two, like you and Rose. But it's more conservative to say ten souls to a fam-

ily : you see at once how many families there
are ?"

"And every family must have an oil-can ?" cried
Miss Maria.

"Ah ! but wait," Charles said. " That's the country population. Now the number of villages in the
United States where they don't have gas— You see
what I am trying to get at ?"

" Why, of course !" his aunt said. " Why, here is
Old Chester, for instance ; I'm sure Matty would
take two. We must give one to Dr. Lavendar,
Charles ; he mustn't buy it."

Charles, proceeding with his calculation, did not
stop to think of the profit on Mrs. Barkley's purchase.
" We can reckon certainly on such and such a number to be sold in small villages, to say nothing of the
poor people in cities."

" Can't we have some cheaper for the poor ?" Miss
Maria asked, sympathetically.

But Charles would not stop to answer questions.
"You see," he said, "it's perfectly easy to figure the
profits !"

Edith was so excited that she began to laugh
hysterically, and Miss Maria caught up the youngest
from the floor, and cuddled him, and kissed him, and
bade him go to sleep :

> "And when you awake,
> You shall have a cake,
> And a coach and six little horses !"

sung Miss Maria, " because we are all going to be rich,
you precious little Theodore !" And the fifth, being so
named because he was, Charles said, "a gift from God,"
cooed and gurgled, and everybody was very happy.

Except Rose. Rose had shown no inclination to trust the oil-can; not because she had any superior wisdom, but just because Charles advocated it.

"But never mind, my darling child," Miss Maria said; "when my profit comes in—Charles says it will be certainly ten times what I invest—I will give half of it to you!"

"Oh, Rose don't believe in any of my projects," Charles said, in a wounded voice. "Rose thinks, Edith, that we ought to stay in the tavern, instead of visiting Aunt Maria."

"Oh, now, my dear Charles," protested poor Miss Welwood, putting the gift of God down on the floor —"my dear children, please—"

"Well, Charles, I must say," Rose retorted, "I don't see how you can be under such obligations to Cousin Maria."

"Oh, my *dear* Rose," sighed Miss Welwood, "please—"

Edith, as usual, began to weep. "Charlie always paints a picture for aunty when we've been making her a visit," she defended her husband.

"It is very sweet to me to owe everything to aunty," Charles said, stung and helpless. "Where one loves, one can accept."

"Well, you must love a good deal," Rose flung out.

"I do," Charles declared. "And just let me say, Rose, that it is the little nature that is afraid of an obligation. Aunt Maria has made me what I am ; I admit it—I am proud to admit it. And when the money comes in, it shall all be hers."

"Oh, but Charlie," Edith whimpered, "sha'n't we have a little ?"

At which there were tears and protests and explanations, and Rose went whirling out of the room, angry and ashamed, her young heart bursting with the sense of her own dependence.

III

It was in February that these dreams of affluence first began to dazzle Miss Maria's eyes; and they grew more dazzling as the spring went on. Charles had gone back to Mercer, so that he might be "on the spot," to look after the family interests, and Edith had been sent South to escape the March winds. As Charles had pointed out, the expense of her journey would be covered ten times over when the first dividend came in. When Miss Maria repeated this to Rose, the girl dropped down upon her knees beside the little, trim, upright figure, and hugged her.

"And in the mean time you pay her expenses?" she said.

"That has nothing to do with it," said Miss Maria, affronted.

"It strikes me that it has a great deal to do with it," Rose retorted. "Cousin Maria, what should you do if—if the oil-can exploded?"

"Oh, it is to be very strong," Miss Welwood explained.

And then Rose explained: "I meant if it failed, dear?"

"Oh, Charles says it can't fail!" Miss Maria declared, cheerfully. "Charles says it's absolutely sure."

"But if — *if?*" Rose persisted, patting Miss Maria's hand, and putting it up against her cheek.

"Nonsense!" cried the other, and then bade Rose move back a little from the fire. "It's bad for your complexion to scorch your cheeks, my dear. When I was young, we were never allowed to come nearer the fire than the outside edge of the hearth-rug."

"Is that the reason your complexion is so pretty?" said Rose.

And Miss Maria said "Nonsense!" again, and blushed, and said that once Mr. Ezra Barkley had paid her a compliment on her color. "He was re-marking upon the number of tons of roses used every year, and he said something about my cheeks. Of course he said it in a very polite and genteel way."

"Why, Cousin Maria!" cried Rose. "Well! When is it to be?"

"Fie, fie!" protested Miss Maria. "At Miss Brace's, Rose, we were always told that jests upon the affections were indelicate. Not that you meant it so, my darling, of course."

"The question is, what does Mr. Ezra mean?" said Rose. "I shall certainly ask him his intentions."

Miss Welwood gasped with dismay. "Miss Brace used to say that any allusion to matters of the heart was 'exceedingly unladylike,'" she declared; but she half sighed. "He's always very kind, Rose, but he is too superior for—for such things. I think learned men are apt to be."

It seemed as though her fresh face fell into lines of age, and Rose, looking at her, felt a sudden pang of pity. "Let's talk about the oil-can," she said; and Miss Welwood was ready and eager for the sub-ject.

Indeed, as the spring went, Miss Welwood talked of little else. Her confidence grew with the season ; in May she was eager to give Charles still another thousand dollars for the enterprise, which "needed pushing," the profits being, Charles said, merely a matter of proportion.

"The more you push, the more you'll get," he said. "It's self-evident."

"Why, *of course !*" said his aunt. "I think, Charles, I'll put in two thousand instead of one ; it seems foolish to simply cut off future profits because of a little present inconvenience."

"That's perfectly true," he told her, admiringly, "but there are very few women who would have the business keenness to see it. Still, dear, you must be your own judge. I consider you quite as good a judge in business matters as I am, and I wouldn't urge you for the world."

"Do you hear that, Rose?" cried Miss Maria. "Charles says he considers me as good a judge in business matters as he is (of course I'm not) ; but what do you think of that?"

"I think that Charles is quite right," Rose said, dryly.

However, the two thousand dollars were given, and still another two. By this time more than three-quarters of Miss Maria's eggs were in one basket —from which, indeed, no chickens had yet been hatched; hence the "present inconvenience" became very obvious, not only to Miss Maria and Rose, but to Mrs. Barkley—and consequently to Mr. Ezra, who played with the paroquets, and listened, and at last gratified Mrs. Barkley by nodding silently when she observed that if Rose were married, things would be easier for Maria.

MISS MARIA

They were sitting in the grape-arbor, with a little table between them; it was just after dinner on Sunday, and, as was Mrs. Barkley's habit when the weather permitted, the coffee had been brought out to this shady place, and now it was being stirred and sipped, and the sermon discussed. A little later, when the sun should burn through the leaves and look in at the western end of the arbor, Mrs. Barkley would grow drowsy, and pick up her religious paper, and go off to take a nap; but just now she was alert. She had said what she thought of Dr. Lavendar's sermon, and added, significantly, that though he was growing old he was remarkably edifying in matters of doctrine. Then she said that she declared it was too bad, Maria Welwood hadn't got a new bonnet yet!

"I don't know where this is going to end," said Mrs. Barkley. "Maria is really pinched for money. Rose is a good, economical girl, but she does eat, and she has to have clothes." Mrs. Barkley's eyebrows twitched, and she looked at her brother-in-law with anxiety.

Ezra took off his glasses and examined them; then he rubbed the bridge of his nose thoughtfully. "Were you aware, Matilda, that glass was discovered by the accident of—"

"No, I wasn't. Now, Ezra, I'm always perfectly open with you, so I'm going to give you some advice. I never shrink from giving advice. Some people do. I once heard Dr. Lavendar with my own ears say he did not like to advise people. He said he always 'hoped they would do the other thing'—which was very foolish in him, for why shouldn't he advise the other thing, to begin with? However, I only wanted to say that you are really getting on in years yourself; and—and Rose Knight is certainly a superior girl. A very superior girl, Ezra!"

Ezra breathed on his glasses and polished them with his handkerchief, and then held them up to see if they were bright.

"She's twenty-five. I call that just the right age for a man of fifty, Ezra; and she's a good, capable girl, and she has about as much religion as you like. (Dear me, Ezra—you know my prayer for you in that regard?)"

Ezra coughed.

"I mean, she isn't like Grace Smith, running to church all the time, when she ought to be at home looking after things."

"You may be interested to know," said Mr. Ezra, mildly, "that the scientific researches of Bishop Colenso prove that the children of Israel could not have—"

"Ezra!" said Mrs. Barkley, with proper indignation, "not in my presence, if you please! *I* avoid 'profane and vain babblings, and oppositions of science *falsely so called!*' (You'll find that somewhere in 1st Timothy, Ezra; I advise you to look it up.) But to go back to Rose: Maria has brought her up to have the greatest respect for you; I've heard her myself tell Rose that your conversation was most improving."

Mr. Ezra was plainly gratified, though he pooh-poohed the compliment. "I fear that I can scarcely hope that my conversation would be of interest to so bright a young lady as Miss Rose."

"Fiddlesticks," said Mrs. Barkley. "Of course it is. What you said at breakfast to-day about chairs being used in Egypt 3300 years before Christ would interest any young person who is quick to learn, as Rose is. No, Ezra ; Rose is all I could expect to find in any girl out of our own family. And if she were married, Maria could live with her—at least until she gets back that oil-can money that that Charles has stolen! I call it stolen. I told Rose so frankly. I'm perfectly open with Rose about Charles."

Mr. Ezra recalled, silently, the reply that he had heard Miss Rose make to this remark—"As for getting back the money for the oil-can, I'm afraid she *can't!*" And then Rose had flung up her head and laughed; and Mr. Ezra believed that there was a joke somewhere. But just now his heart was heavy at the thought of Miss Maria's troubles.

"Do you apprehend," he said, laboriously, "that Miss Welwood's circumstances are really, as you might say, straitened?"

"I *know* they are!" his sister-in-law said, her eyebrows twitching. "Ezra, she's sent away Jane. You know Jane's been with them since—why, it's seventeen years if it's a day!—and Maria and Rose (good, capable girl!) do all the work. Maria looks worn out," said Mrs. Barkley, nearly crying, "and it's all that Charles! Somebody ought to do something. Of course we can't give Maria money ; she wouldn't take anybody else's money, though she thinks it's all right for that boy Charles to take hers. But then she likes to be imposed upon. Oh dear ! Well, she is a perfect fool. I've told her so. Well, Ezra, I'm going up-stairs to lie down. But just remember, Rose is a superior girl. It's queer no man has had sense enough to take her. But men haven't any sense !" ended Mrs. Barkley, with a snort.

As for Ezra, he went and got his cat, and settled

back in his chair, rubbing Pussy's ears with an absent hand, and reflecting. It was warm and still in the arbor; a honeysuckle swaying in some warm, wandering breath of wind threw a lacing shadow over the pool of sunshine that, at the western end, began to widen over the uneven flags.

"Well," said Ezra Barkley to himself, "it is certainly very distressing—very distressing;" and after a while he added that it certainly would be very pleasing to have an agreeable young person in the house. And so Miss Maria had brought her up to have a great respect for him? The thought increased his respect for Miss Maria. It occurred to him that if Rose liked "facts," he could certainly interest her. He decided to make researches in the line of ladies' clothing; he would tell her when gloves were introduced into England; he would divert her with the height of the head-dress in the fifteenth century. Yes, it would be very agreeable indeed to have a bright young creature like Rose eager to listen to his facts. Poor Miss Maria! she was anxious, no doubt, and was worrying over money matters. "Ladies ought not to have such anxieties," thought Mr. Ezra. "Poor lady! Well—it was very hard. Yes; something must be done—something must be done." His eyes narrowed with thought, and he sighed once or twice. He scratched the cat under her chin, which caused her to shut her eyes and wave her tail and purr loudly. The pool of sunshine widened to his feet; the arbor was hot and still, and the heavy fragrance of the tall white lilies crept like some tangible sweetness into the shadows under the grape leaves. Mr. Ezra nodded a little; his hand sunk into the soft warm fur, and he and the kitten slept soundly.

MISS MARIA

The summer passed, and still Miss Maria did not get a new bonnet. Indeed, the time of new bonnets seemed postponed and postponed. However, four of Charles's children came to pay her a visit, as, in the business anxiety of the last month, Charles had felt unequal to the care of them ; and Edith was preparing for another gift from God, and so really could not ("and should not," Miss Maria said) have the burden of her entire household on her shoulders. It was while they were with her that the oil-can exploded, to use Rose's metaphor.

When their father's letter came bringing news of the catastrophe, there came also a little package ("Charles never forgets these darling children !" said Miss Maria)—a doll for small Edith, a book for one boy, a transparent slate for the other, a rattle for Theodore. The distribution of these gifts delayed the reading of the letter with its big engraved heading, " The Universal Oil-Can Co." The children had been painting : it was a rainy afternoon, and Miss Maria had rummaged in the garret among the possessions of her youth, and brought down her old paint-box, and the four little people had been very happy over it. Dear me ! don't we all know those old paint-boxes of our maiden aunts—with cakes of dried and flaked water-colors, rubbed down, some of them, sidewise, or with holes worn through them by pointed feminine brushes—and the saucers, with their cracked films of crimson lake or gamboge still clinging to them !

" I used to paint when I was a young lady," Miss

Maria said ; "I studied the Berthollet method at Miss Brace's. Dear me ! I'm afraid I've forgotten a great many things we learned at Miss Brace's. We used to have a class in making alum baskets, and we painted on velvet. It was certainly very elegant. I don't believe there are such schools nowadays. My paints are nearly worn out, but these precious children won't mind that—will you, my darlings?"

The children did not mind in the least ; so they were all put down around the dining-room table, each one with an old magazine full of wood-cuts, which gave great choice as to the subject to be colored. They were hard at work when Charles's letter and the package of presents arrived. At the mention of presents the four artists, greatly excited, slipped from their chairs, leaving the pictures of "Little Dorrit" half finished, and their brushes standing in dauby tumblers of colored water. Rose, on her knees among them, looked at the dolly's shoes, and drew on the transparent slate, and promised to read the book aloud, all the while raging at the tender father who bought presents out of Miss Maria's money (and yet he was a tender father—nobody could possibly deny that). Miss Maria, smiling at the children's joy, and cuddling Theodore, read the letter with a startled look that changed into absolute bewilderment : The enterprise had failed ; Charles was bankrupt ; the money was lost—her money (and Charles's time as well). She read with Theodore clinging about her neck, and had to stop to kiss him, and listen to his rattle, and cuddle him, yet her bewildered eye followed Charles's bold handwriting with dreadful clearness.

"Rose," she said tremulously, " I'm afraid it's bad news, my dear ; I'm afraid it's a little serious."

Of course then it had to be read aloud to Rose. This was a terrible task—Rose kneeling on the hearth-rug, playing with Charles's children, and saying not one word; but Miss Maria saw the girl's cheek grow rigid over her set teeth, and little Edith shrunk away from her, frightened at the anger in her eyes.

"Yes, it is a little serious," Rose said, grimly. The children, squabbling joyously over their possessions, felt the sudden cloud, and looked up, wondering.

"Of course it's serious; but never mind, my dear," Miss Maria said; "we'll get along." Then, her hands shaking, she opened the letter again and tried to take in the facts: an infringement; a miscalculation as to the amount of alloy in the metal, necessitating a much higher price than had been reckoned; the plant now almost worthless; unfortunate litigation necessary. Possibly, only possibly— "but we must leave no stone unturned," Charles said, courageously —possibly a little more money might set the thing on its feet. ("But I *haven't* any more," said Miss Maria to herself.) However, that it was the Lord's doing Charles had no doubt. "Dear boy! what a lesson he is to me!" said Miss Maria, her eyes full of tears. "What should I do if he were rebellious, or did not put his trust in his Heavenly Father?" The submission in her face silenced Rose's bitter tongue. The girl squeezed her hands together, and did not open her lips.

"He bears it so beautifully," said Miss Maria, wiping her eyes. "Did you notice, Rose, on the third page, where he says—let me see, here it is— 'but we know the Lord will provide'? Dear, precious boy! What an example he is!"

"What kind of an example?" Rose said, curtly; and then burst out crying, and knelt down at Miss Maria's side, and put her arms around her waist, and asked to be forgiven. "*You're* an example! I wish I were a quarter as good."

As for Miss Maria, she was afraid she had been harsh, and kissed Rose's brown head, and said: "Come, come! Never mind; it will all be right!"

But Rose could not hold her tongue.

"Charles meant well, I suppose, Cousin Maria; but it isn't enough in this world just to mean well. I hate him! How could he let you suffer?"

And then Miss Maria had to scold her again, and then apologize again, and then bid her cheer up and look after those precious children. After that she went up-stairs to her bedroom, leaving the children to Rose and their toys. She wanted to be alone and get her breath. It was growing dusk, and the vines grew so close about the windows, drooping even in a green fringe from the lintels, that the room was dark —too dark to read again the bleak facts of Charles's letter, or the words of sacred comfort that she had known and lived on these many years—long enough before Mr. Charles Welwood had adopted them as his own.

"I haven't any more money; and what are we go- ing to do?" she said to herself, in despair. And then she remembered what her nephew had said. "Yes, He *will* provide; these darling children are His," said Miss Maria, and got up in the dark- ness, and knelt down beside her big four-poster, and hid her face on the soft, lavender-scented pillow. When she got up—rather stiffly, for she had knelt there a long time—she wiped her eyes, and went smiling down-stairs to the children and Rose.

"My darling Rose," she said, "of course it's unfortunate. But it isn't the worst thing in the world. Suppose some of you were dangerously sick! Would I think of mere money then? No, indeed! We'll get along nicely; and—and we mustn't let Charles know how serious it is; he would feel so badly. Besides, it isn't so very bad, so never mind! Now don't let's talk about it any more. These precious children must have their supper and play with these nice presents their dear father has sent them, and have a happy time. When they've gone to bed, we'll talk it all over."

V

At first Miss Maria shut the appalling fact that she was penniless in upon herself and Rose. Charles came flying down to Old Chester to explain and to protest at fate. He made no excuses; why should he? He, too, had lost everything he possessed, although a new baby came just at that moment to comfort him—a new baby that was to be called Maria. He had lost all he had in the world, so he certainly was not to be blamed, he told his Edith; besides, as she would remember, he had distinctly said he would not urge his aunt Maria to invest. "It was her own judgment, you know, Edith," said Charles; "I really can't feel myself responsible."

Charles was in hopes of getting a place as a clerk in a railroad office. But before going to work he came (on borrowed money) to condole with his aunt and to advise. He thought it would be well, he said, for her to mortgage her house and invest the money, living on the interest, less the interest on the mortgage.

"I'm sure I could get ten per cent. for you on some perfectly conservative stock," he said.

"But mightn't there be a *little* risk, dear Charles?" Miss Maria objected, mildly. "Not that I don't trust your judgment absolutely," she added, quickly, for she thought he looked hurt.

"But what are you going to live on?" Charles faltered, his blue eyes staring at her in dismay; "what are you going to do?"

Alas! how many times had Miss Welwood asked herself that very question, her gentle heart sinking lower and lower at the blank reply of silence in her own mind. She did not consult any one, but she spent a good deal of time on her knees beside her high bedstead; and of late she thought a glimmer of light had fallen on the subject.

"You've got to have something to live on," Charles repeated, in a bewildered way.

"Well, I have an idea," she said. "No, I am not going to tell you; it shall be a surprise. But I'm sure it's going to be a good thing."

She had told Rose her "idea"; she had to tell her, for the girl had been in a frenzy of anxiety to do something; "anything," Rose said, and meant it—for she had a very determined plan of going to Mercer, to get a place in a shop. "There's nothing in Old Chester for a girl to do," Rose said, impatient, and loving, and raging at poor well-meaning Charles.

It was to prevent this Mercer project that Miss Maria confided her idea. "For you can help me, my

darling," she told the girl ; " indeed, I couldn't do it
without you—you are so much fresher in some of the
things than I am. For instance, Rose, what is the
length of the Amazon River ? I'm ashamed to
say I've forgotten." And then she explained her
plan.

Miss Maria had hoped, at first, to keep the knowledge of the catastrophe to herself, thinking in some
irrational, tender, feminine way that if she gave no
reason for her project of self-support, Charles would
not be connected with it, and so would not be
blamed. But of course the disaster had to be known.
By its very nature an oil-can does not explode in the
dark. In a week Old Chester knew that Miss Maria
Welwood had lost almost all her money.

"And what's she going to live on ?" Old Chester
said, with a gasp of dismay. "What on earth is she
going to live on ! What is she going to do ?"

It was poor Miss Maria's question over again :
" *What am I going to do to earn my living ?*" Now
this question, asked by the suddenly impecunious,
middle-aged, unmarried woman, is ghastly ; it was
especially so in a place like Old Chester, where
the demand for women in the industries was unknown. It is a wretched enough question even in
the great busy world, where there is so much to be
done, but where, alas ! this frightened feminine voice
is lifted up in such a gathering chorus. No one can
quite understand the misery, the sick hopelessness of
the inquiry but the woman herself. She begins by
reckoning up her abilities : She can sew ; yes, but
who wants her sewing ? Nobody ! She can keep
house, in a small way ; yes, but for one such position a hundred applicants are already entreating—

younger, cleverer, better-looking, perhaps. Nursing; yes, in the tender, ignorant, old-fashioned way. But see the crowd of women educated in the science and business of caring for the sick : who will take her, when a dozen trained nurses are ready at every doctor's elbow ? Teaching ? Yes ; but come now, can you or I, at fifty, remember the multiplication table ? And contrast the curriculum of the private school to-day with that which prevailed fifty or sixty years ago ! No ; we middle-aged folk have the education of life, truly ; we know the multiplication table of anxieties and sorrows, the subtraction table of loss, the division table of responsibility. Deportment and religion we might, perhaps, impart ; but who is ready, at a moment's notice, to instruct eager and irreverent youth in—dear me ! what does not youth study nowadays ? Yet it was to teaching that Miss Maria Welwood looked to provide bread for herself, and bread and butter for Rose, and bread and butter and jam for Charles's children.

"There's nothing else I can do, Matty," she pleaded to Mrs. Barkley, who sat snorting with anger and misery.

"Maria," said Mrs. Barkley, her eyebrows twitching violently, "you are a perfect fool !"

Miss Welwood had sought to soften the blow which she knew the knowledge of her poverty would be to Mrs. Barkley by bringing a little present with her. It was no more than a slipper-bag, which, before this grim fact of poverty had taken possession of her thoughts, she had made for her friend ; since then she had been so anxious and confused she had forgotten to present it.

"I promised it to you a month ago," she said, "and

I am ashamed to say I forgot to bring it over,
Matty; but here it is now."

"You needn't apologize," said Mrs. Barkley. "I've
lived all my life without a slipper-bag; I guess a
week or two more won't hurt me. Besides, I don't
wear slippers. Still, I'm obliged to you."

"I've had so much on my mind," said Miss Maria,
nervously; and then confessed.

Poor Mrs. Barkley! She was so angry and so
wretched that, for once, she could not speak; so
Miss Welwood got in her explanations and intentions almost without interruption. She and Rose
were going to support themselves by teaching.
Then it was that Mrs. Barkley called her a fool.

"In the first place, all the children go to Miss
Bailey's, or else to the public school," she said, with
two little hot tears trickling down her nose. "I
wish Charles Welwood had to go out and break
stones! But you'll see that he has his trips South,
and all his children dressed in—in gold," said Mrs.
Barkley, in a flight of angry and terrified fancy, "but
you, you poor, dear Maria—" and then Mrs. Barkley
snorted, and wiped her eyes on the slipper-bag,
and observed that, for her part, she never could
waste her time making things like that! Miss Maria
came and put her arms about her neck and kissed
her.

"Oh, Matty," she said, "what should I do without
you? I do thank my Heavenly Father that I've got
such a friend!"

"Well, then," retorted Mrs. Barkley, "be guided
by me. Come and live here. It will be a blessing
to me. The greatest blessing. Maria, I shall think
it all providential if you'll only come."

"Matty," said the other, the tears running over her cheeks, "it's worth while to be poor! But I couldn't come here; no, dear Matty, no; you must not urge it. As for Miss Bailey, I wouldn't interfere for the world; I don't mean a child's school. I mean an academy for young ladies. You know Mrs. Dale had to send Ellen away to boarding-school; and Mrs. Wright told me herself once that it was a great expense to her to have to educate Lydia away from home, and she didn't know how she would manage with Mary and Agnes; and then the new people have girls, the rich Smiths have two; and Rachel King would send Anna, I know."

"Did you mean to have a boarding-school?" Mrs. Barkley demanded.

"I mean an academy, dear Matty, on the lines of Miss Brace's; of course it never could be so fine, but I'll do my best. The young ladies may board, or they may return to their families at night, if their parents prefer." And then Miss Maria produced her trump card: "In fact, Matty, my dear, I have arranged an advertisement of the school, and it is to appear in the *Globe* next Saturday. This is a proof. (The gentleman to whom I gave my notice called it a 'proof'.)" She fumbled in a reticule at her side—a black bag with a band of flexible bead embroidery representing flowers and blue stars—and produced the notice; the bit of paper was flimsy and inky, and it had several typographical errors, but it displayed the advertisement, enclosed in a black border of inverted urns, which, in an upright position, formed the usual frame for the funeral notices in the *Globe:*

MISS MARIA

"You know, Matty," Miss Maria said, eagerly,
"we had all those things at Miss Brace's. Dear
me! can't you just see Miss Brace when she opened
the classes in September, with those white curls and
her turban! Oh, my gracious, how we girls used to
shiver when she pointed her forefinger at us! I
sha'n't do that, anyhow."

"Nobody would shiver if you did," Mrs. Barkley
assured her. "Miss Brace was very genteel and dig-
nified; but if you think, Maria Welwood, that *you*—"

"Oh," Miss Maria said, with eager humility, "of
course not! but I've got my notes, and I'm going
to say just the same things. I was looking over her
remarks on art this morning—I took 'em down in
my commonplace-book—and I've committed 'em to
memory : ' *The making of wax flowers is an art most
suitable for young ladies ; frost and snow may reign
around us, and nip the tender blossoms in our gardens,
but our homes may still be made elegant by delightful
representations of Flora's children.*' We began with

the pomegranate flower," Miss Welwood ended, with a happy sigh of memory.

"Well," Mrs. Barkley said, morosely, " I don't be-lieve anybody would pay twenty-five cents to learn how to make a pomegranate flower, nowadays; *I* wouldn't. Anyhow, I don't believe you remember it, Maria. I tell you, the only thing for you to do is to come here. Now, Maria—I—I—wish you would," said Mrs. Barkley, with a sob.

But Miss Welwood only patted the hard old hand, and said, cheerfully: "Of course I shall have to brush up a little. I wasn't quite sure about the alum baskets, but I tried one to-day, and it came out pretty well. History is the only thing I'm ner-vous about, but Rose is pretty fresh in that. As for arithmetic, of course I'll have all the answers in the book, so I can tell when the sums are not right."

"Well—" began Mrs. Barkley, slowly, and then burst out: "Suppose Rose were to get married? You couldn't get along by yourself, so what's the use of beginning?"

"Rose get married?" said Miss Maria. "Well—I don't see any prospect just now; not but what any gentleman might be glad to have her."

" If she did, you'd go and live with her," said Mrs. Barkley, decidedly, "so why not both of you come here until then?"

"I wouldn't think of living with her," cried Miss Maria, with spirit; "no, indeed! If my darling Rose gets married, and leaves the academy, I'll—I'll just get something else to do. Or maybe by that time I'll have brushed up so I can keep along by myself. But no young gentleman is waiting on

Rose. Why, there aren't any young gentlemen in Old Chester !"

Mrs. Barkley took off her spectacles, and looked at Miss Maria sidewise.

"Suppose Ezra took a fancy to Rose ?'

"To—*Rose ?*" Miss Welwood looked at her open-mouthed.

"Yes, Rose," Miss Barkley repeated, with a snap. "That's what I said."

"Rose !" Miss Maria faltered. And then she said, with a certain sharpness, "He's twenty-five years older than Rose."

"Well, well," Mrs. Barkley interrupted, crossly, " I only said '*suppose.*'"

Miss Maria, with the color hot in her face, said again something of age and youth ; " and, anyhow, they never, either of them, thought of such a thing !"

"Well," said Mrs. Barkley, " very likely I was mistaken. I was only supposing, anyway. But there's another thing (somebody's got to talk sense to you !) —I don't believe you'd get pupils enough to pay for your shoestrings. Miss Brace was very superior, of course, but schools are very different now—I've been told."

"True," Miss Welwood admitted; " too true ; and it is high time that things should improve. If I may be the humble instrument in educating young women as we were educated, Matty, to respect their parents, and honor their God, and learn how to walk across a room properly, and remember dates—(Do you recollect, ' Now Semiramis, Beautiful Sinner '— that stood for 1050 B.C., you know—N.S.B.S. Think how I've remembered that out of Miss Brace's old chronology)—if I can teach them these things, I shall feel that the Lord had a purpose in taking away my money."

"The Lord," cried Mrs. Barkley, angrily; "don't put it on the *Lord's* shoulders!"

Afterwards, when she repeated this conversation to her brother-in-law, Mrs. Barkley added that it was bad enough to think that the Lord was responsible for creating "that Charles!—though maybe He isn't," said Mrs. Barkley, in a deep bass; "maybe its Somebody Else!" Which bold theology was quite startling, even to a man who had gone so far towards infidelity as to say that the size of a whale's throat would have precluded the passage of a man of average size—"And we are not told in Holy Writ that Jonah was a dwarf," Mr. Ezra had said, in one of those rationalistic flights which so shocked Old Chester.

"That Charles!" said Mrs. Barkley. "Think of Maria, at her time of life, having to earn her own living!"

Mr. Ezra frowned and sighed. "I fear," he said, "that Miss Welwood will not find that appreciative demand for—"

"An academy?" Mrs. Barkley finished. "Of course not!"

"—demand for alum baskets," Mr. Ezra continued. He had not meant to finish his sentence in that way, but it was as good as any other; and it was his own. "But I cannot but admire," he proceeded, "Miss Maria's desire for independence; it commands my respect. Were you aware that the number of school-teachers in the United States was—"

"Ezra," said his sister-in-law, slowly, looking at him over her spectacles, "to be perfectly open: if you are thinking of settling, I must say that Rose is a girl in a thousand. I don't want to urge or influence you, but I must say that !"

And Mr. Ezra listened.

VI

Mr. Barkley came home from his office early in the afternoon. He had a careworn expression natural to a man who has a heavy task before him ; he stopped to look at the paroquets, climbing with beak and claw up the wires of the cage and squeaking shrilly at his approach ; but he did not give them any sugar or scratch their heads. He was thinking to himself that in two hours—it would be over ; he would be back again, and could sit peacefully down in his arm-chair, and let the parrots walk about over his shoulders and knees.

"I do not," he thought, "understand this feeling of enlargement in the region of my throat. And my respiration is hastened. I think I am indisposed. At such a moment I should be especially calm. Perhaps it would be well to arrange the interview to some extent."

Any immediate action is a relief ; and Mr. Ezra went up-stairs to his room, to get his brief together, so to speak. He dressed slowly, and just before he put on his coat he opened his watch, and standing before the little tipping glass on his high bureau, so that he might watch his expression, timed himself :

"I will open the subject by remarking upon the weather. 'These October days are very agreeable.' 'Yes, Mr. Ezra,' she will reply. 'I trust your occupations do not keep you in-doors too much?' I will say. Here I might introduce some interesting data as to exercise. (Allow a minute.) Then I will try and bring up financial matters, and speak, perhaps, of the hardships of life. (Allow five minutes.) And then I must"—the perspiration started to Mr. Ezra's brow—"I must remark that I should be pleased to smooth the path of life for her feet. Ending with the request that she should accept my hand."

Mr. Barkley looked at his watch. Fourteen minutes. Very good. Her reply would no doubt take another minute—allowing for the ladylike hesitation which would probably precede it. Mr. Ezra grew more careworn every instant.

However, he had to go. It was already a good half-hour later than he had planned to start. So he took his stick, and set his teeth, and, opening the front door, let himself out into the still October sunshine. His sense of the seriousness of his object imparted dignity to his rotund and somewhat jaunty figure; he wore a full-skirted frock-coat, and his high, bell-crowned hat was set just a little on one side. As he walked he kept repeating to himself the form of his proposal. When he reached Miss Welwood's gate he had only gotten so far as the "hardships of life," and he debated with himself for a moment as to whether he had not better walk on and finish his silent rehearsal before he put it to the touch. But while he stood hesitating, Rose came down the garden path, and when she saw him there came that flicker of fun into her eyes that was so disconcerting to Mr. Ezra. "You'll find Cousin Maria in the parlor, Mr. Barkley," she said. "Oh, quite so, quite so," replied Mr. Barkley, alarmed, but so polite

ROSE MET HIM AT THE GATE

that before he knew it he found himself ushered into the parlor and into Miss Welwood's presence.

Miss Welwood was seated at a spindle-legged table drawn close to the window, struggling, it appeared, to make wax flowers. She was deeply depressed. Her advertisement was to come out in two days, and the academy was to open in less than a month, and here she was "brushing up" her accomplishments, only to discover that her hand had lost its cunning ; for even Miss Maria could see that the heavy dark red spirals stuck to shaky green stems were as unlike the flowers she meant to make as the painty smell of the wax was unlike the fragrance of roses. Her fingers were clumsy and trembling, and a dull feeling of fright was growing up in her breast. Suppose she should find she had forgotten the use of the globes ? Suppose that she could not remember Berthollet's method ? Suppose she should not be able to recall the ornamental needle-work with which young ladies should be taught to while away the time ? She looked over at the whatnot, where a little air-castle, made of squares of perforated card-board, worked in single zephyr and caught together at the angles, was dangling from a knob on the top shelf ; how was it made ? Miss Maria sobbed under her breath.

Then she looked up and saw Mr. Ezra stumbling among the chairs and tables, for the room was shadowy, even though the autumn nights had thinned the vines about the windows, and some of the broad five-fingered leaves of the Virginia creeper were stained crimson.

"Why, Mr. Ezra !" she said, " it is indeed a compliment to have a call from a gentleman in the afternoon. How is dear Matty ?"

Mr. Ezra Barkley took off his hat and wiped his forehead. "I fear I am interrupting your delightful work," he said, politely.

"Oh no, indeed," she said. "You couldn't interrupt me, Mr. Ezra. I am making wax roses. I hope you think they're—pretty good?" She looked at him wistfully.

"Oh yes; just so; quite so; most beautiful;" he assured her, kindly. "These—ah—October days are very agreeable, Miss Maria?"

"Yes," she agreed, "I suppose they are, but I've had a good deal on my mind; I have not noticed them, I am afraid. You know I am going to open an academy, Mr. Ezra?"

"Yes," he said, eagerly; this was more direct than he could have hoped—the reference to exercise might be omitted, and he could proceed at once to financial matters and the hardships of life. This he did, with several statistical allusions to which Miss Welwood listened with deep attention.

"Dear me," she said, "if I only had some of your learning, Mr. Ezra, I am sure my academy would be successful!"

"Well, now, for the matter of the academy," said Mr. Barkley, changing color violently, "may it not be possible that some other arrangement may be made? In fact, I had in mind a—ah—plan which would make it possible for you to give it up. It is of this I came to speak this afternoon." (Here Mr. Ezra looked at his watch.)

"If you mean coming to live with Matty," she said, touched and smiling, "it's just the kindest thing in the world for you both to think of it; but indeed I couldn't do it. Why, what would become of Rose?"

MISS MARIA

"Oh, Miss Rose would be there too," Mr. Ezra said, warmly; "in fact, personally, I would find her presence a most agreeable addition to the household."

Miss Maria smiled, but shook her head. "You are both of you just as kind as you can be; but I'm going to work, Mr. Ezra." Miss Maria took up a strip of pink wax, and rolled it into a coil for the heart of a rose. "Indeed I do appreciate what Matty offered," she said; "I shall never forget it. And —and your kindness, too." She looked at him as she spoke, and her lip quivered.

"Miss Maria," said the little gentleman, "I was not referring to Matilda's plan."

"Oh," said Miss Maria, blankly.

"No, ma'am," said Mr. Ezra; "I have an idea of my own, which seems to combine my sister's wishes, with greater, as I may say, convenience, and—and suitability. Miss Maria, you may not be aware that the average life of the married man exceeds that of the bachelor by some years? And I—it—my sister—" Mr. Ezra was very unhappy; he turned red, and put on his hat; stammered, and took it off again. As for Miss Welwood, she sat up very straight, and squeezed her hands together under the table. She had forgotten Mrs. Barkley's suggestion about Rose, but it all came back to her: he was going to offer himself to Rose! Her face grew white, but she did not speak. Mr. Barkley continued, bravely: "I have given the subject much thought, and I am convinced that my — my plan will be a desirable arrangement. I venture to hope that Miss Rose will not object to it, if you do not."

"Rose is very young," Miss Welwood said, in a

low voice. "I'm sure I don't know her—her sentiments."

"Very well, then," said Mr. Ezra, and drew himself up, and looked at her with a kindly eye. "Miss
Welwood, I have long felt the deepest esteem for
you, and your present courageous attitude in this
distressing financial crisis has added admiration to
esteem. Miss Welwood, though in matters so delicate as the affections I dislike haste, the exigencies
of the present moment must be my excuse for so
abrupt a statement of my—my—of my—ah—as you
might say, regard. Miss Welwood, will you do me
the honor to accept my hand?"

Miss Maria put down the roll of wax on the table,
and stared at him.

"You see," he said, "it will be—to me, an agreeable solution of this somewhat difficult situation.
May I hope that your sentiments towards me are
not unkind?"

"Why," she said, in a whisper, "I don't—understand!"

"I am aware that my request may seem sudden,"
Mr. Barkley explained, "and I should have been
glad to lead up to it with proper decorum; but I
assure you, Miss Maria, of the warmth of my—my
sentiments." There was silence for a moment. Mr.
Ezra's face was red and anxious. "I trust I have
not offended you by the—as you might say, blunt-
ness of my address?"

"No; oh no," Miss Maria assured him, faintly.
Then she added, in a low voice, "But Matty?
perhaps Matty would have wished — something
else?"

"Miss Rose will live with us," said Mr. Ezra, with

calm directness; "that will be a gratification to Matilda, beyond a doubt."

"I don't know what to say," Miss Maria said, beginning to roll a piece of wax in her trembling fingers. "I never thought of such a thing—at least—not lately."

Then suddenly she put her head down on the table on the strips of red and pink wax, and covered her eyes with her shaking fingers. It had come—her long-delayed romance. Her little hope had risen on glittering wings out of the amber of the past, where it had lain so long. Mr. Ezra had spoken!

She looked over at him, and put her hand out across the table and touched his arm timidly. "Ezra," she said, "you do—care for me?" It seemed to Miss Maria, in the stress and reality of her calamity, that this was all unreal—all a sort of play; as if she were looking at Mr. Ezra through the wrong end of a magnifying-glass.

Her poor little words pierced the haze of Mr. Ezra's mild and kindly wish with a shock; he, too, looked at her, silent.

"Why—" he said, and stopped. After all, the days when such a question would have had meaning for Ezra were very far back; perhaps there never had been such days;—kindly, silent, dull, with few thoughts and many facts, perhaps he never knew the answer a man might make to such a question. All he knew now was that here was a *fact:* a lady for whom he had great esteem was in need. But as he looked at her, suddenly he blushed, and breathed a little more quickly; a break came in his calm, kind voice. "I hope you will think favorably of my offer?" he said. He took her hand and patted it, with evident agitation. "I entreat you, Miss Maria," he said.

And Miss Maria smiled through her tears.

Mrs. Barkley nearly swooned, she told Miss Welwood afterwards, when Ezra came home and told her; and she added that, to be perfectly frank, Ezra was as stubborn as a mule. "But upon my word," said Mrs. Barkley, "I believe he was right! Everybody is sometimes right, by chance; and I think, after all, that this is the best arrangement. But why didn't I think of it myself? I was a perfect fool!"

As for Rose, the gayety leaped back into her voice, and she laughed with all the old flashing looks and rapid words, and declared that she was ready to say, "Bless you, my children," right away.

But all the same she held on to a quiet plan of her own in regard to some work Dr. Lavendar had proposed for her, which later was, it must be admitted, a blow to Mr. Ezra.

Charles was delighted. He sent his aunt a wedding-present, bought from her last loan to him, and wrote her a most beautiful letter, which he ended by protestations of unaltered affection, and the statement that, as things had turned out, it proved just what he had said : "*The Lord would provide!*"

THE CHILD'S MOTHER

THE CHILD'S MOTHER

I

THE winter of the "long frost" has never been forgotten in Old Chester. The river was frozen over
solidly from the frightfully cold Sunday, just after
Christmas, when Dr. Lavendar stayed at home and
Sam Wright read the service, until the February
thaw. Not that the thermometer was unreasonable;
once in a while, to be sure, it did drop below zero,
but for the greater part of the time there was only a
dark, persistent cold, with high bleak winds; it was
too cold for the soft silencing of snow-storms, though
the flakes came sometimes, reluctantly, in little hard
pellets, which were blown from the frozen ruts of the
roads in whirls of icy dust. It was a deadly sort of
cold that got into the bones, the old people said.
Anyhow it got on to the nerves; certainly there
never was a winter in Old Chester when so many
things went wrong. There were happenings among
his people that bowed Dr. Lavendar's heart down
with sorrow and pain. Brave, high-minded, quick-
tempered old James Shields died. The Todds quarrelled violently while that black cold held; and
the eldest Miss Ferris was very, very ill. It was
that spring that the "real Smiths'" eldest son

brought disgrace upon their honest name ; and that Miss Jane Jay, to the scandal and grief of her sisters, made up her mind not to go to church any more. And in the midst of all this perplexity and pain Mrs. Drayton, a little foolish hypochondriac with a bad temper, became so anxious about her spiritual condition that she felt it necessary to see her clergyman several times a week. To be sure, her solicitude for her soul was checked by Dr. Lavendar's calling her "woman," and telling her that it was more important to be amiable in her family than to make her peace with God.

"He has no spirituality," Mrs. Drayton said, weeping angrily ; and did not send for him again for a fortnight.

It was early in December that old Mrs. King died, and though that meant that her daughter Rachel might draw a free breath after years of most wearing attendance, it meant also the grief of the poor daughter, whose occupation was gone.

Yes, it was a hard, dreary winter, and the old minister's heart was often heavy in his breast ; and when one day there came to him a sorrow and a sin that did not concern any of his own people, he had a curious sense of relief in dealing with it.

"It doesn't touch any of 'em, thank the Lord!" he said to himself. Yet there was a puzzle in it that was to grow until it did touch—and very near home, too. But Dr. Lavendar did not see that at the beginning, fortunately.

It was one Monday. Dr. Lavendar never had "blue Mondays"—perhaps because he preached old sermons ; perhaps because he was so dogmatically sure that the earth was the Lord's, and so were all the perplexities in it, and all the sorrows, too. On this particular Monday, just after dinner, he sat down by the fire (he had been out all the morning in the sleet and snow, so he felt he had earned a rest); he put on his preposterous old flowered cashmere dressing-gown, and sat down by the fire, and lighted his pipe, and began to read *Robinson Crusoe*. Dr. Lavendar had long since lost count of the number of times he had read this immortal book, but that never interfered with his enjoyment of it; he had lost count of the number of times he had smoked his pipe, if one comes to counting things up. He had a way of sniffing and chuckling as he read, and he was oblivious to everything about him—even to the fire going out sometimes, or his little grizzly dog climbing up into the chair beside him, or the door opening and shutting. The door opened and shut now, and he never heard it; only, after a while he felt an uncomfortable sense of being watched, and looked up with a start that made Danny squeak and scramble down to the floor. A girl was sitting opposite him, her heavy eyes fixed on his face.

"Why—when did you come in?" he said, sharply. "Who are you?"

"I'm Mary Dean, sir. I come in a few minutes ago. I didn't want to disturb you, sir." She said it all heavily, with her miserable eyes looking past him, out of the window into the falling sleet. It was plain what was her trouble, poor child! The old man looked at her keenly, in silence; then he said, cheerfully:

"Come, come, we must have a better fire than this. You are cold, my dear. Suppose you drink a cup of tea, and then we will talk."

"I don't want no tea, sir, thank you," she answered. "I thought you might help me. I come from Upper Chester," she went on, vaguely. She looked about her as she spoke, and a little interest crept into her flat, impersonal voice. "Why are them swords hangin' over the mantel?" she asked; and then added, sighing, "I'm in trouble."

"How did you come down from the upper village in such weather?" Dr. Lavendar asked her, gently, after a minute's pause.

"I walked, sir."

He exclaimed, looking at her anxiously. "You must have dry clothing on, my child," he said, "and some food, before you say another word!"

The girl protested, weakly: "I ain't cold; I ain't hungry. I only thought you'd tell me what to do."

But of course she had to be taken care of. If his Mary had not had thirty years' experience of his "perfectly obsolete methods," as the new people expressed it, she might have been surprised to find herself waiting on this poor fallen creature, while Dr. Lavendar urged her to eat and drink, and showed her how Danny begged for bread with one paw on his nose and one outstretched. Afterwards, when, fed and clothed, the girl was comforted enough to cry, the old man listened to her story. It was not a new one. When one hears it, one knows the heads under which it divides itself: vanity first; love (so called) next; weakness in the end. It is so pitiful and foolish that to call it by the awful name of sin is almost to dignify it. The girl, as she told it, brightened up; she began to enjoy what was to her a dramatic situation; she told him that she "had always been real respectable, but she had been deceived"; that she hadn't a friend in the world—"no-body to take no interest in her," as she put it—for her father and mother were dead ; and, oh, she was that unhappy ! "I 'ain't slept a wink for 'most a month. I cry all night," she burst out. "I just do nothing at all but cry, and cry !"

"Well, I guess it's the best thing you can do," he answered, quietly.

Mary looked disappointed, and tossed her head a little. Then she said that of course she hadn't let on to anybody in Upper Chester what was wrong with her, because all her lady and gentlemen friends had always respected her. "That's why I come down here ; I didn't want anybody at home to know," she explained, rocking back and forth miserably.

And then, perhaps because his face was so grave, she said, with a little resentment, that, anyway, it was her first misstep ; "there's lots of girls worse than me ;—and he's a *gentleman*," she added, lifting her head airily. Her glimmer of pride was like the sparkle of a scrap of tinsel in an ash heap. He would have married her, she went on, defending her-self, only he was married already ; so he really couldn't, she supposed.

Dr. Lavendar did not ask her the man's name, nor suggest any appeal to him for money ; he had cer-tain old-fashioned ideas about minding his own busi-ness in regard to the first matter, and certain other ideas concerning the injury to any lingering self-respect in the woman if the man bought his way out of his responsibility. He let her wander on in her vague, shallow talk. It was hard to see what was romance and what was truth. She had so far re-covered herself as to laugh a little, foolishly, and say once more she "had made a mistake, of course," but if Dr. Lavendar would just help her, it should never happen again. "This time I'll keep my promise," she said, beginning to cry.

"*This* time?" said Dr. Lavendar to himself. "Ho!"

"But what am I going to do?" she said. "If my mother was to hear it, I suppose she'd kill me—"

"Your mother?" he repeated. "You said—"

But she did not notice her slip.

"Oh dear! I don't know what's going to become of me, anyhow. And I haven't but ten cents to my name!"

With shaking fingers she opened her flat, thin pocket-book, and disclosed a few cents. This, at least, seemed to be true. "I'd die before any of my friends should know about it!" she sobbed.

Dr. Lavendar let her cry. He looked at her once or twice gravely, but he did not speak; he was wondering what woman in the parish he could call upon to help him. He was not stern with her, and he was not repelled or shocked by her depravity, as a younger man might have been in his place. He was old, and he was acquainted with grief, and he knew that this poor creature's wretchedness had in it, as yet, no understanding of sin; she was only inconvenienced by the consequences of wrong-doing. But the old man believed that the whip of shame and pain could drive her, as the Lord means it shall, into an appreciation of the expediency of morality—that first low step up to the full realization of the beauty of holiness. Being old, he knew all this, and was patient and tender with the poor fool, and did not look for anything so high, so awful, so deep, as what is called repentance. And then, beside the knowledge of life, which of itself makes the intellect patient, the situation was one which appealed profoundly to this old man who had never known the deep experience of paternity. The woman—so inextricably deep in the mire, the soul of her killed, almost before it had been born, the chances of her moral nature torn out of helpless, childless hands that did not know enough to protect them—a kitten drowned before its eyes were open! And the child—the baby, unborn, un-desired, weighted with what an inheritance! There was no baseness in this poor, cheap, flimsy creature that could arouse a trace of scorn in him. He let her cry for a while, and then he said, mildly:

"Where is your other child?" She started, and looked over her shoulder in a half-frightened way:

"Why! how did you know? Oh, well, my soul! I won't deceive you: I—I left it in Albany with my sister. She's supporting it."

Dr. Lavendar sighed. "It's a pity you can't be truthful, Mary. I could help you better, you know. However, I won't ask you to tell the truth. I'll only ask you not to tell me any lies. That's easier, I guess. Come, now, promise me you won't tell me any more lies, and then I will know how to help you."

Of course she promised, sobbing a little, and finger-ing her poor empty pocket-book. After all, that was the important thing. How was he going to help her? She had no money, and she could not get any work; and if this minister wouldn't look after her, she would have to go to the workhouse.

But he was going to look after her: that was Dr. Lavendar's way. For, it must be admitted, Dr.

Lavendar did not understand many things; he was only a little, feeble, behind-the-times old clergyman. Out of his scanty salary he was half supporting one shiftless woman with an enormous family, and a paralytic old man, and a consumptive girl. He did not stop to reflect that he was inviting mothers to burden society with their offspring, and encouraging old men to become paralytics, and offering a premium to consumption. No; he fed the hungry and clothed the naked, and never turned his face from the face of any poor man. He was not scientific; he was only human. He hoped and he believed that salvation was possible for every one—and so for this poor fallen woman with the empty pocket-book, whom he was going to look after. But he had to think about it a little while; so he bade her wait, while he went and fumbled among his papers and memoranda, and found the address of a worthy woman in Upper Chester who would take her to board and give her the care and attendance that she was going to need. Then he made a little calculation in his own mind that had reference to a certain old book upon Historical Sapphires, that he had long desired to own; then thrust out his lip and said, "Foolishness, foolishness!" under his breath; and brought a little roll of money and put it into her hand.

"You can go back on the stage to Upper Chester, and then you are to go to this street and number, and give this note to the kind woman who lives there. She will take you in, my child, and I will come and see you in a few days."

THE CHILD'S MOTHER

II

If Susan Carr had been in Old Chester that winter, Dr. Lavendar would have handed Mary Dean over to her, but she was paying a long visit in Mercer, and there seemed to be nobody to take care of the young woman but himself. Certainly he could not ask Miss Maria Welwood; she would have been most anxiously, tremulously kind, but her consciousness of the impropriety of the situation would have made her useless. Mrs. Dale was too stern; Mrs. Wright's large family took up all her time; Rose Knight was too young to know about such matters; and so was Sally Smith. Rachel King — well, yes, there was Rachel King. But her mother had just died, and Rachel needed a little time to breathe without any duty.

"Bless her heart!" he said to himself, "she sha'n't have any more work to do for a while, anyhow."

There was nothing for it but to look after the girl himself. So he put her into Mrs. Wiley's charge at Upper Chester, and took the long stage ride twice a week to visit her, and paid her board, and begged baby clothing for her, and watched over her in his queer, kind, dogmatic way.

"He's awful fond of fussin'," the girl said, wearily.

Mrs. Wiley had always a string of complaints ready for him: Mary was such a dreadful liar! She was that ungrateful, Mrs. Wiley had never seen the like of it! She hadn't any decent feelings, anyhow, for she made eyes at the baker's boy till Mrs. Wiley said she'd put her out on the sidewalk if she didn't behave!

"Wait ; wait," he would say. "She'll love the child, and she'll be a better girl."

"It don't follow," said Mrs. Wiley, with a significant toss of her head. " She allows she left her first child in New York with an aunt, and I can't see as it reformed her any."

However, neither Mrs. Wiley's deductions nor the conflict in poor Mary's stories prevented Dr. Lavendar from hoping. After the baby was born, he was eager to see the mother, peering into her face with anxious eyes, as though he thought that the benediction of a baby's hand must have blotted out shiftiness and sensuality and meanness. But Mary only came out of the experience of birth with her smooth, shallow face prettier than ever. Then Dr. Lavendar bade Mrs. Wiley wait yet a little longer. "Wait until she begins to love it, and then we'll see !" he said.

"Oh, she loves it enough," Mrs. Wiley conceded, grudgingly. "I don't deny she loves it. When I take it up, she looks at me just like our old cat does when I touch her kittens. Yes, she loves it fast enough ; but she's a bad girl, that's what she is, Dr. Lavendar !"

As for Dr. Lavendar himself, he was immensely entertained by the baby, though somewhat afraid of it. He used to hold it cautiously on his knee, chuckling to himself at its little, pink, clawlike hands, which grasped vaguely at him, and at its funny, nodding, bald head, and its tiny, bubbling lips. Mary would watch him languidly, and would laugh too, as though it was all an excellent joke.

"If it was a boy, I'd name it after you," she said, with coy facetiousness. At which Dr. Lavendar came out of his sunny mood, and said "Ho!" gruffly, and put the baby down. The girl was so utterly devoid of any understanding of the situation that, in spite of his hopefulness, she shocked him again and again. However, he kept on "looking after her."

The child was baptized Anna, though Mary had suggested Evelina. "Mary," Dr. Lavendar said, solemnly, "was your mother a good woman?"

"My mother?" the girl said, wincing. "She's— dead. She *was* good. My land! if she'd lived I wouldn't 'a' been here!" For once the easy tears had not risen; she looked at him sullenly, as though she hated him for some glaring contrast that came into her thoughts. "That's honest," she added, simply.

"Then we will name the baby after her, because she was good," he said; and "Anna," was accordingly "grafted into the body of Christ's church."

As soon as she was strong enough, he found a place for Mary to work, where she might have the baby with her. "The child and good honest work will save her," he would say to himself; but he used to shake his head over her when he sat smoking his pipe and thinking about his little world. "And that poor baby!" he would say, looking, perhaps, at his wrinkled forefinger, and thinking how the baby had clutched it.

Once he told Rachel King about it all, and how pretty the child was — that was when it was five months old, and the red and clawing stage was past, and the small bald head was covered with shining, silken rings of hair, and its eyes, no longer hid in creases of soft baby flesh, were blue and smiling, and its little mouth cooed for kisses.

"Oh," cried Rachel King, "to think that such a creature should have it!"

Not that Rachel King was hard, or that she had the shrinking that good Miss Maria Welwood would have had; but her whole heart rose at the mention of a baby. "The little darling," she said; and the color came up into her face, and her eyes gleamed. "I don't believe she loves it a bit."

"Oh yes, she does," said Dr. Lavendar, with a sigh; "yes, she does—in her way. And, Rachel, the baby may save her, you know. Yes, I believe she loves it."

"I don't," said Rachel King, stoutly; "not if this last story of her 'keeping company' with somebody is true. Why doesn't she devote herself to the baby?"

Rachel was sitting out in the garden with Dr. Lavendar; he had been smoking and watching the bees, and she had dropped in to gossip awhile. She was a large, maternal-looking woman of thirty-five. Silent and placid, with soft, light-brown hair parted in the middle and drawn smoothly down and back from a wide forehead, under which shone mild and brooding gray eyes—the eyes of a woman who was essentially, and always, and deeply, a mother; that look that can only come from experience.

But what had she mothered in the last nineteen years!

When Rachel was sixteen years old, Mrs. King fell ill; it was one of those illnesses from which we turn away our eyes, shuddering and humbled. Oh, our poor human nature! the pity of it, the shame of it, yet the helplessness and innocence of it! Rachel's mother gradually but swiftly came to be a child—in

146

everything but years. She had lost a baby, and the grief had shaken the foundations of life. They first suspected how things were with the poor mind by the way she pored over the little clothes the dead child had worn, folding them and unfolding them, and talking to them, with little foolish laughter. It was then that some one whispered to some one else that Ellen King was not herself. So it went on, little by little—at first knowing, and rebelling with horror and with disgust ; then, after a while, passively, she sank down into the bog of the merely animal. When Rachel was eighteen the last glimmer of the woman died out ; there was left an eating, breathing, whimpering thing. She had her doll by that time, and Rachel used to tuck a bib under the poor shaking chin and feed her, and push down the naughty hands that tried to grasp the spoon, and wipe the milky lips, and kiss her, and—honor her. This was her baby, her duty, her passionately tender occupation — but it was her *mother;* and Rachel King's days ought to be long in the land ! When she was about twenty-one a lover appeared, but she sent him away. "I can't leave mother. Father can't take care of her, you know, and Oscar is away ; and Willy will be getting married some day. But it wouldn't be right that you should have to live with her," she said, wistfully. The lover protested ; but she heard the weak note behind the affectionate words, and after that she was quite firm. "No ; it can't be. I see that it couldn't possibly be." When he had gone, she went up to her mother's room and put her arms around her, and hid her eyes on her breast. "Oh, mother, mother !" she said, " can't you speak to me—just once ?"

Mrs. King stroked the soft straight hair for a moment, and then plucked at it angrily, and cried and screamed, and said she wanted her dolly. . . . That had been Rachel's life for nineteen years; for Mrs. King had lived, and lived, and lived. All around her in the anxious, heavy-laden world sweet and buoyant and vital souls were sucked down into death; but the imbecile old woman went on living. Mr. King died in the early part of his wife's illness; and about eight years before the end came, William, the only son who lived at home, married, and went to a house of his own. He married a Mercer girl, who commended herself to him by her great good sense. Old Chester was not quite pleased that Willy should leave his mother and Rachel all alone, though it said, approvingly, that Martha Hayes would make the doctor a good wife. But what could the young man do? The sensible Mercer girl said, frankly, that she was very fond of Willy, but she simply *would not* live in the same house with his mother. Indeed, such was her Mercer sense (it certainly was not of Old Chester) that she said, during the latter part of her engagement, that she did not think it was quite prudent for a young married lady to live in the same house with such a frightful old creature!

So Rachel was left all alone with her child. It was a busy life, in its constant attendance; yet somehow it is the busy people who can always do a little more. If there was sickness in a neighbor's family, Rachel King took possession in a tranquil, sensible way; when there was death, her large, gentle hands were ready with those sacred touches that are so often left to hirelings; when there was sorrow, her soft breast was a most comforting pillow. So year

by year went by, until the final flicker of her mother's life dropped into mere breathing—into silence
—into death. And year by year the lines of mater-
nity deepened in the daughter's face, until she was
all mother.

Then, she was childless.

Oh, after such shame, how humanity raises itself
in glorious death! Even Rachel, mourning and bewildered by the loss of occupation, felt it dumbly—
the dignity, the mercy, the graciousness, of death!
And to the poor soul, fettered in gross flesh, stumbling, stifling, struggling, what must it have been
to emerge into the clean spaces of the stars!

After that, of course, Rachel could live her own
life. But there was no question of a lover now; he
had a wife and five children in another State. She
could not go and live with Willy; her sensible sister-in-law (against this day) had for years been saying how foolish it was to live in other people's families; and Rachel had taken the hint. There were
no nephews and nieces to love—nobody, indeed, to
whom she was a necessity. Of all the bitter and
heavy things in this sorry old world, the not being
necessary is the bitterest and heaviest. With a deep,
simple nature, a nature of brooding love, Rachel
King had nothing in her life but the crumbs that
fell from richer tables: the friendly acceptance of
those services she was so happy to give. But she
had nothing of her very own.

"To think that that creature has a baby!" she said.

"Well, well; we'll hope it will save her," Dr. Lavendar repeated.

"But think of the baby," Rachel insisted. "What

kind of a bringing-up will it have?" She sighed as she spoke, not knowing that the necessity of her own empty arms and wide lap and deep soft bosom dictated the words.

"Well, Rachel, if we took the infants away from all the unworthy mothers, we'd have a pretty large orphan-asylum," Dr. Lavendar said, chuckling, "and it wouldn't be only the Mary Deans who would have to give 'em up, either. No, no; I believe the Lord understands this matter better than we do. The baby will make a woman of Mary yet!"

"Suppose she teaches it to tell lies?" Rachel King suggested.

"Ho! Suppose it teaches her to tell the truth?" he demanded. "No, Rachel. That baby is a missionary; a 'domestic missionary,' as you might say. I've great hopes for Mary—great hopes."

III

But Dr. Lavendar's hopes were greatly tried. In spite of the saving grace of a baby, bad reports came from the family for whom Mary Dean worked—she was an inveterate liar; she was untidy, and coarse in mind and body; she was dishonest—not in any large way, but rather in small meannesses.

"The only good thing about her is she *is* fond of that blessed baby," her exasperated mistress said once. "She kisses it sometimes as if she were possessed. But then, again, she'll slap it real hard if it slops its dress, or, maybe, pulls her hair when it's playing. It's a great baby to play," the good woman said, softening as she spoke.

However, Dr. Lavendar kept on hoping. Then came a time when he could hope no longer. It was one night in August — his Mary's night out, as it chanced. Dr. Lavendar came home from Wednesday evening lecture, plodding along in the darkness, a lantern swinging in one hand and his stick in the other. He was humming over to himself, with husky clearings of his voice at the end of each line, the last hymn :

> " The spa—cious fir—mament o-on hi-gh,
> And a-all the blue—ethereal sky—"

Then he fumbled for his latch-key and came up to his own door-step, where was lying a little heap that moved and said, "Goo—oo—oo."

Dr. Lavendar stood still for a moment, and felt very cold. Then he stooped down and held the lantern over the baby's face. At that there was an unmistakable wail of fright—that sharp "*A-a-ach!*" that pierces the unaccustomed ear with such curious dismay. Fathers and mothers bear this cry with equanimity, and even seem to find it a cause for pride, but to the unbabied adult it is so piercing and so unpleasant that it almost seems as though there was something to be said for Herod. Not that Dr. Lavendar had any such inhuman thoughts ; he lifted the baby up and carried it into the study, where he put it down in his arm-chair, and stumbled about for matches to light the lamp. In his anxiety he did not even take off his flapping felt hat, which encircled his face like a black nimbus. Holding the lamp in his hand, he came and stood over the bundle in his chair ; the baby stopped crying and sucked in its lower lip, and returned his gaze. It was Mary's child. He recognized it at once, and did not need the dirty scrap of paper pinned on its breast:

" Mr. Lavendar i cant do for baby no longer it cries nights and do keep me awake and i got to do my work next day all the same and i cant stand it no longer and i cant do for it no longer i am sorrie i pittie poor baby to be left alone and i love my baby just as much as if i was married but i have to put it away i will never come back any more so get it a home and please excuse no more at present from your friend Miss Mary Dean   P S   i have decided to name it Evelina."

He read it, and then he looked at the baby blinking at the lamp-light, in his arm-chair. " If you'll just wait a minute," he said, in an agitated voice, " I'll—I'll get a woman !"

The baby yawned ; he saw the roof of its small pink mouth, like a kitten's. " I'll return immediately," he assured it ; and hurried, almost running, out to the kitchen. But his maid-servant was not there. " What shall I do ?" he said. " Very likely it ought to be fed, or something. Perhaps it wants to be held. I'll get Rachel."

It was easy to get Rachel King, as she lived but a stone's-throw away ; she was locking her front door when, half-way down the street, he called her and waved his lantern ; and Rachel, in her placid mind, foresaw a sudden illness somewhere, and a night's watching before her. His breathless explanation sent her hurrying, faster than he could walk, back to the parsonage. When he got there she had the baby on her knee, and was taking off the faded shawl that the mother had wrapped around it, and mumbling her lips over the little dimpled arm.

"There's a pin somewhere that has scratched her," she said. "There, you little darling. Oh, dear me, Dr. Lavendar, that shawl is so dirty! And look at this scratch on her little hand. There—there—there. Why, her little feet are as cold as stones!" She gathered the small feet into her hand, and cuddled the child up against her breast. "I feel her shiver!" she said, angrily. "I believe that wretched girl has given her her death of cold leaving her on that stone step. There, dear; there—there. Dear baby, bless your little heart! She says she 'was frightened all alone in the dark; frightened 'most to death,' she says. Yes, darling, yes. 'I was scared,' she says, 'and I was drefful cold.' There, now, are your little feet warm?"

Dr. Lavendar stood looking down at her, greatly relieved.

"But what am I going to do with it to-night?" he said, anxiously.

"Oh, I am going to take her home, sir. Dr. Lavendar, *give her to me?*"

"Oh, well, Rachel, I hope the mother will come back, you know. And, in fact, I suppose our first duty is to get hold of her and make her take it."

"What!" she interrupted, "when she deserted her? Give a child back to such a mother? No! she doesn't deserve her!"

"But, perhaps," he ventured, "the work really was too hard? There's her letter. You see what she says. I certainly ought to try to get a different kind of place for her, where she won't have so much to do. It is hard to be kept awake at night and then have to work, you know. We must try to make it possible for her to keep her child, poor girl."

"Dr. Lavendar, any woman who could write such a letter ought not to be allowed to have a child," Rachel said. "But I don't believe we'll ever hear from her again. Anyhow, I'm going to take this precious baby home with me! Little darling! do you want to come home and have some hot milk, and go sleepy? Well, you shall!—there, there, there!"

"I wish you would take her home, my dear, I wish you would," Dr. Lavendar said, "and to-morrow we can decide what we ought to do."

Rachel smiled, her eyes narrowing a little, but she said nothing. She wrapped the child up in her skirt, "I won't have that shawl touch her," she said, decidedly.

"Won't it cry if you take it out in the dark?" Dr. Lavendar inquired, meekly.

Rachel laughed.

"'It'!" she said. "*She* won't cry in my arms."

That night was a wonderful one to Rachel King. The washing of the soft, uncared-for baby flesh; the feeding of the warmed and comforted little body; then the putting the child to sleep, sitting in a low chair, and rocking slowly back and forth, back and forth, crooning, crooning, crooning, her shadow dipping and rising across the ceiling of the faintly lighted room. When the baby was asleep Rachel looked over the rough, grimy clothing, shaking her head, and touching the little petticoats with disgusted fingers.

"Ach—dirty!" she said. "They sha'n't touch her again; she's as clean as a flower now."

And then she took her lamp and went up through the silent house to the garret. Whenever Rachel came up here under the rafters of the old house, she thought what a place it would be for children to play on rainy days. Well, now, perhaps a little child should play here ; a little girl might use that old doll-house set back against the big brick chimney. Rachel's breath quickened as this thought leaped up in her heart. She put the lamp down on a chest, and, from under the eaves, pulled out an old horse-hair trunk ; when she opened it a scent of dried roses and sweet clover came from the clean old baby linen that had been lying there some twenty years. Poor Mrs. King, staggering from reason to imbecility, had put the little clothes away ; and every spring, for her sake, Rachel took them out, and aired them, and put them back again.

On top of the baby clothes lay a battered old doll ; when she lifted it Rachel drew in her breath as though something hurt her. Then she began to sort out the things she needed for the little rosy child of dishonor and sin. The lamp flickered in the draught from the open door, and cast her great shadow across the ceiling as, gently, she took up one little garment after another. As she shook out the knitted shirts and brushed some rose leaves from the folds of the yellowing slips, a sense of providing for her own came warmly to her breast. Her baby ! She took her lamp and went down-stairs again, the pile of clothing on her arm.

The baby slept, warm and quiet, on Rachel's bed ; she bent over it to feel its soft breath on her cheek ; then she gathered its feet into her hand to be sure that they were warm, and lifted the arm which was thrown up over its head and put it under the cover. It seemed as though she could not take her eyes away from the child, even that she might undress and lie down beside it. And when she did it was not to sleep; a dozen times she raised herself on her elbow to look down at the little figure beside her and listen for its breathing, and lift its small relaxed hand to her lips. Sometimes she thought of the woman who had deserted it : but never as if any of her shame were connected with the child's personality. Only with indignation—and thankfulness !

It was a night of birth to this childless woman.

In those first days she did not ask Dr. Lavendar whether he was taking any steps to find the baby's mother, but she lived breathlessly. " I'll *buy* her, if that creature comes back," she said to herself, over and over. But the creature did not come back, though Dr. Lavendar tried his best to find some trace of her, to urge upon her the duty of caring for her child. And after a while Rachel's plan and plea seemed to the old minister the only way out of the matter : Rachel wanted the baby ; and its own mother evidently did not ; so it had best remain with Rachel. Certainly for the child there could be no question as to which lot in life was best for it.

But it was several months before Rachel King felt assured possession. "The mother may come back for it," Dr. Lavendar reminded her many times, "so don't let's be in a hurry." But in the end it was settled as Rachel wished. The mother drifted off into the world ; and the little waif, which had drifted into a home, grew into a flowerlike child, pretty and happy and good.

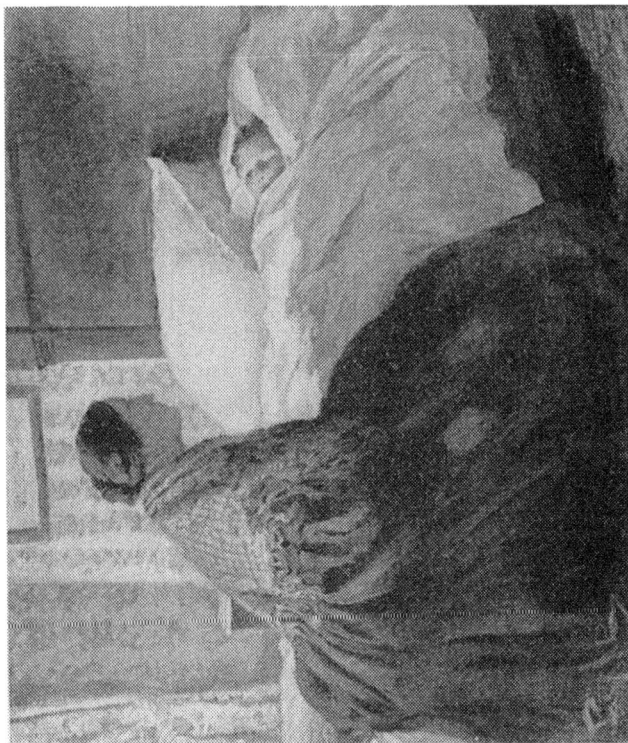

"SHE COULD NOT TAKE HER EYES AWAY FROM THE CHILD"

THE CHILD'S MOTHER

IV

It was a most peaceable Old Chester childhood that came to little Anna, for Rachel preserved the traditions of the town in bringing her up—and that meant love and obedience, and the sweet, attendant grace of reverence, of which, alas, childhood is so often robbed in these emancipated days. In Old Chester the bringing up of their children occupied the women in a way at once religious and intellectual. Practically they had no other interest; individualism and the sense of social responsibility, those two characteristics of the modern woman, were not even guessed at—indeed, they would have been thought exceedingly unladylike. But the care of the individual child and the sense of responsibility for its morals made the interest and excitement and occupation of the mothers' lives. The great fear was that children might be "spoiled"; hence it was a subject for prayer that no sinful human instinct, no mere maternal feeling, should be allowed to interfere with discipline. Infants were punished, children were trained, youth was admonished, with religious devotion. It was a matter of pious pride to Old Chester that Mrs. Dale's first baby had cried himself into a spasm on being forced to drink the skin on scalded milk. It was perhaps unfortunate that Mrs. Dale should have tried to make the child take the crinkling scum in the first place; but having tried, having called in several serious mothers to advise and wrestle with the ten months' baby, having forced teaspoons between small, wet lips, and held little fighting, struggling hands, it was imperative that she should succeed. She succeeded. To be sure, later on, young Eben Dale quarrelled with his mother and sowed enough wild oats to feed the Augean stables; but he reformed in time to die at thirty in the odor of sanctity—his conversion being, Mrs. Dale believed, due to that rigid discipline of his youth (and the mercy of God). Old Chester children were prayed for, and agonized over, and sent supperless to bed, with a chapter in the Bible to be committed to memory by the light of one uncertain candle shining through their hungry tears. And most of them are grateful for it now.

As for Rachel King, she observed these traditions in the way in which she cared for Anna; but it was always with tenderness. And Anna was a dear and happy little child. She never knew that her aunt, as she called Rachel, thought, and planned, and fairly lived in her life. It would have been contrary to Rachel's principles to allow the child to feel herself important; but nothing escaped the kind eyes, the far-seeing love, that punished and praised with that calm justice which children so keenly appreciate. The little girl's physical well-being was of absorbing interest to Rachel, but her spiritual well-being was a religion to the quiet, matter - of - fact woman, who did not look any more capable of spiritual passion than did some gentle, ruminative cow lying under a big tree in a sunny meadow. Anna's possible inheritance was a horror to Rachel, and when the child told her first lie her foster-mother was nearly sick with dismay and anxiety. It was only one of the romancing lies as common to childhood as playing. Anna recited a long tale of how she went to Dr. Lavendar's and rung the bell, and then tried to reach up to the knocker, and tumbled down, and saw a large toad looking at her from beside the front steps, and how she was so frightened she ran every step of the way home. Rachel, when she found this was pure invention, nearly broke her heart. Alarmed and stern, she carried the story to Dr. Lavendar, who chuckled over it, and blinked his eyes, and said:

"And she never left the yard, you say, the whole afternoon? Well, well! what an imagination!"

"But, Dr. Lavendar, it was a lie," Rachel said, staring at him with dismay.

"My dear, you can't say a child of four is a liar. Did you mean to punish her?"

Rachel nodded, and sighed.

"Don't you do it! Laugh at her. That's all she needs. Tell her it's foolish to say things happened that didn't happen. Time enough to punish her when she does it to gain an end. Don't you see it was a tale to the child?"

"But her—the woman who deserted her lied so!"

"Her mother?"

Rachel winced. "Yes, that—that woman."

"That's true; poor Mary didn't seem able to tell the truth. Well, I suppose it's natural for you, Rachel, to be afraid of the inheritance from her earthly mother; but mind you don't forget her inheritance from her Heavenly Father, my dear."

Rachel bent her head, solemnly, listening and comforted.

"Dear me, dear me!" Dr. Lavendar ruminated. "How He has provided for one of the least of His little ones : the deserted child of a woman who was a sinner ! Rachel, I wonder where she is. Suppose she were to come back?"

Rachel King had gotten up to go, comforted and smiling, though the tears were near the surface; her face hardened instantly. "She won't come back; if she did, it would be nothing to me."

"She might want to know about the child—where she is, and all that."

"You wouldn't tell her?" Rachel said, with a gasp.

Dr. Lavendar put his pipe down, and stuck out his lips in a way he had when he was puzzled. "I've never spoken of it to you, Rachel, but I've wondered about it. Not that I think we'll ever hear from her, poor creature—"

"'*Poor*' creature?" Rachel interrupted, violently. "Lost creature! wretch! fiend!" It was like the sudden show of teeth and claws the way in which the face of this slow, mild woman flamed with rage. "I hope she's dead!"

Dr. Lavendar looked up at her, open-mouthed.

"Well, now, Rachel, aren't you a little—harsh, maybe? As for Anna, she is that poor sinner's child—"

"No, no!" Rachel King broke in. "No, Dr. Lavendar, I can't hear you say that; I *can't!* She is my child."

"Now, my dear, you know that is really foolish," he said, shaking his head. "That girl who gave her birth is her mother; ye can't get around that, Rachel."

"That—woman, is only the mother of—of her body," Rachel King said, in a low voice. "I am her mother, Dr. Lavendar. Anna is mine. No; that— creature will never come back; but if she did, it would make no difference; it would make no more

difference to me than it would to Mrs. Wright and
her Lydia, or—or any mother. My child is *mine*."

"I wonder what the law would say?" Dr. Lavendar ventured, meekly.

"The law?" Rachel said. "What do I care for the
law? That's man's word. God gave me that child,
and only God shall take her from me!"

"But, Rachel," he protested, "a mother has a natural right; if she wanted her child (supposing she
could feed it and take proper care of it), I think anybody would agree that she ought to have it."

Rachel King turned on him, panting; her hands
were trembling, and her large face a dull, angry red.
"Is food the only thing she needs, Dr. Lavendar? I
would rather Anna was dead, I would sooner kill her
with my own hands, than have her go to that—
creature!" Without another word she turned and
walked away from him.

As for Dr. Lavendar, he sat still, perfectly confounded by her violence.

"How people do surprise you!" he said to himself
at last. "Well, it appears Solomon knew what he
was talking about. It was the real mother who said,
'in no wise slay it.' Curious how nature can always
be relied on to tell the truth. But how Rachel did
surprise me!"

However, Rachel did not surprise him in this way
again; indeed, though she came to see him on this
matter or on that, things were not quite the same
between them. A deep resentment and distrust
grew up in her mind. Dr. Lavendar had, to her
way of thinking, showed an unfriendly and unfeel-
ing disposition which she had never suspected in
him. She did not speak of this resentment, of

course; but it burned and smouldered, and never quite went out. The anger of slow, mild, loving people has a lasting quality that mere bad-tempered folk cannot understand. Rachel used to reproach herself for the hardness of her heart, and say that she must remember that Dr. Lavendar was getting old, and could not understand things—" or else he would know that God gave Anna to me," she would say, over and over; her simple creed permitting the idea that her Creator had made a depraved mother commit the sin of abandoning her child so that another woman might have a child to love and care for. But she never again let the maternal passion burst out in such fierce words of possession.

Dr. Lavendar, however, pondered those words in his heart. He used to sit blinking at the fire, and rubbing Danny's ears, and thinking about it: after all, to whom did Anna really belong? Over and over he discussed it with himself, but only as an abstract proposition that interested him as any philosophical, impersonal question might. The first mother was gone, having resigned the baby to the chance of kindness; the second mother, so to speak, had taken her empty place, and was doing her neglected duty; thanks to her, little Anna was being brought up as a member of Christ, the child of God, and an inheritor of the Kingdom of Heaven. But to whom did she really belong?

He pottered about over this question with the same mild intellectual enjoyment with which in his salad days he had discussed (and disposed of) the errors of the Socinians and the Pelagians. And by-and-by he made up his mind, and decided, in his dogmatic way, that "there was no question about it":

THE CHILD'S MOTHER

By the inalienable claim of nature Anna belonged to the woman who had brought her into the world.

So little Anna grew into a pleasant child. She was looked after a little more strictly than other children, and perhaps punished more ; but it seemed as though she were loved more too. She had a very happy childhood : sewing on a hassock at Rachel's feet, her hair parted smoothly over her round, pure forehead, and her bright eyes eager as any other child's to be through with her task and get out to play ; romping in the garden with other little girls ; playing with her doll — an old doll given her by Rachel, whose eyes, when she put it into Anna's hands, were wet, and who stroked the dolly's head as if she loved it ; learning to read at Rachel's knee out of a brown book with two fat gilt cherubs on the cover, called *Reading Without Tears.* However, Anna's childhood had its tears, fortunately. Rachel's love was not of that poor fibre that spares the wholesome salt of tears in the bread of life. So little Anna laughed and cried and played, and grew into a dear, good child.

And when she was ten years old, all this was weighed in the balance against the "inalienable claim of nature."

V

It was on Saturday, and the children were straggling up the street to the rectory for their catechism and collect class. Dr. Lavendar had had this class for forty years ; the preceding generation had sat on the little hard benches in the dining - room, and learned that a collect was divided into three parts, the invocation, the petition, and the conclusion, just as this generation was learning it. Fathers and mothers, thirty years before, had recited in concert that their sponsors in baptism had renounced for them the devil and all his works, the pomps and vanities of this wicked world, and all the sinful lusts of the flesh ; and now they were permitting their children to be reminded, once a week, that a like futile renunciation had been made for them.

On this particular Saturday it was raining, and was cold and blustery. But Old Chester children were brought up to believe that they were neither sugar nor salt ; and so, when it was time to start, they trudged along through the rain and mud to the rectory. They were a sturdy, rosy set, very shy, quite clumsy, and stupidly, stolidly silent—except when they were alone ; then they chattered like sparrows. The class met in the dining-room, the table being pushed over into one corner, and some benches placed in two rows in front of a blackboard. There was always a dish of apples on a side-table (or jumbles, if it was summer); and the five or six boys and seven or eight girls kept an eye on it, to cheer them through the half-hour of the old minister's talk. Dear me ! how that dish kept up a sinking heart when its owner was asked (no one ever knew where the lightning was going to strike, so there was no such thing as cramming beforehand), "*What is thy duty towards thy neighbor?*" When collect class was over, the apples or jumbles were handed around, and each child took one, and said, "Thank you, sir." And then Danny was brought in and put through his tricks; and sometimes, if everything had gone very well, and "What desirest thou of God in this prayer?" and "What is thy duty to thy neighbor?" had been answered without a mistake, and Dr. Lavendar was especially good-natured, they were taken into the study and shown the lathe, and the little boxes of garnets and topazes and amethysts; and perhaps — oh, *very* rarely, maybe three times a year — one boy and one girl were chosen, turn about, to put a foot upon the treadle and start the lathe. And then how the collect class stood about, gaping with interest and awe !

This class met at two, and was such an institution of Old Chester that nobody ever thought of calling, or getting married, or being buried, at two o'clock of a Saturday afternoon. But on this rainy January Saturday, a little before two, a carriage drove up to the rectory gate, and a fat, sleepy-looking man helped a very pretty young woman to alight. He held an umbrella over her in a stupid, uncertain way as they walked up the garden path, and she scolded him sharply, and told him to look out, the water was dripping on her hat !

"What's the odds?" he said, good-naturedly. "I'll get you all the hats you want, Mamie."

"Here's the house," the young woman said. "Now, Gus, you sit out in the hall, and I'll talk to the old man."

"Why can't I come in too ?"

"Oh, well, I'd rather see him alone," she said.

"All right," he responded, with a foolish grin.

Dr. Lavendar was in the dining-room, fussing over the arrangement of the little low benches, and printing the collect on the blackboard. The "O Lord" and the "Amen" were always written in very large letters, and the question, "What does Amen mean?" was always asked of the youngest Todd child, who was, poor boy, "wanting," and could only remember that one answer, which he recited as "*Sobeet.*"

"There's a man and woman to see you, sir," Mary said. "I believe they're strangers. I guess they want to be married."

"Ho! What do they mean by coming at this hour?" said Dr. Lavendar.

"I told 'em you had the children coming," Mary defended herself—Mary was always defending herself; it is a characteristic of her class—"but they allowed they had to get back to Mercer to get a train for Australia, and they couldn't wait."

"If they go by rail to Australia they'll do well," said Dr. Lavendar. "Well, I guess I can marry 'em in ten minutes. Just be ready to come in, Mary, will you?"

Then he went shuffling out into the hall, where the man was sitting, holding his hat on his knees.

"No, sir; it's not me; it's my wife wants to see you. She's in beyont."

So they didn't want to get married. Dr. Lavendar saw Neddy Todd coming, rolling and stumbling and grinning, along the street, and made haste to go into his study.

Of course, as soon as he entered the room, Dr. Lavendar knew the woman. She had grown a little heavier; she was very well dressed, and was perhaps prettier than ten years before. It was the same face —mean and shallow and simpering; but there was a hungry look in it that he did not understand.

"I don't know as you recognize me," she began, airily. "I was—"

THE CHILD'S MOTHER

"I recognize you. You are Mary Dean."

"Well, I *was*. I'm Mrs. Gus Larkin now. I'm married." She laughed a little as she spoke, with a coquettish toss of her head. "That's him out in the hall. We're going to live in Australia. We sail on Tuesday. He's a mechanical engineer, and he gets real good wages. Well, he says I can take baby. So I come to get her." Her face, as she spoke, changed and grew anxious, and her breath came quickly. "She's well?" she said. "She's — alive? Why don't you say something?" she ended, shrilly. "My baby ain't—dead, is she?"

"No ; oh no ; no," he said, feebly. Then he sat down and looked at her. Two umbrellas, bobbing against each other, came up the path. Two more children. He wondered who they were.

Mary was instantly relieved and happy. "Of course it's a long time since I've seen her," she began; "but there! there hasn't been a day I 'ain't thought of her. Is she pretty? Well, about two months ago he married me, and as soon as I got a home of my own I just thought I'd have baby. That was my first thought, though of course I was real glad to be respectable. But I'll have baby, I says to myself. Well, he's real kind ; I'll say that for him. And he said I could have her. So I've come to get her. We're going back to Mercer to-night, because we've got to start to-morrow morning. And Tuesday we get on the ship. Baby — well, there! She ain't a baby now ; I suppose she's grown a big girl? She'll be real interested in seein' a ship. I am myself. I never seen a ship—or an ocean. Oh, well, sir, you don't know what it is to me to get my baby back again !"

Her face moved suddenly, with tears, but she smiled. Dr. Lavendar felt a curious faintness; the suddenness of the thing—an abstraction violently materialized, so to speak—gave him a physical as well as a moral shock. The real mother, a married woman, "respectable," as she said, was asking, naturally, simply, for her child. And of course she must have it.

"I do not think," he said, slowly, his voice deep and trembling, "that you really love your child: ten years of indifference to her fate does not show much love!" He began to get his breath, and sat up straight in his chair, glowering at her under stern brows.

"Well," she defended herself, "of course I see how it looks to you. But—there! I couldn't have her with me. Why, how could I? and me—the way I was? Why, I *wouldn't*. I loved her, though, all the time. I don't know as you'll believe me?"

Dr. Lavendar said to himself that he did not believe her; but deep down in his heart, in a frightened way, he knew that she was speaking the truth. "How long have you been married?" he said. She told him; and added that "he" was perfectly respectable.

"What do you call respectable?" Dr. Lavendar said; and even in his alarm and confusion he knew, with shame, that there was contempt in his voice— "what do *you* call respectable?"

"Well, Gus never was took up, and he never kept company with them that was took up," she said, proudly; "and he gets good wages. Before we broke up to go to his place in Australia we had a Brussels carpet on our parlor floor, and a piano—(we were

168

getting it on instalments, but then it's all the same; it was standing right in our bow-window). Baby 'll have a good home. He had twenty-two dollars a week, and he's going to have forty dollars in Melbourne. I'll dress her pretty, I can tell you!"

Respectability: "not to have been arrested!" Well! well! Anna, ten years old, trained in every sweet old-fashioned delicacy of thought and speech, in the nurture and admonition of the Lord, was to be thrown into such "respectability!"

"Mary," he said, clearing his throat, but speaking huskily and with a shaking voice, "you gave your child away. Why do you want her now? She is in a good home, and has good friends. Why don't you leave her there?"

She listened to him in amazement, and then burst out laughing. "Leave her? Well, I guess I won't! I'm willing to pay the folks for her board, if they ask it. But a child don't eat much, and I guess they've made her work; a bound-out child works her passage every time. Still, I'll pay. As for leavin' her — why, I married him more to get her a good home than anything else!"

The room darkened with a splash of rain against the window. Some more children came up through the garden, their umbrellas huddled together, and their little feet crunching the wet gravel of the path. He could hear the murmur of their chatter, and caught Theophilus Bell's shrill inquiry, "'Say, Lydia, 'what is required of persons to be baptisted?'" They came clattering into the hall; and then the house was silent again, except that the man waiting outside coughed, and moved about restlessly.

"I never signed papers to adopt her out—did I?

Well, then, the law 'd give her to me. I'm her mother."

Her mother! Sacred and invincible word! There came keenly to his mind a phrase Rachel had used—"*only the mother of her body.*" Of course Rachel was wrong; but why hadn't she adopted Anna? for in the security of years, foolishly enough, the question of legal adoption had not been raised.

"Mary," he said, "think—think what you are doing!—to take her away from a good home. I—I hope you won't do it?"

She shook her head violently. "You needn't talk to me about good homes; I've got a good home for her. And I'm respectable."

"Oh, do give it up, Mary," he said, his voice shaking with agitation—"do consider her welfare! Mary, let me put it to your husband. He is kind, as you say, to be willing to take her; but let me tell him—"

"No." She went and stood in front of the door, with a frightened look. "No!"

"Let me tell him how it is," he insisted. He had it in mind to offer these people money.

Mary caught him by the wrist. "No, you—you mustn't. He—I told him it was my sister's child. He—don't know."

Dr. Lavendar fell back, but his face cleared. "A lie!" he said. "Mary, you're not worthy of her. What do I care if you gave her birth? You are nothing but her mother! She shall stay where she is!"

Mary turned white; then she dropped down at his feet. "Give me my baby," she said. "Oh, Mr. Lavendar, give me my baby!" She put her arms

" THEN SHE DROPPED DOWN AT HIS FEET "

about his knees and looked up at him, her voice hoarse and whispering. "I must have her—I must have her!" She dropped her face on the floor, moaning like an animal. He looked down at her, the difficult tears of age standing in his eyes.

"Mary," he said, trying to lift her, "stop—stop and think of An—of the child's best good. And, besides, you have another child; why not get it?"

"Dead," she said, brokenly; "dead."

"I believe," he said, solemnly, "it is better dead than with you. Alas that I must say so! And as for this child, that you deserted ten years ago, when I say she must stay where she is, I am not thinking of—of the people she is living with, who would be heart-broken to part with her; I'm thinking of her future—"

"Well, but," she interrupted, passionately, "what about me? Haven't I any future? You've got to give her to me!"

But he knew from her confession that her husband was ignorant of her past, and that he held the situation in his hand: she could not force him to give Anna up unless she betrayed herself; and that, it was plain, she would not do.

"I tell you," she insisted, "I'll give her as good a home as anybody. Oh, my little, little baby! I want my baby! Oh, you haven't a heart in you, to kill me like this! My baby—" Again she broke off, gasping and sobbing. It was horrible and heart-breaking. A timid knock at the door came like a crash into their ears.

"Mamie!"

Mary leaped to her feet, brushing her hand over her eyes, and panting, but holding herself rigid.

("Don't tell him," she said, rapidly;) and then laughed, in a silly, breathless way. "Go 'way, Gus; I ain't through yet."

"I thought I heard you takin' on," he said, peering suspiciously into the room.

"Oh, get out with you!" she answered. "No; I was just talking. Go back, I'll be out in a minute." The man withdrew, meekly.

Dr. Lavendar stood looking at her; he had no doubts now. "Not that which is natural but that which is spiritual," he thought to himself. He wondered if the children had all come; he wondered if Anna was sitting on one of the little hard benches, saying her catechism over to some other child. Mary talked on, passionately, but in a low voice. She urged every conceivable reason for the custody of her child, ending by saying, in sudden anger—for Dr. Lavendar only answered her by a slow, silent shake of the head—

"Well, I shouldn't think, if I'm so bad I can't have her, that the folks that has her would want a child with such bad blood in her!" She was trembling again, and ready for another wild burst of tears.

But as she spoke, Gus knocked once more. "Say, Mame: we've *got* to go; we'll miss the train."

"Shut the door," she said. Then looked full into Dr. Lavendar's face. "*Will you give me my child?*"

"No," he said, pityingly.

She stared at him a moment, her eyes narrowing, hate and fear and misery in her face. "Then—I'll go to hell!" she said; and turned and left him, shutting the door behind her softly.

"Come on," she told the meek husband.

Gus followed her out into the rain.

"Are you goin' after the young one now?" he said.

"No. He won't let me get her. He says she'd ought to stay with the folks that took her when my sister died."

Gus opened the carriage door for her, and chuckled. "Well, now, Mame, it would be quite a change for her. We're strangers to her, and she might be homesick. I didn't let on to you, but I thought of that. I don't know but what the old gentleman is right. And, you know, maybe—" He whispered something, looking at her out of his stupid, kindly eyes, his loose, weak mouth dropping into its meaningless smile.

Dr. Lavendar went to a little closet in the chimney breast, and took out a chunky black bottle and a glass. His hands shook so that the bottle and tumbler clinked together. He had to sit down a few minutes and get his breath and strength; the struggle had profoundly exhausted him; he looked very old as he sat there and swallowed his thimbleful of brandy.

"Solomon didn't know everything," he said to himself; "but may God forgive me if I've done wrong!"

In the dining-room the children were yawning and squabbling and hearing each other repeat the Collect and "your duty to your neighbor." It was nearly three. Theophilus Bell had instituted a game of "settlers escaping from Indians," which involved diving under the table, and leaping over the benches; but the girls felt that such levity was sacrilegious.

"There's prayer-books here," Anna King said, "so it's just the same as church."

"A prayer-book," returned Theophilus, scornfully, "isn't anything but a book; it's the prayers out of it that makes the church, and—" But his voice trailed off into quick subsidence as Dr. Lavendar came in.

"Well, children," he said, "you had to wait. I'm sorry. I think, though, as it's so late, we won't have any lesson—"

("Bully!" said Theophilus, under his breath.)

"—but we'll repeat the Collect, all together, and then you may go home."

"Aren't we going to have our apples?" remonstrated Theophilus.

"Oh, dear me, yes. Yes, yes. Come, Anna, my child, and kneel down here beside me. Children, let us pray:

"*O Lord, we beseech Thee mercifully to receive the prayers of Thy people who call upon Thee; and grant that they may both perceive and know what things they ought to do, and also may have grace and power faithfully to fulfil the same; through Jesus Christ our Lord.*

"*Amen!*" said Dr. Lavendar.

JUSTICE AND THE JUDGE

JUSTICE AND THE JUDGE

I

THE orchard sloped down the hill-side from the Judge's house to the dusty turnpike that bent around the estate like an arm — an arm that ended in a threatening fist where, in Mercer, the road broadened into the square before the court-house and the gray granite jail. The road itself was pretty enough, except where it passed through Mercer's squalid mill suburbs; it kept near the river, wandering across the meadows, and then up and over the hills, through the shadows of buttonwoods and chestnuts; but it lost its prettiness again where, just this side of Old Chester, it held, in a little bend, a cluster of shape-less houses, with patched walls and unsteady stove-pipes, and muddy foot-paths where grunting pigs refused to stir to give room to the passer-by. The men who worked in the brick-kilns lived in this set-tlement, and paid an exorbitant rent to the Judge; their unsightly hovels were not visible from his mel-ancholy old house on the hill, because the road came between them, and then a fringe of elderberries and sumachs, and then the orchard, where the trees, un-pruned for many a year, were thick with bunches of twigs and gray with lichen. The brickmakers' village was not beautiful to look upon, but it meant no irony when it named itself " Morrison's Shanty-town." Indeed, it had a certain pride in having a landlord who was rich and powerful; and it boasted about his money and his "big house" in a way that would have greatly astonished the Judge, who, plod-ding along on his big, rangy Kentucky horse, used to turn his head away when he passed the group of houses self-christened with his honorable name.

It was this neighborly pride, rather than any malice, that made the Judge's orchard a place where Morrison's Shantytown took its outings and its apples. As for the latter, they were poor enough— hard, gnarly russets, or small, bitter rambos. The time was long past since the orchard was in its prime; in those days there had been boys and girls in the "big house," and the Judge himself, the eldest brother, was a serious young man who wore a stock and a flowered waistcoat. The serious young man turned into a serious elderly man, and the brothers and sisters scattered off into the world; and the orchard grew rankly, and the brickmakers began to huddle together at the foot of the hill below the great, dilapidated old house where, with his sister Hannah, the Judge lived, absorbed in his profession, and, when he was not contemptuous, indifferent to all the world besides. If he had a purely human emotion, it was pride that he had never been so great a fool as to care for any human creature; he endured his fellow-beings, and was just to them—he said; but he never knew a man, woman, or child who could not be bought and sold like a bale of cotton. "I could probably be bought myself," he said, "if I could think of anything I wanted enough as a price."

JUSTICE AND THE JUDGE

This was the atmosphere into which Theophilus Bell came to live. A silent child, with mild, wide brown eyes, and straight, silken brown hair parted over his candid forehead. Theophilus's mother had been the Judge's younger sister. He had liked her, in his way; at least, he liked her better than his older sister, Hannah, who, besides being a woman, was a fool — he had so informed her many times. The Judge had supposed that Theophilus's mother was going to keep house for him, and be the meek, subject woman that their mother had been to their father. Instead, when she was over thirty, she suddenly married a poor, good-for-nothing, amiable fellow, an artist—a scallawag, the Judge called him—who had not even kept her alive, for she died in a year, leaving this one child, whom she, with silly, feminine sentiment, had chosen to name after her eldest brother.

"Thinks I'll leave my money to him," the Judge said to himself when he was informed of the compliment that had been paid him; and his eyes narrowed into a sort of laugh.

"You are welcome to call him Theophilus," he wrote the mother, "but I should think the name would kill him. And perhaps I had better take this opportunity of stating he need have no expectations from me; all my money will go in public bequests."

Theophilus survived the name, but his mother did not long survive the letter. As for his father, when the child was ten years old, the poor, gentle, sickly gentleman realized that he too was going to leave the boy, so his future must be provided for. So he gave Theophilus two charges: "Now, boy, remem-

ber, when father isn't here—remember all your life :
'*Don't cry; and play fair;*'" and then he made his
will, bequeathing his only possession in the world,
Theophilus, to the Judge.

He informed his brother-in-law of this fact by
letter. Then he died. The Judge's astonishment
and ire made him take a few days to reflect how
he was to decline this unexpected gift ; and while he
reflected, the scallawag was buried and Theophilus
arrived.

The stage dropped Theophilus at the gate at the
foot of the orchard.

"The Judge lives up on the hill," said the driver,
pointing with the handle of his whip; then the old
yellow coach creaked, and sagged forward, and went
rumbling into the evening dusk.

The little boy stood looking after it with straining
eyes. It seemed to be his last friend disappearing
around the shoulder of the hill.

As Mr. Bell's funeral had been nobody's business in
particular, except an inconvenienced landlady's, who
wished to get it over as soon as possible, and an offi-
ciating clergyman's, who was in a hurry to go to a
parishioner's tea party, there had been nobody who
thought it worth while to prepare Mr. Justice Morrison's mind for his nephew's arrival. The landlady
"shipped" the child the morning after the funeral,
and the undertaker mailed the bill for his services
at the same time. Theophilus was sent through like
an express parcel, and dropped here on the road-
side with his big valise, which held all his belong-
ings—and held also, squeezed into a corner by the
little boy when the landlady was not looking, his

father's old pipe. The landlady missed the pipe afterwards when she evened up her account with the poor deceased gentleman. She said she was sure that the undertaker had stolen it, and she felt an added resentment at Mr. Bell for his inconsiderateness in dying in a boarding-house.

The country road was very quiet; the orchard on the hill-side was full of shadows, and the path up to the house was almost hidden by the fringe of grass on either side. Theophilus wondered if his uncle had any dogs. He thought the orchard looked very dark; he thought the valise was pretty heavy; he— wanted his father. Theophilus hunted in his pocket for his handkerchief. He was a very little boy; he was dressed in an old-fashioned way, and had the nervous and silent exactness of a child who has shared an older person's experiences and anxieties. When he had squeezed his handkerchief against his eyes, and swallowed hard, he folded the small square neatly up and put it back into his pocket; then he tugged at the bag, and got it on his shoulder, and began to climb the hill.

The house loomed up black and desolate in the autumn twilight. Across the closed and shuttered front there was a portico, with wooden columns that had once been white, but from which the blistered paint had cracked and flaked; the ceiling of this porch had been plastered, but the plaster had broken here and there, and fallen, and the laths showed gaunt and dusty; mud-swallows had built their nests in the corners, and a gray ball showed that the paper-wasps liked the crumbling shelter. There had been a garden once in front of the house, but now there was only a vague outline of box-borders,

dead and broken down, or growing high and stiff
in favored spots. There were a good many trees
around the house, and in some places their dense
foliage kept the ground beneath so shadowed that
it was bald and bare, or slippery with green mould.
Theophilus, panting up the orchard path, crossed the
weedy driveway and came up to the porch steps. There
was not a light anywhere in the forbidding front. It
was very still up there on top of the hill, and it is
pretty dark on an October evening by six o'clock.
Theophilus felt his heart come up into his throat; he
stepped stealthily, and started when a twig snapped
underfoot. The dark shuttered house, brooding in
the twilight, and the little boy with his heart in his
mouth, confronted each other. Theophilus looked
over his shoulder breathlessly. Suppose he should
run down the hill just as hard as he could? His
very legs felt the impulse to run! But what dreadful thing might be behind him if he started? He
sobbed once, hauled at the valise, went right up the
steps, and tugged at the bell.

The Judge and Miss Hannah were at supper. The
dining-room was at the back of the house; in fact, in
the liberal days of the Morrison family, before the
Judge got rich, this room had been the kitchen;
now, Miss Hannah did the cooking in the wash-
house, and her brother came in the back way; the
front part of the house—the hall, and the double
parlors on each side of it—had been shut up for
many years.

There was a lamp on the table by the Judge's
book, but the rest of the room was dark. "Don't
waste oil," Miss Hannah had been instructed long

"THEOPHILUS WENT RIGHT UP THE STEP AND TUGGED AT
THE BELL"

ago; so she fumbled about in the dim light, and brought her brother his bread and butter and meat, and pecked at bits from the plates as she carried them in and out, like a thin gray bird with frightened eyes. Then she sat down at the farther end of the table, watching her brother, and ready to jump if he looked up from his book. The Judge's head stood out gray and wolfish against the nimbus of light from the lamp. The wrinkles on his shaven face spread like threads from the corners of his eyes, and were drawn down in deep sharp folds from his nostrils; his cold, mean mouth was puckered, as if a drawing-string had been run around it, then pulled up tightly. The book he read was a French novel. Miss Hannah ate her bread-and-butter, and wondered when he would be ready for his tea.

Then they both looked up with a start.

The rusty wire running along the ceiling jerked, snapped, and the bell at the end of it jangled faintly, and then swung back and forth soundless, as if breathless from exertion. The brother and sister looked up at it open-mouthed.

"What's that?" said the Judge.

"The—bell," Miss Hannah faltered.

"I inferred as much," the Judge said. "Well, go see who it is."

Miss Hannah got up nimbly, as a horse jerks forward at the crack of a whip; she went trotting through the dark hall, but waited a moment before she turned the key in the lock. "Who's there?" she said, faintly.

A small voice answered through the key-hole: "Theophilus."

Miss Hannah caught her breath and stood pant-

ing ; it took her a good minute to draw the bolt and
unlock the door, and when she did, the little boy
fell forward into the hall, he had been so crouched
against the door, for terror of the night, and the
stillness, and the great shadows under the roof of
the porch.

"Does my uncle live here?" said Theophilus, sobbing. At that Miss Hannah knelt down in front of
him and kissed him, and strained him to her with
her trembling old arms.

"I don't know why you're crying," Theophilus remonstrated. "Did I hurt you when I ran against
you? The door opened—unexpectedly. Are you
my uncle's cook?"

At this Miss Hannah got up with a start, as
though she heard the whip crack, and looked over
her shoulder. "Oh dear!" she said, "what shall we
do?" And as she spoke the cold, precise voice called
out :

"Hannah! tell whoever it is that messages come
to the back door. I'm ready for my tea."

"What had you better do?" gasped Miss Hannah.

Theophilus tugged at his valise. "If you'll help
me carry this," he said, politely, "I'll ask my uncle
to pay you. It's very heavy."

"Oh, don't," poor old Hannah entreated. "Oh,
do—oh, my! What will he say?" But she followed,
helping with the valise, irresponsible and inconsequent.

As for Theophilus, he made his way to the room
where the Judge was waiting for his tea.

"Hannah, you are slower than—" Then he looked
up and saw Theophilus.

"Uncle," said the little boy, "father said to tell

184

you that I wouldn't be any trouble. He said I was a pretty good boy," said Theophilus, his voice shaking, "and I've come to live with you. Is that your cook? I nearly knocked her down when I came in; but I didn't mean to. Shall I have my supper now, uncle?"

"Who the devil— Is this that man Bell's brat? Hannah, what does this mean?"

"Oh, brother, it's Mary's child," old Miss Hannah said. "Don't you see?—her eyes! and oh, brother, he was named after you."

"Oh, you're my aunt, are you?" Theophilus inquired. "Father said—" but the tears came at the name; "my father, he said—"

"There, dear; there," Hannah whispered; "don't —do—I wouldn't—brother won't like—"

"I'm not going to cry," said Theophilus; "father told me not to. Uncle, may I have my supper?"

"Hannah, get me my tea. Can't you shut him up? Give him some food and send him to bed. What the devil—" And the Judge took his novel and the lamp and went abruptly out of the room. Miss Hannah and Theophilus, left in the darkness, heard the stairs creak under his angry foot, and then the bang of the library door.

"Oh dear! ought I to take his tea up to him?" panted Miss Hannah, fumbling about for matches and a candle. "Oh, my dear little boy, why *did* you come?"

"He isn't very pleasant, is he, aunt?" said Theophilus. "Father said he was a pagan."

"A pagan!" Miss Hannah repeated, shocked. "Why, no, indeed! A pagan is a heathen, and your uncle is a Christian. You mustn't say such things, my little boy. Pagan! why, not at all—indeed he isn't." Miss Hannah was frightened and ruffled and crying all at once.

"I think," said Theophilus, shyly, "father only meant a brute. I'd like my supper a good deal, aunt."

II

This was the beginning of Theophilus's life with the Judge—or, rather, in the Judge's house. Miss Hannah, palpitating with fright, bade the boy "keep out of brother's way"; and Theophilus was quite willing to do so. The first day or two poor old Hannah scarcely dared to breathe, for fear of reminding the Judge of her existence, and so, incidentally, of his nephew's; she lived in terror of being told that the boy must be sent away—"to the poor-house; or to the devil!" her brother was capable of saying.

For the Judge was sharply angry; all the more so because he found himself unable to dismiss the whole thing by packing the child off. "I don't know why I put up with it," he snarled to himself. "Why should I support other people's brats? And as for leaving him anything—of course that's what Bell was up to—" And then the Judge chuckled, and thought of his will. But in a minute he gritted his teeth with anger. Bell had gotten ahead of him, and he couldn't get at him to express his opinion. "Contemptible!" he said. "These men who go off to play on their golden harps, and leave other men to support their progeny, are religious tramps! One of these days we'll get civilized enough to legislate

on this matter of offspring; every child that can't
be supported properly by its parents will have its
neck wrung! and the father's and mother's too, if I
had my way."

At which Miss Hannah blanched, and hid Theophilus away still more carefully. But that was
how it was conceded that he might remain. So Miss
Hannah got her breath, though she was always looking over her shoulder, so to speak, for fear the Judge
should "legislate."

As for Theophilus, he was very quiet and obedient. He missed his father with all his little mind
and heart, and used to take the pipe out of his valise
every night, and hold it in his hands, and sometimes
he would blink and draw in his breath in the dark,
and remember that he had promised not to cry; but
he never spoke of his loss to Miss Hannah, who said
to herself that she was glad he "had gotten over it."
Theophilus helped her a good deal in her pottering
work about the untidy, dilapidated house, and took
his food in the wash-house when the Judge had finished his meals, and played about by himself, and
crept noiselessly up-stairs to go to bed in a little
closet of a room far away from his uncle's. He
seemed fond of Miss Hannah, and used to sit and
hold her hand, and play with the thin old fingers,
and lean his head against her knee. He did not talk
much, and never about himself; but his soft ways
quite hid from his aunt that he was not a confiding
child.

When the winter came he used to trudge in to Old
Chester every morning to the public school—Miss
Hannah would not have dreamed of asking her
brother for money to send him to Miss Bailey's

little private school. He used to go to Dr. Lavendar's collect class on Saturdays, and he went to church with Miss Hannah every Sunday ; but he made no friendships among the Old Chester children.

" He's so shy," Miss Hannah used to explain. But though Theophilus held her skirt in a nervous grip, he looked out from behind it calmly, with far less shyness than was visible in Miss Hannah's own face. He was perfectly silent, unless spoken to, and then answered in gentle monosyllables.

That winter the Judge hardly spoke to him. The first time he had any conversation with him was once when he found Theophilus in the stable, patting the big Kentucky horse. He began to frown immediately, being especially ready to frown because the horse had gone lame the night before.

" Uncle," said Theophilus, " Jack had a stone in his shoe. I took it out."

The Judge grunted. Then he felt Jack's leg, and thought to himself that it was the only time since the boy had been in the house that he had been good for anything.

" I don't want you hanging round the stable, young man. Do you hear me ?" he said. But he looked at Theophilus once or twice ; and that night he said to his sister, sharply : " Hannah, what the devil do you hide that child away for ? Have him take his meals in the dining-room. Do you hear ? Let him sit with me, or he'll grow up a barbarian, with no manners !"

And Miss Hannah was far too thankful for this grace on her brother's part to feel any humor in reference to manners.

JUSTICE AND THE JUDGE

The Judge's remark about hanging around the stable did not deter Theophilus from playing there all that winter. If grown people will remember, box-stalls are admirable forts in which to hide during the attacks of Indians ; and an old carriage, unused for many years, the cushions slit and dusty, is an excellent vehicle in which to journey to Asia or the north pole, as fancy may chance to drive. Miss Hannah used to wonder sometimes what Theophilus did with himself, all alone in the barn. When she asked him, he would think a while, and then say, vaguely,

"Oh, just play, aunt ;" and Miss Hannah was contented.

She never dreamed of " bringing him up," as Old Chester expressed it; all that the boy did, and the little that he said, were perfect in her mild, frightened eyes. She treated him as an equal, if not as a superior — which, if Old Chester had known it, would have been a cause for anxiety and prayer. She used to talk to him a great deal in her incoherent way, telling him her troubles about the cost of things, and her worries over the Judge's food. And Theophilus listened, and said, " Yes, aunt," and " No, aunt"; and Miss Hannah felt that at last she had a confidant.

After a while Theophilus began to wander down through the orchard and look at Shantytown—dirty, good-natured, friendly Shantytown ; and later in the winter he slipped across the road and made acquaintance with the pigs and chickens, and then with the children, and by-and-by he constructed a society of his own, of which Katy Murphy was the choicest spirit.

The Murphys lived in the second house on the other side of the road. There were seven dirty, happy children, and a big, rosy, comfortable mother, and the usual drunken, bad-tempered father, and two pigs, and a cat, and the hens—such tame hens they were, too, Theophilus noticed, walking all about the room when the family was at table! The house was a series of little pens, without any ventilation to speak of; its earthen floors were laid in refuse bricks, and it was cheerfully and openly dirty. Of course the Murphys ought, by rights, to have been sick. Willy King told Dr. Lavendar that there would be a terrible outbreak of typhoid in Shanty-town some day. But so far it had not appeared; which must have been very mortifying and disappointing to Willy.

Theophilus had made acquaintance with Katy by offering her silently over the gate a tumbler of snow ice-cream. Katy, as silently, ate the slushy mixture of sugar and milk and snow, looking with big eyes at Theophilus. After that they became friends—quite speechlessly, however. It was not until spring, when she showed him how to make licorice-water in a bottle, and he taught her one of the child languages: "willvus youvus playvus withvus mevus?" that their friendship began to be eloquent.

But Theophilus said nothing about Katy or Shantytown to his aunt. Miss Hannah sometimes saw the flutter of a ragged petticoat or a shock of tangled hair under a dirty cap; and once she asked him anxiously if he didn't think perhaps he was seeing too much of those rowdy children?

" No, aunt," said Theophilus; which closed the subject—though Miss Hannah did suggest, hesitat-

ingly, that perhaps he had better not let his uncle
see him playing with the Shantytown children, because he might be displeased.

"He's almost always displeased, isn't he, aunt?"
Theophilus said, meditatively, but had no thought
of committing himself to a promise.

At first all the Murphy children played with him
in the orchard, and there were the usual squabbles
and bickerings. Katy, however, followed Theophilus's lead in all their games, and never had any ideas
of her own. She used to look at him with her mouth
open and her eyes wide with wonder, but she never
made an objection. So, by degrees, Nelly and Tommy and the other children were gently but firmly
dropped. Theophilus found that friendship *à deux*
was quite enough for him, so Katy became his constant companion. It was through this love for Katy
that the Judge first really wounded the child, and
laid up wrath against the day of wrath. It was the
summer of the seventeen-year locusts. Old Chester
will not soon forget that summer. On every leaf,
on every stalk of blossoming grass, on all the clover
tops, were the locusts; the hot, still air was full of
their endless *z-z-z-ing*, like the sharpening of scythes.
The children of Shantytown added largely to family
incomes by collecting the locusts, picking them by
the hatful or the basketful, as though they were
berries, and being paid by the farmers a few cents a
peck. Theophilus, however, forbade Katy's taking
part in this industry; which caused her soft eyes to
well over with tears.

"They kick," said Theophilus; "don't touch 'em."

"They're ateing things up," Katy murmured,
longingly.

The two children were sitting on a stile making bur baskets. Later, these baskets were to be filled with the little whity-green seeds of the mallow, which are "cheeses," and are eaten when one eats the white ends of early grass and calls it celery. Theophilus was frowning with anxiety, because the handle of his basket, made with burs which were showing the blossoming pink at the end, would break, no matter how carefully he lifted it. His head ached with the worry of it, and with the sun, and the smell of the burdocks, so he was glad to think about the locusts. "They are eating things up," he said, "and they are pretty wicked, so I'll tell you what you may do: you may catch a *few;* catch twelve, and put 'em in a flower-pot for a dungeon. And bring 'em up into the orchard this afternoon," he added, as an afterthought. Then he kissed Katy tenderly, and put the bur baskets in the shadow under the stile, and went home to dinner, absorbed in thought.

When Katy met him in the orchard with the imprisoned locusts, he had decided their fate.

"My uncle's a judge," he said, "and he hangs wicked people. So we'll hang these prisoners; for they certainly are bad. Only, first," he said, his face beginning to glow, "we must build the gallows!"

Katy opened her mouth, speechless. Theophilus, however, expected no comment. He led the way, knee-deep through a rustling patch of May-apples, to a shady spot, where he proceeded to drive two laths into the ground as uprights, laying another lath over them for a cross-piece.

"There, now!" he said, breathlessly. "Of course, Katy, we must give them warning first, so that they may prepare to die. My uncle does that when he hangs people. Give me the flower-pot, and I'll tell them." He lifted the shingle which formed the door of the prison, and surveyed the captives, tumbling and crawling over each other, each with the ominous black *W* on its membraneous wings—that *W* which meant *war*, Katy's mother had said. "It means wicked, I guess," Theophilus said, sternly. And then, in an awful voice, he bade the prisoners "prepare to die." "I hope it won't hurt 'em," he added, slowly.

"What, Theophilus?" Katy inquired.

"To hang them, you know."

"Oh !" said Katy.

"Do you think it will ?"

"I don't know just how it do feel," Katy admitted.

Theophilus opened and shut his hands nervously. "I don't like to put the rope around their necks," he faltered.

"Oh, lemme," Katy said.

"It isn't fair to make you do it. Oh, Katy, let's let 'em escape ! If we take the stone off the top of the shingle, they can get out, and we can play it was an accident. Play one of them is a great general ; play he plans an escape—"

"They're wicked, Theophilus," Katy reminded him.

"That's so," said Theophilus, with a troubled face.

"And I don't mind putting the thread on 'em," Katy coaxed.

" 'Rope,' " Theophilus corrected her. "Are you sure you don't mind? Had you just as lieve?"

"I just as lieve ; I *rother*," Katy said, eagerly.

"Well," the little boy said; but his voice was reluctant. "They are wicked—there's no use playing they're not; and if you don't mind touching 'em—"

"I'd like to," Katy said, with animation.

So Theophilus produced a spool of black sewing-silk which he had secured from Miss Hannah's work-basket, and measuring off enough "rope" for each victim, instructed Katy how she should fasten it round what he called the "necks" of the unfortunate insects; then he turned his back, shivering and clinching his hands, his face pale with emotion.

"Katy, don't forget: *they are wicked*," he kept reminding her, "and so they ought to be punished; it's fair. Are the prisoners ready?"

"Yes, Theophilus; I've fixed 'em," said Katy, joyously.

"You must say, 'Yes, my lord,'" Theophilus said, in an imperative aside.

"Yes, my lord," repeated Katy.

Theophilus, with a majestic tread, turned to the gallows, and began to tie each piece of thread to the cross-tree; but his hand shook. "I wonder if uncle says anything to 'em when he hangs them?" he murmured. He was so wretched that Katy was moved to say,

"Theophilus, let me tie 'em up for you? I'd just as lieve."

"No," he answered—"no; I'm a judge, like uncle; and the judge has to hang people; my uncle does it every day." He tied the last thread, and the wicked locusts began to spin round and round in their black silk halters.

The two children were holding the court of justice down in the orchard; it was a still, warm after-

" ' SO YOU'RE HANGING THE LOCUSTS?' "

noon, the sky was deeply blue and without a cloud ; the grass under the apple-tree where the gallows stood was beaten down, but it grew so high outside that they did not see Judge Morrison coming up the path, and he stood still a moment looking at them, and, as it happened, heard Theophilus's last remark. At first he did not understand the laths and the unhappy locusts swinging back and forth ; but his nephew's words enlightened him. He laughed, silently, thinking of his peaceful Orphans' Court. "The Judge doesn't have a chance, unfortunately," he said to himself; and then brought his cane smashing down on the gallows.

"Here, what are you about?"

The two children jumped apart, guiltily.

"Who's this girl?" the Judge demanded.

"It's Katy Murphy," Theophilus said, with white lips.

"Well, clear out," Judge Morrison said. "I don't want you loafing on my place. Do you hear me?"

Katy ducked, and ran as fast as her bare, fat legs could carry her, bounding across the orchard grass, and scrambling over the gate at the end of the path.

"So you're hanging the locusts?" inquired the Judge, contemptuously.

"Oh," said Theophilus, in a low voice, "I do *not* like you;" then he turned and ran after Katy, leaving his uncle feeling as though a humming-bird had suddenly attacked him. His tight, wrinkled mouth relaxed in a sort of smile. "Well!" he said ; "he doesn't like me!" He cackled to himself once as he climbed the hill. He had not been so diverted in a long time.

III

So that was how the Judge began to get acquainted with his nephew. The mimic court of justice in the orchard tickled him immensely, and Theophilus's enraged candor in saying he did not like him awoke a sense of humor that generally only responded to the bitternesses and meannesses of his court-room. "O most excellent Theophilus," he said, "how many people feel that but don't say it!"

He began to watch the boy, and sometimes threw a condescending word at him. As for Theophilus, he spoke when he was spoken to, and once or twice in his small voice, unasked, expressed opinions which were not complimentary to the Judge:

"Uncle, why don't you say 'Thank you' to Aunt Hannah? Father told me always—"

"Hold your tongue!" said the Judge.

"You're not very polite," said Theophilus, his heart beating hard, but his voice calm. The Judge put down his book and looked at him, the drawing-string around his puckered mouth relaxing.

"Well!" he said, with a chuckle. The child's courageous dislike entertained him greatly. As for Miss Hannah, she was so frightened she could only murmur: "My dear little boy! Oh do—oh don't— oh, brother, he doesn't mean it."

Theophilus did not corroborate this statement; he ate his bread-and-butter in silence, and planned his plays with Katy, and thought how pleasant it would be if his uncle should die, and Aunt Hannah should marry some kind gentleman, like father, and have six little boys and six little girls for him to play with. He told Miss Hannah so, thoughtfully; and her old, worn face colored faintly, and she said,

"Oh, Theophilus, now do—now don't—now, you musn't—"

"Well," he said, "I'm going to get married myself; I'm going to marry Katy, and we'll live here and take our meals in the wash-house, and not with uncle; for Katy don't like uncle."

Miss Hannah was horrified; but very likely Theophilus did not hear her agitated reproof; he was arranging a new play. It was of such elaborate character—revolving, as it did, upon the capture of Katy by cannibals, and her rescue by Theophilus—that the next afternoon, when he and Katy acted it out, supper-time came and went and he was all unconscious of it. When hunger and Katy reminded him of this oversight he went into the Murphys' kitchen, and had a piece of fried meat and a potato, sitting by the stove, and waited upon by Mrs. Murphy, who cuffed her children away from his chair, and put a stool under his feet, and told him he was the darlin' boy, if ever there was one.

"Ach, Katy, ye spalpeen, ye! ye've got the fine sweetheart! When are ye's going to set up housekeepin', the two of ye's?"

"Very soon," said Theophilus. "I'd like some more tea, Mrs. Murphy. Katy, we'll get married next week, I think."

Mrs. Murphy winked at her husband, who was filling the room with clouds of bad tobacco smoke, and clapped Theophilus on the shoulder with her kind big hand. "An' what 'll the Judge say?"

"Oh, I don't mind what he says," Theophilus answered, calmly. "Katy and I don't like him. He's

an unjust judge. Father said you must be polite,
no matter how you felt inside. So I'm polite to him.
But he spoke cross to Katy, and I don't like him."
Then he got down from his chair and embraced
Katy tenderly. "It's pretty dark out-of-doors," he
said, with a sigh; and Katy offered to escort him
home. He looked at her longingly, for the shadows
under the apple-trees on the hill were very black,
but shook his head, and went timorously out into
the twilight.

Meantime Miss Hannah had some bad moments:

"Where's that child? Hannah, if that boy can't
be on time for his meals, he can go without. Do
you hear?"

Then the Judge opened his book, and added something in a sharp voice about a boarding-school.
Poor old Hannah's knees trembled; she looked
stealthily out of the window between every mouth-
ful; but it grew darker and darker, and there was
no sign of Theophilus.

"Where is that child?" the Judge said again, angrily. Miss Hannah looked over at him with a start,
her cowering mouth opening in astonishment. *His
voice was anxious!* It was such an amazing revela-
tion that she could not speak. "Why, brother's
worried!" she said to herself.

The Judge did not, apparently, miss her response.
He got up and went out of the room; in the upper
hall he stopped, and, leaning over the banisters, called
down to her:

"Where does that child sleep?"

She told him, tremulously; and a moment afterwards heard him tramping overhead, and then the
door of Theophilus's room opened and shut. Evi-

dently he had thought the boy might be there ; but he came tramping back again.

"Has he come in yet?" he called down.

"No, brother. Oh yes, brother! Here he is. Oh, Theophilus, where—"

The library door banged.

"Theophilus, brother has been asking about you," Miss Hannah said, breathlessly. "My dear little boy, don't you think you ought, perhaps, to be a little more punctual? I've saved some supper for you—"

"I don't want any. Katy's mother gave me some. What was uncle in my room for? I saw the light—" Theophilus was out of breath, for the orchard had been very dark ; but without waiting for a reply he ran up-stairs, and was back again in two minutes. "Aunt, he has taken— He's a thief! He's stolen— *my pipe !*" Then he burst out crying, shaking with sobs, and stamping with anger. "He's a thief! It was on the mantel-piece. It's no fairs, going to my room. He's stolen—my pipe!"

Miss Hannah was at her wits' end. "If brother hears him, he'll send him to school," she thought, in despairing terror. Then suddenly Theophilus was calm.

"I won't cry any more," he said, in a shaken whisper ; "but—"

And Miss Hannah was satisfied, hearing nothing threatening in that "but."

That night, when she was asleep, the little boy arose, and, creeping from his closet of a room across her floor, gained the entry ; beyond, on the right of the wide hall, was the Judge's library. Theophilus

went stealthily over the boards, stopping when one
creaked loudly under his bare feet, and panting—
and then creeping on again. It seemed to the child
that it was after midnight, so long had he been lying
awake, hating his uncle; but it was scarcely eleven
o'clock, and Judge Morrison was working hard over
his papers, with no thought of bed for a couple of
hours. Theophilus softly turned the knob of the
door, and pushed it a little, and then a little more.
The instant blur of light confused him; he had expected to feel about for his pipe in the darkness.
But he did not see his uncle standing in a shadowy
alcove of the room. The Judge was drawing a book
from one of his shelves. As the child entered he
stopped, his hand in mid-air, and watched him.
Theophilus, breathing hard, and clinching his hands,
went at once to the library table. It was piled with
documents; four or five battered japanned filing-
cases held brown linen envelopes tied with red
tapes, and stuffed in, in overflowing and convenient
disorder; in the middle was a dusty inkstand, with
a bunch of quills beside it; in front of it the papers
were pushed to the right and left to make room for
work. Purdon's Digest was open, propped on an
unsteady heap of other books; on the floor, leaning
up against the desk in tottering piles, were stacks of
reports; every chair, except that which the Judge
used, was full of pamphlets, and an old sofa was lit-
tered with bundles of papers; everything was thick
with dust, and in inextricable disorder. The Judge,
being master in his own house, allowed no woman to
"red up"; so he knew just where everything was.

Theophilus opened a drawer in the writing-table
softly, and looked in; and then another; no pipe.

JUSTICE AND THE JUDGE

There was a desk on the table—one of those old-fashioned desks with a flap that folds back, making a slope, covered with frayed and ink-spotted velvet. He tried to lift the inner lid, which stuck—yielded—and then :

"*Well, young man ?*"

The lid dropped, clattering. Theophilus stared at him, speechless. His uncle's eyes narrowed, and he showed his yellow old teeth in a noiseless laugh.

"You are beginning early, most excellent Theophilus ; you'll end as your locusts did." The Judge was more diverted than he had been in many a long day. "Very likely you will come before me, sir ; and you may be sure I will do my duty !"

Theophilus looked as though he were going to faint ; but he did not ask for mercy.

"Yes ; you are beginning early—smoking, housebreaking— What was it, by-the-way, you hoped to steal ?"

"You," said Theophilus, his teeth chattering in his head, "are a thief. You took my pipe."

"Hah !" said the Judge ; "you mean to file a cross suit ? Very good, sir. What is this about a pipe ? I don't allow boys to smoke in my house."

"I don't smoke," said Theophilus, in a whisper.

The Judge dropped his banter.

"Now don't lie. If you're a liar, I'll—"

"Oh," cried the child, "you are certainly a very bad man. You stole my pipe, and say I tell stories. You tell stories yourself ; and you are a thief ; it's no fairs. Give me my pipe or"—the little boy was deadly pale, shaking with anger and hate—"or—very likely I shall—probably—be obliged to—to kill you, you know." Then he burst into a storm of tears.

The Judge looked at him with a sort of pride : courage, temper, truth — he ought to amount to something.

"If you don't smoke, why do you have a pipe?"

Silence.

"Answer me, you cub !"

No reply.

"Answer me, or you won't get your pipe. Why do you have it?"

Theophilus looked at him, but said nothing.

The Judge was more and more pleased. "Well, you can clear out. I shall keep the pipe, and after this I'll lock my door. Clear out! I've had enough of you. Wait a minute. Why were you late for supper? As long as I feed you, sir, you will be on time at your meals. Do you hear? Where were you?"

"At Mrs. Murphy's," said Theophilus.

His uncle's face darkened. "You are not to have anything to do with those people. If I hear of your playing with any of those Shantytown ragamuffins, I'll—I'll attend to you !"

Theophilus shuffled back across the room, and shut the door softly behind him.

The Judge sat down at his table, and his mean, cold face relaxed into something like a smile.

"Spunk !" he said. "Confound him, he'll amount to something !"

IV

"It's my father's pipe," Theophilus told Katy afterwards, "and uncle is a wicked man."

"But if you're not usin' of it, Theophilus," she said, wonderingly, "I wouldn't be takin' on about it."

He looked at her wistfully, but he did not try to explain. Instead, he told her that he wished to get married at once.

"I'd just as lieve," said Katy.

"We'll get married, and I'll keep you up in the garret," said Theophilus. "He'll not know. Then, when I get some money, we'll go away. Let's play this morning that you are a princess turned into a dragon. Play I am a prince coming to rescue you, and you roar and eat me; then you turn into a beautiful princess—no, because where would I be if you had eaten me! Play you roar, and I'll cut off your frightful head; then I'll die, and we'll both come to life, and you'll be a princess."

Katy nodded.

"Play we're dead first," said Theophilus, changing his plot as he proceeded. "We'll dig our graves, and lie down in 'em to see how it feels to be dead."

Katy opened her mouth with interest. Theophilus reflected that it would be hard to dig his grave in the matted orchard grass, and led Katy up into the deserted and neglected garden. It would be easy to make a hole in the soft black earth under the larches, where the grass grew thin and pale. They picked some dandelions on the way, and Theophilus tore the long hollow stems into shreds, and passed them between his lips to make them curl. "They're awfully nasty and bitter," he said; "but I don't mind. Here, let me hang 'em over your ears, Katy. Princesses always have curls." Katy allowed herself to be decorated in silent joy; to feel the dandelion curls brushing against her cheeks made her heart beat with pride. Then she sat down in the grass and watched Theophilus. He grew so happy in his dig-

203

ging that he forgot his wrongs and talked eagerly as
he worked. He said he meant, as soon as he got
time, to dig under a big flat stone in the garden, because he believed there were things buried under it.

"What things, Theophilus?" Katy inquired.

"Oh, dead Indians, and gold," said Theophilus,
impatiently. "It doesn't matter just what. It's
treasures. But I'm so busy I don't get time to dig
'em up."

"An' why was they left under the stone then?"
Katy inquired.

"Well, why shouldn't they be left there?" he retorted, and enlarged so upon the treasures that Katy
was convinced. She leaned her chin in her two little
dirty hands, and crossed her bare feet over each
other, as a duck does, and listened.

"It's pretty hot," said Theophilus; "I guess we
won't each have a grave; we'll just get buried turn
about." And then he stopped, and stood up straight,
and wiped his little forehead, and said, in a manly
voice, "By George, it's hard work. By George."
Then he bade Katy get up and be measured for her
grave, for she was taller than he.

"Don't you think you *could* be buried by putting
your legs under you?" he asked. "It's pretty hot,
digging."

"Honest, I can't," she said anxiously; "my legs
'ain't got no hinge in 'em between there and there;
honest they 'ain't, Theophilus."

"Well," said the grave-digger, bitterly, "I'll make
it a little longer. But it's long enough for *me*, Katy
Murphy!"

Katy was in despair lest she was going to lose her
chance to be buried, and her big, gentle, stupid eyes

filled up ; at sight of which Theophilus sprung from the grave and embraced her.

"You shall be buried ! Now don't you cry, Katy. I don't mind making room for your legs ; only, they are a little long."

Katy cheered up at once, and listened to Theophilus telling his story as he dug—a prince and a princess, a cruel king, a jealous fairy, a poisoned cup, and —an open grave !

"Now it's ready," Theophilus cried, exultant, throwing down his spade and preparing to step in ; then he stopped and looked at Katy. "You may get in first," he said, with an effort : " but you won't stay very long, will you ? Because I did dig it, you know. Still, you may stay as long as you want, Katy."

Katy, with delightful tremors, stepped into the shallow trench and lay down. "Ouch—ain't it cold !" she said. "There's worrums ! O-o-w—"

"Don't talk," said Theophilus, anxiously ; " you're dead."

Katy shut her eyes tightly, and sighed. Then she said,

"May I get out, Theophilus ?"

"Why, don't you want me to shovel in the dirt ?" he reproached her ; but she squealed and scrambled up at the idea of such a thing. And Theophilus, elate and solemn, with shining eyes, stretched himself in her place ; he looked up and saw the fringe of thin grass on the edge of the grave, the dark, drooping branches of the larch, the gray, cloudy sky beyond—

"Theophilus !" whispered Katy. "Oh, my ! here's somebody !"

Theophilus frowned and sat up. It was Judge Morrison.

"Theophilus! who is this girl? Here, you, clear
out! What did I tell you, Theophilus? I will not
have this scum about. Girl, do you hear? Clear
out!" He raised his stick as he spoke. Katy
shrieked, dived past him, and ran. Theophilus came
up to him slowly, then suddenly lifted a trembling
leg and kicked at him. The Judge took him by the
collar and shook him, and then held him off at arm's-
length, and laughed, his eyes lighting with appreciation.

After that there was no question of Judge Morrison's feeling towards his nephew. The boy amused
him, and then interested him ; his courage and candor gave him a thrill of pride ; and by-and-by,
strangely enough, in his withered, mean old heart
there came something which he did not recognize,
having never felt it : to be sure, it showed itself only
in disappointed irritation if Theophilus appeared
stupid ; in impatience if the boy looked tired, which
he did very often ; in anger if he chanced to be late,
as he frequently was, for supper. "Broken his neck,
probably," the Judge would say, and look out of the
window half a dozen times with a snarl of anxiety.
Irritation and contempt are not often interpreters of
love ; certainly it was a good while before the Judge
recognized them. He only realized that he thought
of the child very often ; but he used to tell himself
that that was because Theophilus was a nuisance.

Still, he told Hannah to get the boy better clothes
—though he forgot to give her any money for the
purpose ; and he snapped at her because Theophilus
did not eat enough. Indeed, he watched the child
constantly, his keen cold eyes softening under a sort

of film, as an eagle's, when it looks at its young.
Once, at midnight, he came knocking at Miss Hannah's door. " I want to feel that child's pulse," he
said ; " he looked flushed at supper, and you are such
a fool, Hannah, you'd let him sicken on your hands."

Miss Hannah, palpitating with fright, sat up in
bed and bade him enter.

" I think he's well, brother," she said ; " he said
he was."

" As if either of you had sense enough to know
anything about it !" the Judge retorted. He came
in and went shuffling across the room to Theophilus's
door—a long, lean figure in a gray flannel wrapper ;
he had a palm-leaf fan in one hand, and a red silk
handkerchief, and he carried a tall brass candlestick
—the old-fashioned kind, with a hood, and a spring
inside. He had a vague idea that the boy should be
fanned if he was feverish, and perhaps his head ought
to be tied up. Theophilus was sleeping placidly, the
flush all gone, and his face on its low pillow looking a
little thin.

The Judge came back, blowing out his light as he
walked. "He's to have a tonic. Do you hear ?
Have Willy King see him. A funeral is expensive,"
he ended, with a grin.

Meantime Theophilus paid very little attention to
his uncle ; he did not recognize any overtures for
friendship. Katy had been banished (not that that
made any great difference, because Theophilus could
play down in Shantytown almost as well as in the
orchard) ; Aunt Hannah was scolded ; he himself
was laughed at ; his pipe was gone ; so what did he
care about his uncle ? Indeed, his bitterness grew
as he discovered the practical effect of Katy's fright

the day she had been buried : she refused for a long time to be married. She could not, she said, go and live in the garret, because "He" would find her and lick her. Kill her, maybe. No, she would not get married !

But Theophilus pleaded with her with a passion of entreaty. "Oh, please, Katy. Don't say 'no'; oh, please—*please*, Katy !" And by-and-by there was no gainsaying him.

"Well," said Katy, with a sigh.

"You put on your Sunday dress," her lover told her, "and come to the gate after supper, and I'll be there and take you up to the garret. We'll play it's a railroad journey."

"Father Williams must be gone to first," said Katy.

"Oh, he might tell on us," objected Theophilus. But Katy said again that folks had to go to Father Williams before they were married.

"Why ?" said Theophilus.

But on this point Katy was vague ; she had heard her mother find fault with girls for not "going to the priest" with their sweethearts ; that was all Katy knew.

"Well," said Theophilus, reluctantly ; "it's too late to-day ; but we'll go to-morrow. I'm going to be busy putting the provisions into the garret this afternoon." Then he kissed Katy tenderly, and left her sitting on the fence, scratching her bare legs and reflecting upon her wedding.

The provisioning of the garret was not difficult. Miss Hannah had gone to the sewing society that afternoon, and of course the Judge was not at home ; so the little boy had the gaunt, echoing old house to

himself. If he had not been so interested and excited, he might have been frightened at the silence
and emptiness. Through the wide window in the
upper hall the afternoon sunshine poured in, and lay
in a dusty pool at the foot of the garret stairs ; it
pleased Theophilus to say that he had to wade
through this pool as he carried up his supplies. The
stairs creaked under his eager feet as he lugged up
one burden after another — raw potatoes, a loaf of
bread, eggs, apples, a pitcher of water. Then he
brought some bedclothes from the press in the linen-
closet — his little arms full, and the blankets and
coverlets trailing on the ground, so that he walked
on them and stumbled a dozen times before he
reached the garret.

It was nearly five when all was ready, and then the
impatient bridegroom went to claim his bride.

She was waiting for him at the gate ; she had put
on her red plaid dress, and a little red sack, and her
hat with a feather in it ; her feet and legs were bare,
however, because she could not bring herself to wear
her new shoes when it was not Sunday ; she had an
apple in her hand, and her round little face looked
up trustfully at her bridegroom. Theophilus hurried
her up the path with such anxiety in his manner that
Katy began to be frightened.

"Is He there, Theophilus ?" she said, panting with
their run up the hill.

"Not yet," said Theophilus. "Don't be scared,
Katy. I won't let him hurt you. If he should attack
you, I will throw him down and tie him. Now,
Katy, you climb on the back woodshed, and I'll help
you into the window in my room, and then we'll go
up to the garret."

o   209

Katy was stolidly obedient. It would have seemed simpler to go in the back door and walk up-stairs, but Theophilus preferred this dangerous mode of entering; so she had nothing to say. When she found herself in the garret, however, her eyes widened with interest, and a little stir of imagination made her suggest that they put a chair against the door, for fear the enemy should break in. But Theophilus objected.

"No; if he found the door locked, he'd think maybe we were here; if we hear him coming, we'll hide behind the trunks."

There was plenty of opportunity to hide in the garret. It was a great loft, extending, without any partitions, over the whole house; two chimney-stacks, rough with plaster and gray with dust and cobwebs, stood, half-way from the centre, at each end.

"They are our breastworks to the foe," said Theophilus. However, there was no need to hide, for no dreadful footstep told them of the approach of the enemy. They ate their supper and then cuddled down on the pillows Theophilus had brought, and slept until the eastern window began to grow into a shining blue oblong that opened into heaven.

V

The real alarm did not begin down-stairs until nearly eight, when Mrs. Murphy appeared, apologizing and crying. Was Miss Morrison after knowin' where her Katy was? The young one had lit out, and the holy angels would tell Miss Morrison that Mrs. Murphy didn't know where she was, no more than the dead ; onless she was with the young gentleman, who was after sayin' he was going to marry her.

The Judge, who had been angry because Theophilus was late for supper, was immensely diverted at Mrs. Murphy's tale, and bade her go and hunt for the children in the orchard, promising the boy a caning, and threatening Katy with the House of Correction ; by-and-by he took a lantern and went out himself, looking through the shrubberies, and nearly falling into Theophilus's open grave. The jar and wrench of his stumble, and the flash of remembrance of the little still figure lying there, made him suddenly keenly alarmed, and so, of course, angry again ; but anger did not help matters. All that night they looked, and beat through the woods, and flashed lanterns along the river-bank, and called and shouted ; the Judge was dreadfully silent, and Miss Hannah prayed ; but no children were found.

The next day Theophilus and Katy ate and drank and played—their game being that Theophilus was a hunter, and caught apples in traps in shadowy caves under the rafters, and brought them home to his wife. Katy yawned in the afternoon, and reminded her husband of Father Williams, and began to get rather tired of being married. So, towards dusk, Theophilus said they would try to get out and "go to the priest"; it was as they were coming softly down-stairs that they suddenly heard voices in the library, and darted back for shelter to their garret. But Katy was restless ; in a few minutes she insisted upon crawling out again on to the staircase. Theophilus went after her and plucked at her sleeve.

"He'll catch you! Come away."

"Don't," Katy said, crossly.

Theophilus crept back and sat down on a trunk. The garret was getting dark; those caves under the rafters looked very black; as for what might lurk in them, Theophilus dared not trust his imagination. He felt that if he began to think of their possibili-ties, his mind would decide upon dead pirates. Why pirates, why dead, Theophilus did not know; he only felt that that way terror lay.

"I mustn't get scared," he told himself, breathing hard, and picking with nervous little fingers at the rotting leather of the old trunk. When he could not stand the silence and loneliness any longer, he came cautiously out to Katy again.

"I can hear 'em talkin'!" she whispered, excitedly. "She's takin' on awful."

"Come back," whispered Theophilus; "it's no fairs; they don't know you're hearing them."

Katy looked at him scornfully.

"An' would I be listening if they did? Theophi-lus, she's cryin'!"

And, indeed, poor old Miss Hannah's sobs reached her nephew's ear—for the library door was ajar. At this he took his wife by her arm and dragged her back.

"I must tell Aunt Hannah," he said, in great agi-tation; "I don't want her to cry. When she goes to bed, I'll go down and tell her we are married, and living up here; but she mustn't tell."

"An' leave me alone in the dark?" gasped Katy; and then, suddenly, she began to cry. "I'd 'a' brung a candle 'stead of all them potatoes, if it had been me was doing it," she said. Then she reproached Theophilus for telling her to wear her Sunday clothes. "They'll be shabbying on me," said Katy. She moaned that she did not like living in a garret, and that she wished she had never got married. "I'm going home to my mother," she sobbed.

Theophilus stood beside her in despair. He had never seen Katy in the rôle of her sex. He got down on his knees, and put his little arms around her, and tried to reason with his bride—as other husbands have done before him, and with like success. Katy wept more loudly than ever.

"I don't like being married; and I don't like potatoes that ain't been boiled; and I don't like havin' no bed to sleep in, only them pillows and things which ain't no real bed; and I ain't a-goin' to stay. I'm going home to—my—mother!" Katy's sobs were heart-rending. Theophilus was pale with misery.

"Why, you wouldn't — oh, Katy, you *wouldn't* leave me all alone up here in the dark?" The poor young husband's voice was broken with emotion; he had forgotten the open door, and the wail of Katy's sobs woke only the fear that his domestic happiness was threatened—not that the enemy might hear her.

"I got to, Theophilus; I don't like it. Honest, I don't. Oh, Theophilus, change to Nelly for a wife. She'll do ye; she'll not mind the dark."

"No, she won't do me," he answered, tremulously; "I don't want to change to Nelly; she don't play nicely at all; and she's always talking. I don't want a wife that talks." (Ah, Theophilus, how many men discover this when it is too late to "change to Nelly"!)

"Well, anyway, I'm going home to my mother!" wailed Katy; and this time the enemy heard.

The Judge had been greatly shaken by this day of anxiety; the fact that the children were not immediately and easily found had led to the conclusion that they must have wandered in the darkness along the bank of the river — and the black, deep, quick-flowing little river knew the rest.

"He's drowned," the Judge said to himself over and over when, towards dusk, he sat in his library, his head bent on his breast. "I've lost him," he said, and drew in his lips, and played a tattoo on the arms of his chair. "Lost him — lost him." It was such a wanton and unnecessary loss; if the boy had fallen sick and died, one might say "Providence," and know a sort of dull acquiescence. But this was pure carelessness; there was no need for such a calamity; the child had been neglected. "Hannah neglected him," he said to himself; "the fool! why couldn't she have looked after him? She allowed him to play with that little Murphy devil. I'm glad there's one less of them, anyway; she's drowned, too, thank God! Well, I'll clean that place out. They've killed him—Hannah and those people between them. I wish Mary'd lived; she would have looked after him."

It seemed to him that Mary was somehow responsible; if she had stayed at home and behaved herself, she could have taken care of the child, he thought, dully; so confused by this sudden meeting of love and selfishness, that whirled like two contrary and tumultuous streams through his dry old heart, that he forgot that if Mary had stayed at home Theophilus would not have been at all. He looked up when, with despair in her face, Miss Hannah came in.

"They haven't heard anything yet, brother," she said. "Oh, brother, what do you think?"

"I think that your promising nephew is drowned,

214

my dear sister." His lips curled back from his teeth as he spoke, and there was a gray pallor under his leathery skin.

Old Miss Hannah sat down on a pile of reports, and covered her face with her hands. The Judge glared at her; then he said fiercely, under his breath, "damn you." Yet they had never been so near each other before.

Then, suddenly, from up above them, somewhere in the darkness, a shrill, childish wail wavered faintly, and dropped, and rose again. The two started to their feet together, and listened, breathlessly.

VI

No doubt the reaction from anxiety, and the mortification of remembering how shaken he had been, made the Judge harder than ever. He had no pity; perhaps, even, he had no anger, which would have been humanizing in its way; he had mere disgust and determination. He "cleared that place out" without a day's delay. "Pack!" he said; and the Murphys packed. They did not know enough to use the weapon of the law to make delay; and, besides, who could use the law against a judge?

"He'll be putting us in jail," said Mrs. Murphy, quaking and packing; "and it's your doin', ye spalpeen!" she said, shrilly, to Katy; and cuffed her soundly.

"You are to be off my premises by nine o'clock Saturday morning. I give you twenty-four hours' notice," Judge Morrison had told Mr. Murphy, who was too drunk to do more than hiccough,

"Jest as you say, yer honor ; jest as you—ach !—say."

And Theophilus?

When that little sound of weeping had struck his ear the Judge had hurried, stumbling and breathless, into the garret. There had been a blank minute of rage ; then he had flung Katy to one side, saying viciously something Theophilus did not hear. Then he clutched his nephew's arm in a cruel grip, and storming and threatening for sheer relief, dragged him down to his library. There he spoke his mind.

Theophilus sighed once or twice, and looked out of the window, but said not a word until the Judge had finished. Then, in a voice curiously like his uncle's, he said : "You ain't fair. I am going to tell God on you." And waited for more abuse ; but none came.

"Hold your tongue, and go to bed !" his uncle said; and the boy went. But Theophilus Morrison, alone in his library, put his head down on his hands, and drew a long breath.

Miss Hannah, shaking and crying, led Theophilus to his own little room. She asked her broken questions, and exclaimed and protested and reproached him all at once. Theophilus made no response. When at last she kissed him good-night, and left him in the welcome darkness and silence, it seemed as though some weight was lifted from him. He sat up in bed and bent his face forward on his knees. He did not cry, but sometimes he sighed — a long, broken, despairing breath. He was very white and still all the next day. In vain Miss Hannah tried to make him talk, so that she might comfort him. He ate what she forced upon him, because she cried when he refused. But except to whisper once, "Aunt, I shall tell God on him," he was silent. For Theophilus knew Katy was to be sent away ; they would never see each other again. "Never any more—never any more," he said to himself over and over.

But, spite of the Judge's orders and Miss Hannah's care, Theophilus did see his wife once more. The morning of the Murphys' departure he watched from the orchard the loading of the dray in front of Katy's door, and when he saw that Mrs. Murphy was climbing up, to sit on top of her stove and feather bed, and the children were standing about, ready to be packed in beside her, he went to the wash-house door, and called in to his aunt that he was "going to say good-bye to Katy." He did not wait for her horrified protest, but ran, white and panting, down through the orchard and across the road. Mrs. Murphy screamed when she saw him, and poor swollen-eyed Katy hardly dared look at him, after her first glance. The men who were loading the wagon stopped and laughed—but Theophilus was blind to all but Katy.

The child had been pulled up to sit beside her mother, and, looking down at him, said, trembling, "Good-bye, Theophilus."

"Shut your mouth," said her mother, beginning to cry. "The darlin' boy ; he's that white—"

"Katy," said Theophilus, in a low voice, "as soon as I'm a man, I'm coming for you."

"All right, Theophilus," said Katy.

"You won't forget we're married ?"

"Oh no, Theophilus," murmured Katy.

"Oh, Katy, don't, don't, *don't* go and leave me !" he burst out.

"There, now, dear," said Mrs. Murphy, "don't be takin' on." The big, motherly woman had a sudden impulse to pick him up and pack him with her brood among her pots and pans and feather beds. The little boy did not seem to hear her.

"Katy"—he said, in a low voice, and looked up at her. Then, suddenly, he burst into tears, ran madly at the wagon, and tried to climb up over the big wheels. "I'm going too; I'm going too—" he sobbed. "Take me with you, Katy!" He clung to the wheels, and the men, laughing, pulled him back.

Mrs. Murphy, from her perch on the feather bed, laughed too. "Ain't he comical?" she said; "well, there; bless him! Say, now, darlin' go home. I'll be keepin' your wife for you—"

The wagon started, and Mrs. Murphy forgot Theophilus, and began to weep for her own hearth-stone from which she had been so cruelly torn away. Then she smacked the child whose fault it was, which made Katy weep also, and the wailing chorus rose above the good-byes of the neighbors, who stood about watching the flitting.

As for Theophilus, he was quiet again, only looking with burning eyes at the little figure on the wagon, until a turn in the road carried it out of sight.

Then he went home. Miss Hannah did not tell the Judge of this disobedience, but she reproached Theophilus in her agitated, flurried way.

"Now, my dear little boy, you must—you mustn't —you know brother wouldn't—now you will remember, won't you, Theophilus?"

Theophilus nodded, silently. He was perfectly apathetic. As the days went on he made no complaint of loneliness. He seemed to be just a silent, biddable child. He fetched and carried for Miss

Hannah, and took the tonic Willy King had ordered,
and learned his lessons, and never went down to
Shantytown for play-fellows; but he turned away
his head whenever his uncle spoke to him. If he
was asked a question, he answered briefly; but it
was impossible not to see the shrinking and fear
and hatred on the little mild face. He used to try
to play, at first. He said every day to himself
that to-morrow he would make ink out of pokeber-
ries. He had a fancy for pretending to be an earth-
worm burrowing through miles of clay and rock,
represented by the hay in the loft. But interest
flagged, and he came back and sat listlessly by the
fire in the wash-house, while Miss Hannah's anxieties
about him rippled on with mild incoherence which
never needed a reply. Sometimes after tea, when he
had been stolidly unresponsive, the Judge would go
back to his library with a pang which he supposed to
be anger, and he would tell himself that Theophilus
was as ungrateful as everybody else.

"I would make something of him," he used to tell
himself. "He has brains; he would be a credit to
me." And then he would think to himself, bitterly,
how unjust it all was. "I never cared for a human
creature before," he said, not knowing that this was
his own sentence; "and I'm a fool to care now!" he
added. "Well, he's not worth it. Willy King is an
idiot." In his rage and anxiety he was almost as incoherent as Miss Hannah. Indeed, he made no con-
cealment of his feeling for the boy; he was harshly
and openly anxious about him. He scolded Miss
Hannah because he was pale, and was imperious in
his orders that the child should have this or that comfort, for which, indeed, with anguished reluctance, he

once or twice gave her some money. Over and over he tried to make Theophilus talk. He was eager for a friendly look or word, but none came. The child never forgot. Once it came to the Judge as an inspiration that Theophilus had not forgiven him for taking his pipe; and he called the boy into his library, hopefully.

"Theophilus," he said, "I have something of yours; I'm going to give it back to you. Only you are not to smoke, young man!" he ended, with an effort to be jocose that made the little boy look at him wonderingly; but he would not take the pipe.

"I don't want it now," he said, briefly, and went back to sit with Miss Hannah, leaning his head against her knee, and trying languidly to study his spelling lesson. "I don't like spelling," he said. "There isn't any 'because' in just sticking in letters." This was apropos of "dough" and "doe," which had presented difficulties that had moved Theophilus to tears. "Katy could spell, just as easy!" he said. And that was his only reference to his little tragedy.

Shortly after the rebuff of the pipe the Judge made still another effort. "Here, young man," he said, "is a present for you. Come! what do you say? Don't forget your manners!" He snapped a half-dime down on the table by Theophilus's plate with a little chuckle of generosity.

"Thank you," said Theophilus, listlessly. He slipped the coin into his pocket, but afterwards Miss Hannah saw him fingering it, and looking at it with a gleam of interest. "Does it cost much to take a journey, aunt?" he said. And then he said, with a little animation in his face, "I guess I'll save up." And he even went so far as to put his half-dime into an empty cigar-box, which he said should be his bank. "When that's full I'll have enough," he said. But by-and-by he seemed to forget it.

As the winter passed he grew whiter and stiller. The Judge was bitter to all the world; Miss Hannah had a bad time of it, but Willy King had a worse.

"What are you good for, anyhow?" the Judge used to say, sneering and frightened and angry all together. "What do you suppose I pay you for?"

It appeared that Willy wasn't good for anything. "Some spring has been cut," he said; "the boy doesn't care for anything." Afterwards he said the child had no constitution, anyhow. At the end the Judge was with the little boy day and night, and perhaps the old man's harsh misery softened the child. The last day, when from morning until morning the Judge had sat on the bed (it was his own, into which Theophilus had been put), the child looked at him once or twice, with a glimmer of interest in his face.

" Uncle," he said.

The Judge took his hand, and held it, opening and shutting his lips, and trying to speak.

"Uncle, I—won't—I won't—tell God," he said.

And then he turned his face to the wall.

WHERE THE LABORERS ARE FEW

WHERE THE LABORERS ARE FEW

I

MISS JANE JAY used to think that she discovered Paul Phillips ; but really and truly Dr. Lavendar saw him before she did, and so did her sister, Miss Henrietta.

It was one hot August afternoon that the old minister, passing by the open door of the tavern bar-room, saw a lazy, sweltering crowd gathered inside, where, it seemed, some sort of entertainment was going on. Dr. Lavendar stopped and looked in, his hands on either side of the doorway, his hat pushed back, his face red with heat. He smiled, and blinked his kind old eyes, and then he frowned : an acrobat, in black tights and scarlet breech-cloth, was vaulting over chair backs and making high kicks. His work was done with remarkable grace, but with exertions which it was painful to witness ; for he had but one leg, and had to use a crutch. Still, his face, which was dark and very handsome, and streaming with perspiration, was sparkling with interest and enjoyment.

It was the one leg that offended Dr. Lavendar. " Trading on his infirmities," he said to himself, frowning, and shook his head. Van Horn, who, in his shirt-sleeves, was trying to keep cool in a big rocking-chair, shook his head also, as if to say that he didn't approve, but what could he do? Then he turned his eyes back to the man, who, with astonishing ease, spun round on his crutch and kicked lightly up into the air so far above his own head that he dislodged a hat balanced on top of the clock. There was a round of applause, and the acrobat, panting and leaning on his crutch, bowed and laughed and showed his handsome white teeth. Dr. Lavendar snorted under his breath, and opened his umbrella, and went back into the sun and heat, plodding along towards home. He stopped once to speak to Miss Henrietta Jay, who was coming down the street, her square, faded countenance full of agitation and dismay.

"Oh, Dr. Lavendar!" she said, with a gasp, "have you seen—*have* you seen a large white cat anywhere about?"

Poor old Miss Henrietta's voice shook as she spoke. She had no umbrella, and the sun beat down on her bent shoulders. She wore a faded black dolman which had a sparse fringe of narrow crinkled tapes. Her rusty bonnet was very much on one side, as though the green velvet rosette over her left eye weighed it down. "It's our Jacky," she said, her lip shaking. "He's lived with us fifteen years; and he's lost."

"Oh, lost cats always find their way home," Dr. Lavendar said, comfortingly.

"Do you think so?" she said, in a despairing voice. But she did not wait for his answer; she went on down the street, with wavering, uncertain steps, as though feeling always that she might be going in

226

just the wrong direction. She stopped now and then at a gateway or an alley, and called softly, "Baby! baby!" but no white cat appeared. It was then that she too passed the tavern door and looked in, but only to say to Van Horn, "Have you seen a large white cat anywhere?" Afterwards she remembered that she had seen the acrobat; but at the moment she was blind to everything but her own anxiety.

Dr. Lavender looked after her and sighed; but when he met Willy King coming out of Tommy Dove's shop, and smelling of dried herbs, he burst out with his disapproval of the performance in the bar-room. "There's a man down there at the tavern," he said, "jumping around on one leg to get coppers. I wonder Van Horn allows it!"

And Willy agreed, gloomily: Willy was very gloomy just then, because his wife, very sensibly, was dieting him to reduce his weight. "That kind of beggary is blackmail," he said. "It makes an appeal to your sympathies, and you give, in spite of common-sense. At least, you want to give; but I won't. It's the same thing with these women who knit afghans and things that you can't use. Your mountebank at the tavern ought to be in the work-house."

"As for knitting," said Dr. Lavendar, thoughtfully, "I suppose you mean the Jay girls. Well, poor things! they've got to do something that's genteel; and knitting is that, you know. Jane refers to it always as 'fancy-work,' which soothes her pride, poor child."

"Jane is a goose," said the doctor, irritably. "Maggy is the only one that has any sense in that family."

"Willy," said Dr. Lavendar, chuckling, "you've bought an afghan!—or maybe baby socks?" Willy looked sheepish. "William, you always remind me of the young man in the Bible who said he would not, and then straightway did. Well, I'm glad you did, my boy; they are straitened, poor girls!—very straitened, I fear."

As for Willy King, breathing forth threatenings and slaughter, he went down to the tavern to drop in his quarter when the mountebank's hat went round. But when he got there the crowd had dispersed and the man had gone.

"Well, Willy," said Van Horn, who had known the doctor when he was a boy and used to steal apples from the tavern orchard, "I swan, that was the queerest fish! He hadn't only but one leg and a crutch, and he kicked as high as your head, sir. Yes, sir, as high as your head. And then, I swan, when the show was over, if he didn't turn to and preach to them there fellers; preach as good a sermon—well, now you won't believe me? but it was a first-class sermon! Well, sir, them fellers listened. Tob Todd listened. Yes he did. He listened. And that man he told 'em not to patronize my bar, so he did. Well, for the soakers, I hold up both hands to that. But to see a one-legged dancing tramp setting up to preach in a bar-room—I swan!" said Van Horn, who could find no words for the occasion.

The doctor looked disgusted, and put his quarter back in his pocket. "You'd better keep your eye on the till," he said, briefly.

But Van Horn was doubtful. "Seemed like as if he was all right," he ruminated; "still, you can't never tell."

So it happened that Willy King had his views about Paul when Miss Jane Jay came, white and breathless, to tell him that the poor man had "hurt his limb" on the road near her sister's house, and would he please come and fix it? "At once, Dr. King," said Jane, agitatedly, "at once!"

Miss Jane was the youngest of the Misses Jay. There were three Misses Jay, who lived "the Lord knows how!" Old Chester used to say, in their tumbled-down old house on the river road. Dr. Lavendar had referred to their circumstances as "straitened," but he had no idea of the degree of their straitness. Nobody knew that but the Jay girls, and they kept it to themselves. The family had known better days two generations back; indeed, many a time, when their dinner was inadequate, the Misses Jay stayed their stomachs on the fact that they were Bishop Jay's great-granddaughters. Besides that, their father had been a clergyman; so they had, poor ladies! in the midst of their poverty, that gentle condescension which is the ecclesiastical form of Christian humility. They took a great interest in church matters, and they were critical of sermons, as behooved those who knew the dark mysteries of sermon-writing. Still, they were kindly, simple women, who tried to do their duty on a very insufficient income, and to live up to their clerical past. This family pride was most noticeable in fat Miss Maggy—there are people who would be fat on a straw a day; Henrietta, the oldest, devoted to her cat and her canary-bird, and the real genius of the family in regard to afghans, read her Bible through twice a year on a system arranged by the bishop, and merely echoed Maggy's views; little Jane realized her birth, but with a vague discontent at its restrictions. Indeed, she and Henrietta, without Maggy's influence, might even have slipped down into what Miss Maggy called "mercantile pursuits." They would have been dressmakers, perhaps, for Henrietta had a pretty taste in turning dresses wrong side out, right side out, and wrong side out again; and Jane might have trimmed bonnets with (she used to think to herself) a "real touch." But Miss Maggy was firm. "I am sure," she said, "I have the greatest respect for working persons. Great-grandfather Jay wrote a tract for them—don't you remember?—'The Virtuous Content of Poor James, the Brickmaker.' But still, I know what is due to our station. And besides," she ended, with that pathetic shrinking of elderly, genteel poverty, "if you trimmed hats, Jane, everybody would know that we are—are not well off." The other sisters sighed and agreed, and were somehow oblivious of the fact that Willy King had no need of a dozen pairs of baby socks, and that Mrs. Dale's order of an afghan every year implied either that these brilliant coverings wore out very quickly, or else that Mrs. Dale's purchase was only—but it would be cruel to name it!

"We do fancy-work," Miss Maggy said, "for recreation; if our friends need the product of our needles, well and good. Were our circumstances different, we would be glad to give them what they wish. As it is, we make a slight charge—for materials."

So the Misses Jay knitted and crocheted; and one day in the year put on their shabby best clothes and made calls; and one day in the year entertained the sewing society, and lived on the fragments of cake afterwards as long as they lasted. It was a harmless, monotonous life, its only interest the anxiety about money—which is not an interest that feeds the soul.

On this hot August afternoon—the afternoon following, as it chanced, the meeting of the sewing society, the Misses Jay's ancient cat, disturbed, perhaps, by the excitement of so much company, had disappeared. Henrietta had hurried into the village to look for him, and Jane had gone out in the other direction; Maggy stayed at home to let him in if he came back. But Jane did not go far; not that she was not anxious about Jacky, only "there's no use getting a sunstroke," she said to herself, wearily. However, she did look, and called among the bushes, and then, feeling the heat very much, in a hopeless way she gave it up.

There is a wooden bridge across a shallow run just beyond the Jay house, and Jane thought how cool it would be in the deep shadow underneath it, where the run slipped smoothly over wide flat stones, or chattered into little waterfalls a foot high—and perhaps Jacky might be down there, she thought. So, holding on to the bushes and tufts of grass, she climbed down the bank and found this dark shelter, with the cool sound of running water. "Jacky! Come kitty!" she called once or twice; and then she sat down on a water-worn log washed up under the bridge and caught between two stones; there were tufts of dried dead grass here and there, swept sidewise by the winter torrents, and left above the shrunken summer stream, bleached and stiff with yellow mud ; overhead were the planks of the bridge, with lines of sunshine between them as thin as knitting-needles. Once, as she sat there, a wagon came jolting along, and the dust sifted down and spread in a flowing scum on the water. It was very silent, except for the run, chattering and bubbling, and chattering again ; sometimes, absently, she picked up little stones and threw them into the water : she was thinking of an afghan she was making for Rachel King's little adopted baby. But Miss Jane had no interest in her work ; it was something to be done, that was all. Indeed, she was tired of the touch of the worsted, and of the hot smoothness of the crochet-needle, slipping in and out, in and out. She dabbled her fingers in the water, as if she would wash the feeling away. She thought vaguely of the years of afghans and socks and endless talk about colors ; there was never anything more exciting to talk about than whether pink and blue should be used together, or the new fashion of using green and blue, which Miss Maggy declared to be shocking ; nothing more exciting, except the sewing society meeting once a year ; or, now, Jacky's getting lost. Nothing rose up in the level dulness of her thirty-four years—not even a grief !

As she sat there listening to the low chatter and whisper of the run, there came to little Miss Jane a bad query—"*what is the use of it all ?*" I suppose most of us know the peculiar *ennui* of the soul that accompanies this question ; it is a sort of spiritual nausea which is never felt in the stress of agonized living, but only in sterile peace ; indeed, that is why we may believe it to be but the demand of Life for living—for love, or hate, or grief. Miss Jane, thinking dully of afghans, made no such analysis ; she was not happy enough to know that she was unhappy. She only said to herself : " I wonder what's the matter with me? I guess it's Henrietta's cake."

She sighed, and dropped her chin into her hand, leaning her elbow on her knee. Her face was thin, but it had a delicate color, and her eyes were violet, or blue, or gray, like changing clouds ; her pathetic mouth, drooping and patiently discontented, had much sweetness in its timid way. But there was no touch of human passion about her. She was fond of her sisters, she told herself, as she sat there wondering what was the use of it all, but nothing stirred in her at the thought of them. " If somebody told me just now, here under the bridge, that something had happened to sister Maggy, I don't believe I'd really mind. Of course I'd cry, and all that — but it wouldn't make any difference. I just *don't care*. And I don't care whether Jacky comes back or not."

Some one came down the road whistling. Jane lifted her head and listened ; when the walker reached the bridge there was a curious sound : a footstep, then a tap ; a footstep, then a tap. The dust jolted softly down, wavering across the strips of sunshine, and then vanishing on the flowing water. " It's a lame person," said Miss Jane, listening. A footstep, then a tap—then a snap, a crash, a fall ! Jane jumped up, breathlessly ; from a knot-hole in the planks above her a broken stick fell clattering on to the stones ; it had a brass ferrule and ring. " Some poor man has broken his crutch," Jane thought. " Wait a minute, and I'll bring it up to you !" she called out, and began to climb up the bank, the end of the crutch in her hand.

As for Paul, when he had pitched forward into the dust, he was so astonished that for the moment he did not feel the keen pain of a wrenched knee. But when Miss Jane, out of breath, with the end of the crutch in her hand, appeared over the edge of the bank, his face was white with it.

"Oh, you've hurt yourself!" said Miss Jane.

"Yes, 'm," said Paul; "but never mind!" His brown eyes smiled up at her in the kindest way.

"Oh, you are—lame," she faltered.

"Yes; but that's nothing," Paul said, the color beginning to come back into his face; "I guess I put the end of my crutch into that knot-hole. I was whistling away, you know, and I never took notice of the road."

"I heard you whistling," said Miss Jane; "but— what are you going to do?"

"Oh, somebody 'll come along and give me a lift," he said; then he looked ruefully at the parted strap of his knapsack, which had burst open, scattering his possessions in the dust.

"You can't stay here in the sun," she protested, "and so few wagons come along this road."

"If I could get over there to the other side," he said, "there's a good lot of shade, and I could just sit there until a cart comes along. I'll get 'em to drop me at one of these barns. I'll get a night's lodging in the hay, and my knee'll be all right to-morrow." He tried to scramble up, but the effort made him blanch with pain.

"Oh, do let me help you," said Miss Jane, her color coming and going. "Oh dear, I know it must hurt! Do put your hand on my shoulder; do, please!" Paul assented very simply; with a gentle, iron-like

234

grip he took hold of her thin little arm ; but it was so little and so tremulous that he let go almost instantly, and would have had an awkward fall but that she caught him ; then he got his balance, and leaning on her shoulder, sweating and smiling at the pain, he managed to get to the other end of the bridge.

Miss Jane, standing up beside him, in her striped barege dress, and her hat, with its flounce of lace around the brim, pushed back from her flushed and interested face, began to protest that she must get some help immediately. But even as she spoke Paul suddenly turned his head a little and fainted quite away.

So that was how it happened that (a man and cart coming along most opportunely) he was not carried to a barn to nurse his sprained knee, but to the Jay girls' house, where he was put down on the big horse-hair sofa in the parlor, and given over to the ministration of Willy King.

II

William King was not sympathetic. He said the man had hurt his knee badly, and had better be sent to the workhouse to recover. " He ought to be in jail," Willy said to Miss Maggy, who lifted her hands in horror at the word. " He's a vagrant. I'll send some kind of conveyance, and have him taken to the workhouse. It's too bad you should be bothered with him, Miss Maggy."

Then it was that Jane, standing behind her sister, and quite hidden by her ponderous frame, said, in her light, fluttering voice : " Poor man ! I think it would be wicked to send him to the workhouse."

Dr. King shrugged his shoulders. "Oh, of course it is just as you and Miss Maggy say. You'll be very kind to keep him for a few days; but I hope you'll not be repaid by having your spoons carried off."

Miss Maggy's mouth grew round with dismay. "But ladies in our position cannot refuse shelter to a poor man with an injured limb," she said.

"And his only limb, too," Jane added, with some excitement.

As for the danger to the spoons—"We haven't but six," said Miss Maggy, sighing, "and we can hide them under the edge of the carpet in Henrietta's room. Go and meet her, Janie, and tell her about the poor man."

Henrietta was coming up the road, her bonnet still very much on one side, and her old face quivering with anxiety. "Did you find him?" she called out as soon as she saw Jane, who shook her head, and began to tell her own exciting story. Miss Henrietta listened, absently.

"His name is Paul," Jane ended; "a very romantic name, I think. You don't mind his remaining, do you, sister Henrietta?"

"No, I don't mind," said Miss Henrietta, sighing. "Is he a circus actor? One of the servants took me to the circus once, when I was a little thing. Janie, ask him if he saw a large white cat as he came along. Poor man! I'm sorry he hurt himself. Oh, Janie, Jacky may be hurt! I keep thinking that he may be suffering," she said, her poor old eyes filling; then, as they came up to the door, she called again, faintly: "Baby! baby! Come, pussy; come, Jack!"

As for Miss Maggy, when it was settled that the man should remain, she thought of the pantry and sighed; but it was she who informed him that he might stay until his "limb" permitted him to walk.

Paul, however, had his own views, "No, 'm," he said, "thank you; but I see you have a stable back there behind the house; I'll go there, and lie in the hay till my knee clears up. Then I'll go along."

"But you can just as well stay here," Jane said.

Paul shook his head with cheerful stubbornness. "No, ma'am; I'm much obliged to you, but I'll go to the stable."

"As you please, my good man," said Miss Maggy.

But Jane still protested. "Oh, a stable!" she said; "I wouldn't do that."

"There's been One in a stable, ma'am, that didn't think it beneath Him. I'm right apt to think about that, sleeping round the way I do," the man said, simply.

The two ladies stared at him with parted lips.

"It must have been a pretty sight," he went on, thoughtfully. "When I'm lying up on the hay, I get the picture of it in my mind real often—just like as if I saw it. There's the cows standing round chewing their cud; and maybe some mules—you'd hear them stamping. And the oxen would be rubbing up against their stanchions. I always think the door was open a little crack, and you could see out—the morning just beginning, you know. And there'd be a heap of fresh manure outside, smoking in the cold. And there, in the manger, Mary and Him. I like to think that to myself—don't you?"

"Why—yes; I don't know—I suppose so," Jane said, breathlessly.

"My great-grandfather wrote a sermon on the

Nativity," Miss Maggy said, kindly ; "I'm sure he would think it very nice in you to have such thoughts."

But after that they did not oppose his plan of leaving the house. The butcher - boy was asked to help him limp out to the stable, and some hay was shaken down for his bed.

"He talks like a Sunday-school teacher," the boy said when he came back for the five-cent fee that had been promised him ; "but I don't mind. And you'd ought to 'a' seen him jump—down at the tavern ! My !"

And indeed, with open pride, the acrobat himself bore testimony to his ability. "I get a good living out of this leg," he said, "and I don't know what I should do if it was to stiffen up on me." He sighed and looked anxiously at Willy King, who had come in to see how he was getting along.

"If you keep quiet, you'll come out all right," Willy said, gruffly ; "but if I were you, I'd try to find a more decent way of earning my living."

Paul laughed. "It's decent enough," he said, "so long as I'm decent. That's the way I look at work —your trade's decent, so long as you are. It isn't being decent troubles me ; though I will say I don't like to hand round the hat. Not but what I've a right to ! I do good work ; yes, sir, first-class work. There ain't a man in my class with two legs, let alone one, that can touch the notch I do. No, sir ! I'm proud of my profession ; but the trouble is—"

"Well, what's the trouble?" the doctor said, crossly.

"Why, it's so uncertain," the man said. "I have got as high as $1.75 at a performance ; and then, again, I won't get but twenty-five cents. But if this darned knee was to stiffen up on me—"

"It won't," William King said; "but I should think you could do something better than this, anyhow."

Paul looked perfectly uncomprehending. "But I'm A 1," he insisted. "Before my accident I was 'way up in the profession. Of course this is a come-down to travel and hand round the hat; but I'm mighty lucky I've got a profession to fall back on to support my little sister; she's an invalid. And then, I do get good opportunities," he added.

"Opportunities to perform?"

"No, I didn't mean that," the man answered, briefly.

"What was your accident?" said Willy King. He was sitting on a wheelbarrow, and Paul was stretched out in the hay in front of him. The barn was de-serted, for the cow was out at pasture; now and then a hen walked in at the open door, and pecked about in a vain search for oats; on the rafters overhead some pigeons balanced and cooed, and from a dusty, cobweb-covered window a dim stream of sunshine poured down on the man lying in the hay. Willy King took off his hat and clasped his hands around one fat knee. "How did you hurt yourself?" he said.

"Trapeze. That was my line. Well, it wasn't just an accident. There was a rope cut half through—"

"What! You don't mean on purpose?"

"Well, yes," the man said, easily. "I guess there was no doubt of it. Well, I was up there right by the main pole— My, that's a sight! I suppose you never was up by the main pole during a perform-ance?"

"Well, no," the doctor admitted.

"Yes, it's a great sight. You sit up there on the trapeze, and look down at all the rows and rows of faces, and you can't hear anything but a kind of hum, you're up so high—right up under the canvas; you can hear it, though, flapping and booming, cracking like a whip once in a while! Half of it may be in the sun, and then a big shadow on half of it; and all the people looking up at you, and the band squeaking away down below for your money's worth! Yes, it's a sight. Well, that's all there was to it. I saw the rope giving, and I jumped to catch a flyer; and I missed it. But I wasn't killed. Well, it was wonderful; I wasn't killed!" He smiled as he spoke, but there was a brooding gravity in his face.

When Willy King left his patient, he stopped at the Jay house to say that Paul was getting along very well; he must have said something else, too, for when he went home he presented his wife with a sofa pillow. "Now, Willy!" said poor Mrs. William, "this is the sixth! Indeed, I do think it is wrong in you to encourage the Jay girls to make things nobody needs. I think it would be more truthful to give them the money outright than to pretend you want a sofa cushion."

"It would hurt their feelings," the doctor objected.

"My dear, truth is more important than feelings," said Martha, decidedly.

William changed the subject hurriedly. William was blond, and fat, and very amiable, and with a great respect for his Martha's common-sense; but common-sense does pall on a husband sometimes.

III

Paul improved very slowly; the fact was the barn was comfortable and the perfect cure of the knee important, so with simple confidence in the hospitality of the three ladies, he gave himself up to the pleasure of convalescence. And it certainly was pleasant. The Misses Jay were very kind to him. Miss Henrietta visited him every morning, bringing his breakfast, and telling him many times how, when she was a little girl, she had been taken to the circus. "I saw a young lady ride on a horse without any saddle," Miss Henrietta would say; "it was really wonderful; I've never forgotten it." And then, after this politely personal reminiscence, she would talk to him about her poor pussy, whose affection and intelligence gradually assumed abnormal proportions. Sometimes, as she carried his plate away, she would stop and call feebly, "Jacky, Jacky! You know he might be lying sick under the barn," she explained to Paul, who was very sympathetic. Miss Maggy went every day before dinner to inquire for his "limb." As for Miss Jane, she came to the barn door upon any excuse. Into the starved, thin life of little Miss Jane had come suddenly an interest. Perhaps that reference to the stable in Bethlehem had first given her something to think about. It had been startlingly incongruous, but there had been nothing offensive in it, because it was so simple; indeed, that it was the natural tenor of the man's thought was obvious at once. The first morning, when Miss Henrietta took his breakfast out to him, she found him reading his Bible. The next day,

Miss Maggy, hunting for eggs in the shed, heard some one singing, and listening, heard:

"Guide me, O thou Great Jehovah,
  Pilgrim through this barren land.
I am weak—"

Then there was a pause. Then a joyous burst: "yes; but Thou art mighty (I bet Thou art!);" and then the rest of it:

"Lead me with Thy powerful hand!"

Miss Maggy, who had the unreasoning emotion of the fat, repeated this with tears to her sisters, and added that perhaps it might help the poor man in his effort to be a Christian to give him one of Great-grandfather Jay's sermons to read. Miss Henrietta agreed vaguely, and then said she knew that he was a good-hearted person, because he had sympathized so about Jacky. But Miss Jane, crocheting rapidly, thought to herself how strange it was that a man who had been a circus rider should be—religious! The fact caught her interest, just as sometimes a point in a wide dull landscape catches the eye—perhaps the far-off window of some unseen house flaring suddenly with the sun and speaking a hundred mysteries of invisible human living. The commonplace, healthy way in which, once or twice, Paul spoke of those things which, being so vital, are hidden by most of us, was a shock to her which was awakening. It was like letting hot sunshine and vigorous wind touch suddenly some delicate, spindling plants which have grown always in the dark. But it attracted her with the curious fascination which the unusual, even if a little painful, has for all of us. So she went

very often to the barn to inquire about his health.
Sometimes she took her knitting and sat on the barn
door step, and tried, in a fluttering way, to make
him talk. This was not difficult; the acrobat was
most cheerfully talkative. Propped up in the hay,
he watched her, and sometimes held her big loose
ball of double zephyr in his hands, unrolling a length
or two in answer to her soft jerk; he told her about
his "business" and the difficulties of his "profession," and once in a while, very simply, there would
come some allusion to deeper things. But for the
most part he talked about being "on the road." He
blushed all over his dark, handsome face when he
said that he had to hand round the hat after a performance; "but it's for sister Alice," he explained.
He had a good deal to say about this sister. She
lived out in Iowa, he said, and he didn't believe he'd
ever take another long tramp so far east as Pennsylvania. "It's too far away. Alice is kind of sickly,
and if she was to be taken bad, I might not be able
to get back in a hurry; I mightn't have my car-fare.
I'm going to tramp it home in October, and then
I guess I'll dwell among mine own people, as David
says." One day he showed her a little dog-eared account-book in which he kept the record of his re-
ceipts and expenditures. "In a town, I've got to put
up at a tavern over-night, and that counts up.
That's why I like to go to little places where there
are barns. Now there's Mercer on that page: I had
to pay for a license in Mercer; and the barkeepers,
they charged too; so I only made $1 the first day,
and 75 cents the next, and $1.20 the last day. You'd
'a' thought I'd done better in a city, wouldn't you?
On that page opposite is my expenses. See? At

the bottom of the page is what I sent Alice—$3.25 that week. I have sent her as high as $5 once."

It was raining, and Jane was sitting just inside the door; she ran her hand along her wooden knitting-needles, and then took the account-book, holding it nervously, as though not quite certain what to do with it.

"I made most of that $5," said Paul, "in a saloon that was run by a man named Bloder."

"I shouldn't think," Miss Jane said, hesitatingly, "that it would be pleasant to—to perform in saloons."

"Oh," he said, eagerly, "they're just my place! I'd rather go to a saloon than have three open-air turns."

Jane Jay shut the little book and handed it back to him, a look almost of pain about her delicate lips. The acrobat glanced at her, and then his handsome face suddenly lighted. "Oh, not the way you think —bless you, no! I get more men in a saloon, that's why; and when the show's done, I get a hack at 'em. I believe that when I go into a saloon, dirty, like as not, with old musty sawdust on the floor all dripped over with beer, and a lot of fellows just shaking hands with the devil—I believe I'm preaching to the spirits in prison."

"Why, do you mean," she demanded—"do you mean that you talk—religion in those places?"

"Yes, ma'am."

"Why, you ought to be a clergyman!" she said, impulsively.

"I wish I could be," he said, with a sigh. "Of course that's what I aimed for; but you see, with Alice to look after—no, I don't suppose it'll come about. This is the best I can do—to talk after the performances. But it isn't like having a church with red seats and a pulpit. But my vow was to be a preacher, ma'am."

"And then you decided to be a—to—to give performances?"

"No, ma'am; 'twas like this," he said. "I was doing trapeze business. Well, I was advertised all round; you ought to have seen the bill-boards, and Signor Paulo, in his great act, shooting down with his arms folded—this way—across his breast! That was me. I got good pay those days; and—and I was—well ma'am, I was a great sinner. I was the chief of sinners. Well, I had enemies in my line: a star always has. The greater you are," said the acrobat, with perfect simplicity, "the more folks envy you. So somebody cut a rope half through right up under the canvas. The ropes are tested before every performance, so it must have been a quick job for the fellow that did it. I was sitting up there, and I seen the rope giving. Well, I don't know; I don't know;"—his voice dropped, and he looked past her with rapt, unseeing eyes—"it was a vision, I guess:—*I seen my sin.* 'My God!' I said, out loud. I don't know to this day if it was because I was scared of being killed, or scared of my sin. Of course nobody could hear me—the horses tearing round the ring, and mademoiselle jumping through fire-hoops, and the band playing away for dear life. Well—it was jump, anyhow; so I just yelled out, ' *You save me, and I'll give You the credit !*' Then I jumped."

"Oh!" said Jane, panting, and knitting very fast.

"Well, that was all there was to it. He saved me. And there was my bargain with Him. At first, seeing that my leg had to go, I wasn't just sure we was even ; and then I says to myself : 'Yes ; He saved me. He only just gave me a pinch in the leg, for fear I'd get too stuck up, starring, and forget my bargain.' I don't know as I would have seen it right off, but a minister came to see me a good deal in the hospital, and he gave me a lot of ideas. He just pointed out that so long as my life was saved, my bargain was good. 'You give God the glory wherever you go,' he said—which is the church way of saying give Him the credit, you know. Well, at first I took it to be that I'd preach, respectably, in a church ; I've a good deal of a gift in talking. But it wasn't to be," he ended, with a sigh.

"Why not ?" Jane demanded, boldly. In her interest she rolled her work up in her black silk apron, and came and sat down beside him in the hay. Paul turned a little on his side, and leaning on his elbow, looked up at her, his dark, gentle eyes smiling. She would not have known how to say it, but she felt a dull envy of the passion and emotion that had illuminated his face. She wished he would talk some more about—things. It was as if her numb, chilled mind tried to crouch closer to the warmth of his vital personality. She bent forward as she talked to him, and her breath came quicker. "I don't see why you shouldn't be a clergyman," she said.

"Well, I haven't any education," he explained. "I couldn't stand up in a real church, with nice red cushions, and talk. You see, I don't know things that church people want to hear. I don't understand about election, and foreordination, and those things. You've got to have an education for a church ; and an education costs money. And then there's Alice : I can't stop earning, you see." He lapsed into silence,

" 'THE GREATER YOU ARE,' SAID THE ACROBAT, 'THE MORE
FOLKS ENVY YOU ' "

and Jane was silent too. But she looked at him again sidewise, and the beauty of his large frame—the broad, deep chest, the grace and vigor of the long line from the shoulder to the knee, the powerful arm and wrist—held her eyes.

"My knee's getting on," he said, suddenly; "and I think I can make a start in another week; but before I go I want to have a performance for you and the other two ladies—and any of your lady friends you'd like to invite in. I'll give you the best show I've got," he said, his face eager and handsome, and all alert to return favor with favor, and to reveal the possibilities of his profession.

"Oh, you are very kind," Miss Jane said, with a start; "I'll tell my sisters. They'll be very much interested, I know; but—but I'd like it better for you just to preach."

"I guess you ladies don't need my kind of preaching," he answered, good-naturedly; "you're 'way up above that, you know. You're all ready to hear about the Trinity, and how much a cubit is, and what a centurion is, and free will—and all those things. If I ever get my education, and know 'em, I'll invite you to come to my church. But now I'll just have to stick to the gospel, I guess."

IV

Those were strange days to Miss Jane Jay. Into the even dulness of knitting afghans, and bemoaning Jacky, and wondering whether the weather would be this or that, had come the jar of vigorous living, as vulgar as the honest earth—loud, courageous, full of

toil and sweat and motion. Once, walking home in
the rainy dusk, she stopped before a deserted cow-shed
by the road-side, on which, long ago, had been pasted
a circus advertisement. It was torn at one corner,
and was flapping idly in the wind The colors were
washed and faded by summer rains, and some boys
had thrown mud at it, but Miss Jane could still see
the picture of a man hanging by one arm from a
trapeze, ready for the downward dive

"Mr. Phillips used to do that," she thought. She
called him Mr. Phillips now, not Paul, as the others
did in familiar and condescending kindness She
was glad he did not do those things now the preaching lifted him to another plane in her mind.

The other sisters were interested in Paul too, but
the atrophy of years cannot be easily vitalized, and
they did not think very much about him. Henrietta
was patiently trying to accustom herself to Jacky's
loss. She used to sit making baby socks hour after
hour, her poor vague fancy picturing the pussy's
wanderings and sufferings, until for very wretchedness the slow painful tears would rise and blur the
crocheting in her wrinkled hands Still, she listened
when Jane told her this or that of Mr. Phillips; and
she and Maggy were especially moved when they
heard of his desire to preach the gospel.

"I think he'd make a good clergyman—he's kind
to animals," said Miss Henrietta, sighing. "I saw
him patting Clover the other night. Oh dear, how
he would have loved Jacky!"

Miss Maggy nodded approvingly, and said again
that it was very nice for a poor person to be religious. "Perhaps I'll copy one of Great-grandfather
Jay's sermons for him, and he can take it away with

him, and read it aloud after his performances—
though perhaps he ought to have a license for a
bishop's sermon," she added, doubtfully. "As for
his performing for us"—for Miss Jane had repeated
Paul's offer—"I suppose it would seem ungracious
not to let him do it."

But when the day came that Paul's knee was
strong enough for gymnastics, the two older ladies
were really quite interested in his "show," as he
called it. "He is going to do it to-night," Miss
Maggy said ; "and he says that it will be in the finest
style ! He said he would wear tights. I didn't like
to ask him what they were, as it is not, I think, delicate to refer to any special garment of a—a gentleman's wardrobe ; but I did wonder."

"It means stays, I suppose," said Miss Henrietta.
"I don't see why he mentioned them, I'm sure."

"Oh, well, a person in Paul's walk of life does not
realize the impropriety of such an allusion before
ladies," said Miss Maggy, kindly "You can't expect
him to make delicate distinctions. I hope he's not
disappointed because we are not asking any one in ;
but we couldn't do that. Henrietta, would you put a
white border on this baby blanket, or a blue one ?"

"I think," said Jane, breathing quickly, "that Mr.
Phillips is just as delicate as any one."

"I like blue best," Miss Henrietta said.

Jane's hands trembled, and she put her knitting
down. "I'm going to ask him if he doesn't want another lamp for to-night. We can let him have two,"
she said, indifferent to poor Miss Maggy's sigh that
it would use up a good deal of oil. She went swiftly
down the garden to the stable, where Paul welcomed
her with enthusiasm, and asked her if she didn't

think he had made things look pretty nicely. " I feel nervous about my knee," he said, " but I'm mostly worried for fear I won't do my best before the ladies. It's more embarrassing to have a little select audience like this, than a big dress circle." His tone seemed to range her on his side, as opposed to the " audience," which gave her a new and distinct feeling of responsibility that was almost anxiety. She told him about the lamps, and advised him as to which end of the open space between the stalls and the feed-bins should be the stage. She laughed, in her flurried way, until the tears came into her eyes, at some of his jokes, and she asked questions, and even made one or two suggestions. Perhaps she had never been so excited in her life.

Then she went back to the house. " We'll put on our best dresses," she said to her sisters, in a breathless way.

" Oh, Janie, not to go and sit in the barn ?" protested Miss Maggy.

" I will," Miss Jane said, with spirit. " I think it's only polite. And please, girls, each of you bring your bedroom candle over with you. He says he wants as much light as possible. Oh dear ! he is so superior to his profession !" she burst out, her face flushing.

The best clothes were wonderingly conceded by the two older sisters, and after tea, in the September dusk, before the moon rose, the three Misses Jay stepped out across the yard to the barn. Each had a lighted candle in her hand, and each held up her petticoats carefully, and walked gravely, with a troubled consciousness of the unusualness of the occasion.

WHERE THE LABORERS ARE FEW

The barn was very bright : Paul had borrowed some lanterns from a neighbor, and added two or three he had found in the loft, and all the lamps Jane could bring him from the house. The narrow space in front of the stalls was swept and garnished, and at its farther end were three chairs, each with a bunch of golden-rod tied on the back. The lanterns swung from the rafters, and the lamps stood on the top of the feed-bin, and the three bedroom candles were deposited, at Jane's command, on three up-turned buckets in front of what was evidently Paul's end of the open space. When the sisters entered there was a rustle among the pigeons overhead, and the cow, rubbing her neck against her stanchion, stopped, and looked at them with mild, wondering eyes, and then drew a long, fragrant sigh, and went on chewing her cud.

"This is very strange," said Miss Henrietta.

"It is very exciting," murmured Miss Maggy, nervously.

The gleam of all the lights, the candle-flames bending and flaring in wandering draughts, the gigantic shadows between the rafters, the silence, except for Clover's soft breaths, Paul's impressive absence— were all strange, almost alarming.

As for Miss Jane, she looked around her but said nothing.

"Shall we sit down?" Miss Maggy asked, in a whisper. "Where is he, Janie?"

"He will come in a few moments," said Jane. "Yes, sit down, please."

She went over to the bin to turn up one of the lamps, and looked, with anxious responsibility, towards the unused stall which Paul had told her was

251

to be his dressing-room. Suppose he didn't do well? She was nervous to have him begin and get through with it.

Suddenly, back in the shadows, Paul began to whistle :

> " I'm dreaming now of Hallie
> Sweet Hallie, sweet Hallie ;"

then he came bounding out, bowed, whirled round on his crutch, and stood still, laughing. Jane caught her breath, her feet and hands grew cold ; the other sisters murmured, agitatedly. Paul was clothed in his black tights and scarlet breech-cloth; a small scarlet cap was set side-wise on his head, and his crutch was wound with scarlet ribbons.

"Ladies," he began, " I shall have the pleasure—"

" I really think—I really feel—" said Miss Maggy, rising.

"I—I'm afraid, perhaps—such a costume—" murmured Miss Henrietta.

Paul looked at them in astonishment. " Is anything wrong, ladies ? If you'll just be seated, I'll begin at once."

"Do sit down," Miss Jane entreated, faintly ; " people always dress—that way."

The two older sisters stared at her in amazement. " But, Janie—" whispered Miss Henrietta.

"You can go," said Jane, " but I shall stay. I think it's unkind to criticise his clothes."

"If he only had some clothes," Miss Maggy answered, in despair. But they sat down. They could not go and leave Jane ; it would have been an impropriety. As for Paul, he plunged at once into his performance, with his running commentary of fun and jokes. Always beginning, " Ladies !" Once inadvertently he added, "and gentlemen," but stopped, with some embarrassment, to explain that he got so used to his "patter" that he just ran it off without thinking. His agility and strength and grace were really remarkable, but Jane Jay watched him with hot discomfort; once, when he turned a somersault, as lightly as a thistle seed is blown from its stalk, she looked away. But the rest of the "audience" began to be really interested and a little excited. "Just see that!" Miss Maggy kept saying. "Isn't it wonderful!"

"But if any one should call," Miss Henrietta whispered, "I should swoon with embarrassment. Still, I am sure it's very creditable. Once, when I was a child, I went to the circus, and saw a man jump that way."

Jane's face was stinging. "I don't like it at all," she said, under her breath. She looked at one of the lamps on the feed-bin until it blurred and made the water stand in her eyes. "Oh, I wish he would stop!" she said to herself.

"If," said Paul, "any lady in the audience would care to hold a hat up above my head, I may demonstrate a high kick!"

"I will, Mr. Phillips," Miss Jane said, briefly.

"Oh, Janie—" said Miss Henrietta.

"Oh, my dear, really—" murmured Miss Maggy.

"If you'll stand on this bin, ma'am," said Paul, taking off his cap with a sweeping bow.

For just an instant Jane hesitated, which gave Miss Maggy the chance to say, "Oh, Jane, my dear—really, I don't think—"

"I don't mind in the least," said Miss Jane, breathlessly.

"Well, wait," Maggy entreated; "if you must do

it, let me run back to the house and bring over one
of my skirts.   I'm taller than you are, and if you put
it on, it will be longer and hide your feet."

Miss Jane nodded.   "I'll come in a moment, Mr.
Phillips," she said, in a fluttered voice; and when
Miss Maggy, very much out of breath, brought the
skirt, she slipped it on, and, climbing up on to the
bin, stood, the long black folds hanging in a clumsy
and modest heap about her feet, and held out the
hat.   Her face was stern and set; she was miserably
ashamed.   The two other sisters gaped up at her
apprehensively, but with undisguised interest.   Paul,
however, did not share the emotions of the moment;
he leaped over three chairs arranged in a pyramid,
twirled round on his crutch, and then, with a bound
up into the air, lifted with his foot the hat out of
Jane's nervous hand.   Then he stopped, by force of
habit, to wait for applause; the two ladies before
him said, faintly, "Dear me!"   But they whispered
to each other that it was wonderful.

Jane, gathering up the long skirt in her hands,
looked down at him, and said nothing.

He turned, kissed his hand to her, and bowed so
low that the scarlet cockade on his cap swept the
floor; his dark eyes, looking up at her, caught the
flare of the candle-light in a sudden flash.

Jane Jay's heart came up in her throat.

That was the end of the show.   The three candles
of the foot-lights were burning with a guttering
flame; the cow had gone down on her knees, and
then come heavily to the floor, ready for sleep.
Paul, out of breath, but very much pleased with the
condition of his knee, sat down on one of the overturned buckets and fanned himself.

"This is the time you preach, isn't it, Mr. Phillips?" Miss Jane said. It was as if she were trying to bring him back to his true self.

"When I get through a performance? Yes, ma'am. People are pretty good-natured then, and willing to listen, you know."

He laughed as he spoke. There was always a laugh ready to bubble over when he talked.

"It is a pity," said Miss Henrietta, vaguely, "that Paul's circumstances in life did not permit him to study for the ministry."

"That's so," said Paul; "but my folks couldn't have afforded it when I was growing up, even if I'd had a mind to—which I didn't, till I was converted, and I was twenty-four then."

"It isn't too late yet, is it?" said Maggy, sympathetically. "Perhaps Dr. Lavendar could help you to get a scholarship somewhere. I know he wrote letters about a scholarship when the Smiths' oldest boy wanted to go to college."

Jane's face flushed suddenly. "I never thought of that! Why, Mr. Phillips—why shouldn't you study now?"

Paul had stopped fanning himself, and was listening. "I've heard of scholarships," he said, "but I never had anybody to put me in the way of them."

Miss Jane, in her excited interest, had not noticed that her sisters had risen and were waiting for her. "Come, Janie," they murmured; and Jane came, reluctantly. "You must see Dr. Lavendar to-morrow," she said, as they drew her away. "Oh, I believe, I believe you can do it!"

And as the three sisters, with their empty candlesticks in their hands, walked back in the moonlight to their own door, she said again and again, "Yes, he must be a clergyman—he must!"

Miss Maggy smiled indulgently, and said that she supposed Janie had it in her blood to work for the church. "Great-grandfather Jay was always encouraging young men to enter the ministry," she said, "and Janie inherits it, I suppose." And then Miss Maggy said that she was worried to death because she didn't think the new pink worsted was a good match for the pink they had been using.

When Miss Jane went to her room she was too excited to go to bed ; there was a spot of color in her cheeks, and her eyes shone ;—a clergyman ! yes ; why not?

It seemed to Miss Jane, because of the beating of her heart and the swelling of her throat, that her hope for Paul was desire for the Kingdom of God. How much good he would do if he only were a clergyman ; if he had a church, and wore a surplice ! He would talk differently then, and not say "ain't"; and he would take dinner with Dr. Lavendar, and go to Mrs. Dale's for tea ; he might even be assistant at St. Michael's ! For Dr. Lavendar was getting old, and by the time Mr. Phillips took orders, there would have to be an assistant at St. Michael's. Jane Jay sat down and leaned her elbows on the window-sill, and looked out into the misty September night. She could see the black pitch-roof of the stable, where a lamp was still burning. It came to her that perhaps Paul was kneeling there. Something lifted in her like a wave. She felt a strange longing for tears ; she, too, wanted to pray, to cry out for something— for pardon for her sins, perhaps, or for death and heaven. She said to herself that she loved her

Saviour;—this was what Mr. Phillips called "conversion," she thought. "Oh," she said, in a broken, breathless way—"oh, I am a great sinner! He has converted me." She murmured over and over that she had sinned; in the exaltation of the moment she did not stop to search the blank white page of her life to find a stain. Through her numb thoughts, this sword-thrust of emotion had pierced to the very quick. She suffered; and began to live.

She covered her face with her hands, and knelt down and prayed passionately.

V

Paul Phillips was to set out on the road the next day; but the hope that had leaped up at Miss Maggy's words made him eager to follow the suggestion of seeing Dr. Lavendar.

Jane Jay, her face pale, but full of some exalted consciousness, went early to the rectory and told the story of Paul and his aspirations. "It is very interesting," Dr. Lavendar said, "very interesting. Of course I'll see him. Jane, my dear, it is wonderful, as you say. The Lord is able to raise up children to Abraham out of—anything! Send him along. Tell him to be here at ten o'clock."

Jane went back to the stable and gave Paul the message. He was kneeling down, packing his few possessions in his knapsack, unwinding the scarlet ribbons from his crutch, and taking the cockade out of his cap. He looked up anxiously. "Does he think—" he began.

"You are to go and see him at ten, Mr. Phillips,"

she said; "and—you will be a clergyman!" Paul drew a long breath and went on with his packing; but there was a light in his eyes.

"Do you know," he said, "sometimes it seems to me that our disappointments are His appointments? Just drop the *dis*, you know. It makes 'em real pleasant to look at them that way. It was a disappointment to wrench my knee; there's no use denying it; and yet look what may come out of it!" He gave a smiling upward look of the frankest, most good-humored affection, as though communing with Some One she did not see.

Miss Jane watched him without speaking. She stood leaning against the feed-bin, twisting a bit of straw nervously, looking at him, and then looking away.

"You will be a clergyman," she said again, in a low voice. "But I want you to know now,—I want to tell you—"

Paul had risen, and gotten his crutch under his arm; but there was something in her voice that made him look at her keenly; then, instantly, he turned his eyes away.

"I want you to know—that I—oh—until you came I never thought anything—mattered. I never really cared; though I went to church, and my father was a clergyman, and Great-grandfather Jay was a bishop. But I—I didn't really—" She faltered, trembling very much, her throat swelling again, and her face illumined. "You've made me—religious, I think," she ended, in a whisper.

"I thank the Lord if He's spoken a word through me," the man said, tenderly; but he did not look into her face.

Miss Jane went away hurriedly, running, poor girl! the last half of the way to her own room ; there she lay upon her bed, face downward, trembling. She was very happy.

When Paul came limping into the rectory, the old clergyman gave him a steady look ; then all his face softened and brightened, and he took his hand in both his own. "Sit down," he said, "and we'll have a pipe. Well, you had an ugly fall, didn't you? How's your knee ?"

"Well, the darned thing's all right now," said Paul, with his kindling smile, "but it's been slow enough. I don't know what I would have done if the ladies hadn't been so kind to me."

"And you are starting out again now, are you ?" said Dr. Lavendar. "Oh, that's my dog, Danny. Danny, give your paw, sir, like a gentleman."

Paul seized the dog by the scruf of the neck and put him on his knee. "Ain't he a fine one ?" he said, chuckling. "Look at him licking my finger! Yes, sir ; I'm going on the road again ; but Miss Jane Jay, she told me that maybe you could put me in the way of getting an education, so as I could be a preacher."

"But I understand you do preach now ?" said Dr. Lavendar.

"Yes, sir ; but not properly. I just talk to 'em. Plain man to man. I get at them after I've given a show on the road or in the saloons. But—it's a hard line, sir. I—used to be a drinking man myself," he ended, in a low voice.

The old minister nodded. " You go right into the enemy's country ?"

"Yes," Paul said, briefly.

"It gives you a hold on 'em?" Dr. Lavendar suggested.

"That's so," Paul said. "I sometimes think if I hadn't been there myself I wouldn't know how to put it to them. Still," he said, thoughtfully, "you can't apply that doctrine generally. It would be kind of dangerous. We don't want to sin that grace may abound. Well, it's mixing. You see, that's where I feel the need of an education, sir. That, and people going down to the pit : the pit ain't just according to my ideas of fairness."

"How do you explain those things?" asked the old man.

"Oh, well, I just say to myself, '*He understands His business.*'"

"The Judge of all the earth shall do right!" said Dr. Lavendar. "Tell me some more."

So Paul, stroking Danny's shaggy little head, told him, fully. Dr. Lavendar got up once, and tramped about the room, with his coat tails pulled forward under his arms, and his hands in his pockets ; once his pipe went out, and once he took his spectacles off and wiped them.

When the story was finished he came and sat down beside the younger man, and struck him on the knee with a trembling hand. "My dear brother ! my dear brother !" he said. "Go back to the roads and the saloons ; and prepare the way of the Lord, and make straight His paths !"

Paul put Danny down, gently, and looked up with a puzzled face.

"Sir," said Dr. Lavendar, "the Lord has educated you. You don't need the schooling of men. See

what a work has been given you to do : Paul, a minister to the Gentiles !"

"Yes, sir," said Paul, "if I can just get some education. If I can know a few things."

"My dear friend," said the old man, smiling, "you
know what is best worth knowing in the world :
you know your Master. He's put you to do a work
for Him which most of His ministers are not capable
of doing. You have a congregation, young man,
that we old fellows would give our ears to get. Who
would listen to me if I went into Van Horn's and
talked to them ? Not one ! They'd slink out the
back door. And I can't get 'em into my church—
though I've got the red cushions," said Dr. Lavendar, his eyes twinkling. "No, sir ; your work's been
marked out for you. Do it !—and may the Lord
bless you, and bless the word you speak !" His face
moved, and he took off his glasses again, and polished
them on his big red silk handkerchief.

Paul's bewildered disappointment was evident in
his face. So evident that Dr. Lavendar set himself
to tell him, in patient detail, what he thought of the
situation ; and as he talked the light came. "I see,"
the young man said once or twice, softly, as though
to himself ; "I see—I see." It came to him, as it
comes to most of us, if we live long enough, that
when we ask for a stone, He sometimes gives us
bread—if we will but open our eyes to see it.

But when he rose to go, there was a solemn moment
of silence. Then the old minister, with his hands up-
lifted above the young minister's head, said :

"*Almighty God, who hath given you this will to do
all these things, grant also unto you strength and power
to perform the same, that He may accomplish His*

work which He hath begun in you, through Jesus Christ our Lord."

Paul, leaning on his crutch, covered his face with his hands, and said, passionately, *"Amen."*

When he went back to the three ladies, the uplifting of that moment lingered in his eyes. He came into the sitting-room, where Miss Henrietta and Miss Maggy were at work; it was a cool September day, and a little fire crackled in the grate. The room was hot, and smelled of worsted; Miss Henrietta's canary hung in the sunny window, cracking his hemp seeds, and ruffling his feathers after a splashing bath. The two ladies were rocking and knitting, and Miss Henrietta had been saying how much she missed rolling her big pink ball along the floor for Jacky to play with. "Though he didn't play much," she said; "he was getting old."

"I used to think he was lazy," observed Miss Maggy, comfortably.

"No, he wasn't," Miss Henrietta retorted. "You never appreciated Jacky."

"Yes, I did," Maggy remonstrated; "only I never called him human."

"Human? Well, I think that some cats are nicer than most people," old Henrietta replied, with heat.

It was just then that Paul came in to report the result of his interview with Dr. Lavendar. He was very brief about it, and as he talked the solemn look faded, and he spoke with open cheerfulness, though with reserve. "I guess he's right," he said; "the place for me is the place where I'm put; I guess he's right. Well, ladies, I came to say good-bye, and to thank you, and—"

"Do you mean," said Jane, from the doorway behind him, "that Dr. Lavendar won't help you to be
a clergyman?" Her face was pale, and then flooded
with crimson; she was trembling very much. "It
is wicked!" Her voice was suddenly shrill, but
broke almost into a sob. "You ought to be a clergyman!"

Paul held up his hand with a certain authority.
"I have been called to do my own work," he said.

"I guess Dr. Lavendar's right, Janie," Miss Maggy
said, soothingly. "Paul, I'm going to give you one
of Bishop Jay's sermons. I've copied it out, and I'm
sure you will make good use of it."

Then she asked some friendly questions about his
route, and brought him the sermon, and a little
luncheon she had prepared; and then Paul began
to make his adieux. He said much of their kindness
to him, and his wish that he could ever have the
chance to do anything for them; while they politely
deprecated anything that they had done. Miss Henrietta shook hands with him, and said that if he
should meet a white cat anywhere, to be sure and
see if he answered to the name of Jacky. Miss
Maggy bade him be very careful of his limb, and
hoped he would find his sister better. "And if you
ever get so far east again, you must come and see
us," she said, kindly.

Jane gave him her hand; but she let it slip listlessly from his fingers, and she did not lift her eyes
to meet his; a brother's eyes—pitying and brave.
"Good-bye," she said, dully.

Paul, shouldering his knapsack, waved his hat gayly and started off, limping down the path to the
street.

"Well, now really, for a person in his position," said Miss Maggy, "he has behaved very well, hasn't he?"

"Yes, indeed," old Henrietta agreed; "and he was so sympathetic, too. See, Maggy, this needle does make a looser stitch—don't you think so?"

Jane leaned her forehead against the window and looked down the road, where there was a little cloud of dust for a moment; then it disappeared.

SALLY

SALLY

I

"When I'm a man, Sally, and you're a big girl,
we'll get married," Andrew Steele used to say to his
little neighbor across the fence of their back yards.
And Sally would respond, cheerfully, "Yes, Andrew;
when we get big, we'll get married."

In those days they lived next door to each other,
and they talked across the fence, and played, and
went to school together, and said they would be
married when they grew up. But when Sally was
seventeen, and Andrew was seventeen and a half,
there was suddenly a break in their friendship. Sally did not look at Andrew in church, though he sat
just across the aisle. Andrew hung back, and did
not walk home with her in the old matter-of-fact
way. They stood apart for the first time in their
lives, these two young things, regarding each other
in shy silence ; and then, as suddenly as the simple
melody of their friendship had faltered and died
away, just so suddenly the music burst out in the
profounder harmony of love.

They told each other about it, standing shy and
blushing on the wet flag-stones in Andrew's greenhouse. Sally, a little plump body, with a freckled

nose and pretty red-brown hair; Andrew, very tall
and lanky, all wrists and ankles, with a mild, strong
face. They scarcely dared to look at each other—
the color coming and going in the boy's face just
as in the girl's. And when Sally had half whispered—her head turned away from him, and her little
fingers pleating and crumpling the big leaf of a be-
gonia—"Yes—Andrew; I—I do—care," Andrew
had said, in his simple way, pretty much what he
had said when they were children: "As soon as we
are old enough, we'll get married, Sally. Because
I've loved you all my life." And Sally's little heart
beat so hard that she could not speak for happiness.

"When you are twenty-three and I'm twenty-
three and a half," Andrew said, "we'll be married."

And Sally said, "Yes, Andrew."

He kissed her, and the color flooded up to her
temples; then the boy lifted his face and looked up,
silently; but his lips moved.

All this was just after Andrew's mother had decided to go and live in Upper Chester; and though
Andrew was to come back and forth every day to
the greenhouse, the moving meant to these very
young people the tragedy of separation. Very likely
it was that that brought matters to a head and revealed to them that they loved each other. Except
for this moving away, however, the course of true
love, for once in this rough old world, ran pretty
smoothly. No cruel elders, with the common-sense
derived from experience, declared that calf-love did
not last, and with the parental right to break hearts,
forbade, and, separated, and all the rest of it. The
fact was, Sally's mother, a vague, somewhat foolish
little lady, never dreamed of interfering with her

"THEY TOLD EACH OTHER ABOUT IT"

children—especially not with Sally, who was the eldest girl; a reliable, sensible, responsible child, who,
when her father died, really assumed the care of the
noisy, headstrong family of brothers and sisters. So
when Sally said she was engaged to Andrew, Mrs.
Smith never thought of objecting, though she did
not, she said, like Andrew's mother. "But you're
not going to marry her," she murmured, vaguely.
Then she kissed Sally, and cried a little, and said it
was too bad to think that she would have to go and
live in Upper Chester with Mrs. Steele—"unless she
dies first," said Mrs. Smith, hopefully.

When the young fry heard the news, they teased
her, and Robert, who was next in age to Sally, cried
out,

> "Handy Andy,
> Jack-a-dandy,"

and referred to the lovers as "the long and the short
of it." Which was considered an exquisite form of
wit in the family circle.

On Andrew's side there was no objection. "Sally's mother is a goose," said Mrs. Steele, "but it
doesn't *follow* that Sally is. And I think it is a good
thing for a young man to form an attachment early
in life; it keeps him steady." Then she reminded
her son that he hadn't any money of his own, and
he was too young to think of getting married. "But
if you like to say you're engaged, it doesn't hurt the
greenhouse," said Mrs. Steele.

But, of course, there was no question of their
being married. They knew they were too young,
and they knew that until Andrew could earn more
they were too poor. In their sensible way they had
made up their minds to all that when Sally said "yes."

Of all those good-looking Smith children, Old Chester's favorite (next to Sally) was Robert. He was
a handsome boy, with good manners and a quick
tongue, that, because of its wit, was forgiven many
things. Everybody had a good word for him, for
his behavior, his intelligence, his sweet temper; and
when Robert said he wanted to go to college, Old
Chester said that Mrs. Smith ought certainly to
manage to send him, because he had more brains
than all the rest of the children put together (except Sally).

"I think he ought to go, Andrew," said Sally.
Andrew came to supper at the Smiths' on alternate
Sunday nights, riding back and forth from Upper
Chester on the shaggy, heavy little horse that did
the carting for the greenhouse. This was his night,
and the lovers were alone for their usual half-hour
before tea-time; after that, Andrew would go into
the sitting-room to talk to Mrs. Smith and the two
younger girls, and play with the little boys, and
listen to Robert's views on many subjects—most of
all upon the necessity that there was for him to go
to college. So now in the parlor—which was chilly,
because it was hardly worth while to light a fire just
for that half-hour's talk—Sally confided to her lover
her belief that the boy ought to have his wish.

"Can you afford it, Sally?" Andrew asked.

"Yes," she said, smiling; "I guess we can afford
it; if it's best. But do you think it is best, Andrew?"

"Well," the young man said, "I'm inclined to
think it would be a good thing. Though your
mother 'll miss him when you are married. It's only
eighteen months and five days now, Sally?"

"Yes," she said; and then : "I mark the days off on my calendar, you know, Andrew."

Andrew had one arm around her waist, and held her left hand in his ; after this one tender allusion they talked in a commonplace way of how Sally must economize to manage Robert's education ; and of the greenhouse; and of the condition of what Andrew called "The Fund"—which meant his savings, that were to be devoted one of these days to house-furnishing—and of anything else that came into their heads. But Sally was marking the days off on the calendar !—and it was only eighteen months and five days until she should be twenty-three, and he twenty-three and a half.

He kissed her when it was time to go out to the family, and she put her arms around his neck for a minute ; but there were no raptures.

So it was decided that Robert should be sent to college ; and all Old Chester applauded, and said it was very proper in the real Smiths to make such an effort, and it believed that the boy would be a credit to them one of these days.

Robert entered the university that autumn, and Sally was to be married when he came home in June for the summer vacation. And so the time passed. Andrew's mother really grew fond of Sally (in her way); "the only thing I don't like about her is her mother," said Mrs. Steele ; and also, she had her opinion, she said, of two people who were going to marry on air. "That's about all Andrew's father ever got out of the greenhouse—air ! and damp air, too. Well, Andrew needn't look to me to do anything for him ; I've told him that. They'll have to board here, because I can't get along without Andrew. But I won't have this house overrun by the girl's brothers and sisters. Miss Sally Smith can just understand that !"

Miss Sally Smith understood it perfectly, and felt very sorry that Andrew's mother should be so ill-tempered. But, all the same, her calendar showed a growing expanse of diagonal lines over the days ; and by-and-by it was only three months before "the day" should be reached ! Then Mrs. Smith asked Sally if she didn't think perhaps she ought to be getting her wedding-clcthes ready—which was an astonishingly practical remark from Mrs. Smith. Sally did think so. And so the younger sisters and the mother and Sally all cut and stitched and fitted ; and Andrew came regularly every other Sunday night ; and everybody was very happy.

Sally and the girls were sewing away in the dining-room the day the letter with the bad news came from Robert. It was a May morning, warm, but with a cold edge in the wind ; and just outside the dining-room window was a peach-tree, all shimmering pink. The long dining-room table was heaped with white nainsook and edgings, and there was even a little narrow Valenciennes lace, which was the apple of Sally's eye.

" Real Val, for trimming !" she said. " Mother, I declare it's robbery to take it from you."

" Why, Sally," Mrs. Smith said, "it has been lying there in my piece-box for six years ; I don't see why you shouldn't use it, I'm sure. I got it to trim a baptismal robe for David ; and then I couldn't afford to buy the robe ; so I never used it."

" Well, girls," Sally announced to the other two

sisters, "when your turn comes, I'll give it back to you."

"Pooh!" said Esther, scornfully. "I'm not going to be married. I'm going to be an artist. And when I get rich, I'll buy you all the Valenciennes lace you want, Sally."

Little Grace lifted her serious face, and watched Sally measuring off the precious lengths, and put in her disclaimer too: "I won't want any lace. I'm not going to wear things like that. I think they are worldly."

"Do you, dear?" Sally said, in her kind voice, that never held any disrespect. "I don't. Oh, it is a pretty good old world, after all!" she ended, joyously, looking out at the rosy torch of the blossoming tree, and beyond it, into the soft blue sky. And then one of the little boys came in with Robert's letter.

It was to Sally, not to his mother, as usual, which surprised the elder sister enough to make her put it in her pocket unopened, though Mrs. Smith said, with a little note of disappointment in her voice, "Oh, I thought it was from Robert?"

Then some one asked for a spool of 90, which, not being in the family work-basket, Sally was obliged to run up-stairs to her own room to fetch. Sally never thought of asking either of the girls to do anything she could do herself; which was a pity for the girls.

She must have had to search for the spool a few minutes, for she did not come back immediately.

"Mother says, 'Look in the second drawer of her work-table,'" Esther called up to her.

"Yes," Sally answered, briefly. When she came

down with the spool her face was very much flushed, and her hands were not steady.

"Why, Sally," her mother said, "you are all out of breath. I wouldn't run up-stairs that way, my child."

"No, ma'am," Sally answered, obediently, and put her hand in her pocket and squeezed the letter. She did not talk very much after that, though the girls kept up their pretty chatter of wedding clothes and spring weather and the glow that the peach-tree made, standing so warm and rosy right up against the dining-room window. After a while she said she thought Andrew was out in the greenhouse, and she would run across and speak to him. So she folded up her sewing, and said she would be back in time to bring her mother her beef-tea at eleven, and went, bareheaded, out into the cool sunshine of the back garden and across the road to the greenhouse. Andrew was at the farther end of the nursery behind the greenhouse, and when he saw her coming he stopped his work and stood still and watched her, his plain, kind face, breaking into a contented smile. Sally's hair was blowing all about her forehead, and her fresh calico dress rustling in the wind; and to Andrew's eyes she was the prettiest girl in the world.

"Well, Sally?" he said. And then he added, anxiously, "You're worried?"

"Yes, Andrew." Her color came and went, and her eyes filled. "Oh, Andrew, Robert has been cruelly, cruelly treated! He— Oh, Andrew, what shall I do? *People suspect Robert!*" she burst out— "our Bobby! They say he is—a thief! That he has stolen something from one of the tutors. Robert!" she ended, with passionate contempt.

"SALLY WENT ACROSS THE ROAD TO THE GREENHOUSE"

Andrew's face grew anxious. " Sally, first of all,
are you sure he didn't ?"

" Why, Andrew ! you—doubt Robert ?"

" No," he said, slowly ; " not any more than I would
doubt myself, or anybody. But I can't say it isn't
possible. I can't help seeing that side of it."

" Oh, Andrew ! don't—don't ! He is innocent ; he
couldn't do—*that !*"

" I don't think he could, Sally ; he's your brother,"
Andrew said, simply. Then she gave him Robert's
letter. It was a letter full of blustering indignation — a boy's letter, Andrew said ; incoherent,
protesting, angry, frightened. Andrew sighed and
shook his head when he folded it and handed it back
to her. "I'll start to-night, Sally. I'll get a line
from Dr. Lavendar to the president, just saying he
has known Robert all his life—"

" And he will vouch for him," Sally broke in, with
a sob. If she had not been a sweet-hearted woman,
she would have added, " if you won't !" But that
was not Sally's way. Andrew looked around for a
moment, because his gardener might be somewhere
about ; and then he kissed her. And she reached
up and clung to him, and cried, and felt certain that
he would make everything right.

" Vouch for Bobby ?" said Dr. Lavendar, very red
and angry when he heard the story Sally and Andrew told him. " Of course I will vouch for Bobby !
Sally, my child, don't worry. Andrew will right the
boy in five minutes. If he doesn't, I'll go myself ;
I'll send the Bishop !"

" Oh, Dr. Lavendar," Sally said, the tears rolling
down her cheeks, " it is such a comfort to hear you
talk !"

"Well, come, come! you mustn't cry! Here's Andrew looking as though he were going to be hung at the sight of those tears. How are the wedding clothes coming on? There! That's better!" For Sally blushed as happily as every young thing should, and Andrew gazed at her in open pride and joy.

"Andrew will make it all right, I know," Sally said.

It was very satisfying to Dr. Lavendar to see how they loved each other.

So Andrew went. And while he was gone—indeed, it must have crossed him on the way—another letter came. Alas! alas! Poor Sally, stumbling through its maze of excuses and explanations and accusations, read, at last, confession:

"*I only meant to borrow it, of course. It was only* $100. *Why did he leave it in his desk if he didn't want anybody to take it? I believe it was a trap; but I only borrowed it. I meant to put it back as soon as you sent me my allowance. If you weren't so mean about my allowance, I wouldn't have had to borrow. There's no use making a fuss about it.*"

Sally read the letter, and then sat and looked at it. "Our Robert," she said, once or twice. "Father's son—"

After a while she gathered up her courage, poor child, and went to break the dreadful news to Robert's mother.

Later in the day—the restless, hopeless day—she told Dr. Lavendar. But his amazement and grief, his shame, even, because Robert was one of his children, he said, gave Sally only a dull sense of pity for him. For herself she had no words; she sat and looked at him, and wondered, vaguely, why he talked;

she could not talk. Only when, out of his humilia-
tion and sorrow, he came to face the practical neces-
sities did she seem to listen to him.

"Sally, my child, tell me what you are going to do."

"Andrew will see the President. I think Robert
won't be expelled. But he will come home, of course."

"No, no," he said quickly; "don't spare him; let
the university expel him! Oh, my child, the Lord
in his mercy sends consequences to our sins, or there
would be no health in us. Let Robert be *ashamed*,
if you would save his soul alive!"

Sally looked at him in dull and miserable astonishment; he was so insistent that poor Robert should
be punished. ("As if the doing it wasn't punishment
enough!" she said to herself.)

"I don't understand, Dr. Lavendar; but, anyway,
I can't have father's son expelled for—for what Robert has done. I know he didn't mean to do wrong;
it was a sudden temptation, and he didn't realize—"
Poor Sally broke down and cried. "I'm going to
have him come home, and—take care of him. And
love him. And I think people needn't know."

"You can't love him too much," he said; "but
love him enough to let him suffer, Sally. Shame
is wholesome."

She shook her head. "No, no," she said, passionately; "people sha'n't know!"

The old man looked at her pityingly. "Ah, Sally,
my girl, when you get old you'll know the worth of
pain. Poor child, you can't see the blessing in it
yet, can you? Well, well; we won't tell any one
about it, if you and your mother think best; but I
think you're wrong; mind, now, I think you're wrong.
Now, what about the money?"

" I have sent it to his tutor."

" Well ?"

" I don't know what you mean, sir," she said, wearily.

" I mean, how is Robert to pay it back ?"

" I've paid it, Dr. Lavendar, she explained again. And once more he checked her, this time sternly:

" Sarah, Robert must pay it back. He must earn it. Let his body teach his soul its lesson. Let him work hard, and live plainly. Let him go as a hand in the mills. My child, don't you interfere with Robert's Heavenly Father, and try to make the way of the transgressor easy !"

Her outcry of pain and entreaty did not move him.

" Do your duty, Sarah," he said, frowning. And then he added, softening a little : "And after all, Sally, he might as well go to work now. When you and Andrew get married in June, you can't have him tied to your apron-string. You'll have to leave him then."

" But we won't be married in June," said Sally.

III

" I hope you won't disapprove," Mrs. Smith said to Dr. Lavendar, when he came and sat beside her in a long, kind, comforting silence, "but we are going to have Robert stay at home. Sally thinks it is best ; he is going to help Andrew in the greenhouse, and Sally can look after him all the time. You know they are not going to be married this summer."

" Why not ?" said Dr. Lavendar.

" Oh, I couldn't do without Sally," the poor lady

said, shrinking and whimpering. "Sally saw that herself. She knows I couldn't get along without her, now. She can manage Robert better than I can. He always had so much will," she ended, sighing, and looking tearfully at the initial on her handkerchief.

Dr. Lavendar shook his head sadly.

"You think I'm doing wrong, sir?"

"Yes, ma'am."

She wept a little, and tried feebly to argue it with him. "He might have some temptation if he went away from us. Oh, dear, dear, dear!"

But Dr. Lavendar spoke his mind: "Set Bobby to work; put him on his own legs. He needs some hard knocks! Andrew's greenhouse is too easy for him. And, I tell you, it isn't right for Sally and Andrew to wait, ma'am; it isn't right."

"Well, I don't know," she said; "perhaps it isn't. But I couldn't get along without her, you know."

And Dr. Lavendar sighed, and gave it up.

And by-and-by they all settled back into a sad sort of acceptance of the situation; Robert was sullen and mortified, but, alas, not ashamed.

Now there are certain great angels which meet us in the way of life:— Pain is one; Failure is one; Shame is one. Pain looks us full in the eyes, and we must wrestle with him before he blesses us. Failure brings in his stern hand the peace of renunciation. Shame bears to us the sense of sin, which is the knowledge of God; his hidden face shines with the mercy of Heaven—and well for us if we may look into it. But, alas, poor Robert looked only at himself; he had nothing but a small and worthless mortification, which was only wounded vanity. He knew that his sister's marriage had been put off for his sake, and he was angry that it was so ; he knew that Sally watched him with hopeful love, and he was angry at the hope and love ; he knew that he had disgraced his family, so he was angry at his family.

Dr. Lavendar watched him, sick at heart. The fact is, theft means a moral *kink*, which is probably congenital (to speak spiritually), and leaves small ground for hope. The tendency may be checked, or at least covered up, but it is sure to break out again, some day, if the man lives long enough. Not that Dr. Lavendar was hopeless ; he was never hopeless of anybody ;—I used to think he had expectations for Satan — but he was wise ; so he was deeply discouraged. And he was very much troubled to have Sally's marriage delayed.

Andrew, however, had conceded almost immediately that under the circumstances it was Sally's duty to defer her marriage. " I can see her mother's side of it," he said. Mrs. Smith was so broken by this disgraceful trouble that it would be cruel to take Sally away from her. Perhaps in a year they could be married ; that was what Andrew counted on.

But that year of waiting was not like those first, young, sweet years. Mrs. Smith was more helpless than ever ; the great shock of Robert's fault seemed to have cut some spring ; she was never the same woman again. " Sillier than ever," Mrs. Steele said. Certainly she was a little more vague, a little more querulous ; perhaps a little dulled to everything except her love for her oldest son. She was sensitive to any remembrance of his wrong-doing, and quick

to resent what seemed disapproval or even anxiety
on Sally's part.

"You act as if he was the wickedest person in the
world!" she would say. "He shouldn't have done
it, of course; but he was thoughtless. And he meant
to pay the money back. I don't see anything so *very*
wicked in that," she would sigh, with that singular
moral obliquity which in money matters seems to
belong to feminine love.

However, the days came and went, and the months
slipped into each other, and the year of watching
over Robert was nearly ended. But Mrs. Smith did
not grow any stronger, or any more sensible; so,
by-and-by, when nearly another year had gone, Sally
began to say that she could not go away from home
until Esther was old enough to take her place.
"When Esther is eighteen, Andrew, she can help
mother. That's only two years more," she said,
with courage.

"But you took charge of everything when you
were seventeen, Sally," he reminded her, moodily.

"Yes, Andrew; but that was different. I had to.
And I can see now I really was too young. Now
wasn't I?"

And Andrew, with reluctant truth, was obliged
to admit that he thought she was. "A girl oughtn't
to have such responsibilities," he said; "I can see
that side of it, Sally." Then he stopped and calcu-
lated for a minute. "Well, Sally, when you are
twenty-seven, and I am twenty-seven and a half—"

"Yes, Andrew."

So the definite period of postponement was faced,
and the days went bravely. That winter Robert
had a chance to read law in an office in Mercer,

which gave him some sort of hold on life again, while at the same time it lifted the cloud of his idle and discontented presence at home. Grace and Esther shot up into big girls. Esther drawing and painting, and calling herself an artist, according to Old Chester lights ; and Grace, a queer, morbid, anxious child, who was always fumbling about in her mind for a vocation. "Isn't it strange?" Sally confided once to Andrew ; "when I was a girl I never was thinking what I was going to do. Why, there isn't anything special to do—except just grow up, and please mother, and make the little boys happy, and go to church on Sundays. It seems to me that's enough," Sally said, thoughtfully. "But I suppose that's because I haven't any talents."

"Esther will be seventeen the 5th of next month," Andrew reminded her. "A year and one month more, Sally !"

"Yes, Andrew ; only a year and one month. Oh, Andrew, did you see her last picture? It's wonderful!" And Sally, with careful pride, displayed a drawing of Clytie. "She copied it from that Parian marble one in the parlor, you know. Miss Annie Shields says she ought to go and study drawing at the School of Design in Mercer. She's wild to! And I don't know why she shouldn't, if we can afford it."

"Well, now, Sally," Andrew said, "why can't she? Let me help."

And such was the simplicity of Sally's love that she saw no reason why he should not help, if help were needed. "But I don't need it, Andrew. I think I can manage her board ; and the tuition is free, you know. But—but do you think it would be well, Andrew?" she said, with a sudden break in her voice. "You know—"

"Yes; but Esther is different. I would trust Esther anywhere."

He saw his Sally's eyes fill at the remembrance of how together they had planned that other flight into the world. Poor Robert! It had cut deep, that stab of shame and sorrow. Andrew took her hand in his and kissed it; and she put her head down on his shoulder, and knew he understood.

So it was settled; and when the fall term opened, Esther, excited, eager, hopeful, started out to "study art" for one year.

"She has *great* talent," Miss Annie Shields told Sally, with enthusiasm. "We'll hear from her one of these days! She'll be in Paris in one of the studios before we know it."

"In Paris?" Sally said, with a startled look.

Miss Shields laughed a little, and put her arm about her. "My dear, Esther is going to be an artist, and that means a long road to travel."

"Why, yes, of course," Sally agreed; "but—" Then she stopped, and her open face clouded a little.

But whatever her disturbed thought was, she banished it. Esther was going to have a winter at the School of Design; then she would come home, and Sally would get married.

That was a very peaceful winter to the "real Smiths." As early as January, although the family laughed at her a little, Sally began to plan her wedding clothes again, and the unfinished wedding dress was taken from its wrapping of silver paper to be altered, so as to be in the fashion, and finished—for the wedding was to be in June. Esther's visits, and

her work, and her "standing," were weekly interests.
There were good reports of Robert from the lawyer's office in Mercer. The two boys David and
John were vigorous, open-air little fellows, who kept
Grace and Sally busy mending and brushing, and
helping them with their lessons. Grace was more
contented, too ; which was a great comfort to Sally.
The child began to read devout books and have intense religious experiences ; and she would have
gone to church three times a day,—if only Dr. Lavendar had been of the same mind in regard to services. But when she said to him once, with timid
passion, that she wished he would have church on
all the saints' days—he only replied, cheerfully, that
every day was a Saint's day for staying at home and
helping her mother and Sally. "Don't ye forget
that, Gracie, my dear !" he said, his kind eyes twinkling at her in such a friendly way that the snub did
not hurt her feelings ; perhaps it would have been
more wholesome if it had.

"She's a little saint," Sally told Andrew. "Oh,
Andrew, that child makes me really ashamed of myself ; she's only fifteen, but she cares more for—for
things like that than I ever did in all my life."

"I think she is a good child," Andrew agreed ;
"but you're good enough, Sally. I don't think I'd
want you to be any better," he said, thoughtfully.

"I'm not good at all !" she said, laughing. "I'd
never have the patience to read all those books
Gracie does."

"Well, it isn't all books,—religion," Andrew said.
They were standing by the bench of seedling carnations in the greenhouse, and Sally had been watching him splitting down the stems in search of a fat

SALLY

white grub that was turning all the cool gray-green
into a sickly yellow. Andrew touched his flowers
as if he loved them, and when he tore open the heart
of a carnation to discover the enemy, his mild face
puckered with sympathy. It was a sunny winter
morning, with a glare of snow outside ; but in the
greenhouse the air was moist, and warm, and full
of the scent of roses and wet earth and growing
things. There was a soft green mould on the azalea
pots and on the curb of a little pool, which was sunk
in the flag-stones and bordered by callas ; the water
was still and dark, with a sudden glitter now and
then in its placid depths, when a goldfish turned his
shining side, or came up to the surface for a fly.

Suddenly Andrew put down his knife and twine,
and took Sally's two hands in his. "Oh, Sally," he
said, "you are good ! Sometimes I think if you
weren't so good we would have been married by this
time !" His face quivered as he spoke. Sally slipped
her arm through his silently. "We've waited so long,"
the young man said, with a hard note in his voice.

Sally put her cheek against his shoulder. " Yet I
couldn't leave mother, could I, dear ?"

Andrew took up his knife and twine again with
a long sigh. " No, Sally, no. I can see that side
of it. But—"

IV

Robert did so well in the lawyer's office that by-
and-by his good-humored assurance came back to
him, his old intelligent certainty of ability. And on
the strength of it—plus his allowance from the family purse—he got married.

285

He did not see fit to notify his family, however, until the deed was done, and a smart, pretty Mercer girl, "of no family whatever," Old Chester said, his wife. It would be interesting to know why, occasionally, a person of decent and refined traditions commits, without cause, the vulgarity of a secret marriage. However, nobody can say there is anything actually wrong about it; unless bad taste is wrong. Sally and her mother may have felt hot and ashamed, but they kept their own counsel, and said they were glad to have Bobby have a home of his own. Grace looked grave and troubled; but Esther spoke out her angry thought : "Robert ought to do something for mother, instead of getting married in this low, underhand way !"

"Don't you think, Esther," Sally suggested, "that perhaps you ought to live with Robert now, in Mercer, instead of boarding? He spoke of it to me. It would help him a little, and—it would seem kinder."

"Indeed I won't !" Esther declared, hotly. "I'm ashamed of him, Sally. I don't want to have anything to do with him, or his wife either. I know she's horrid, or she wouldn't have married him."

This decided expression of Esther's will troubled the elder sister, and it came upon another trouble which was heavy on her heart, and which must be told to Andrew.

It was dusk, and they were walking along the river road; Sally was very silent, which was not usual, and Andrew was talking a good deal of their own little comfortable commonplace interests. They stopped on the bridge for a few minutes, and leaned on the hacked and whittled hand-rail, looking sometimes at the dark, smooth current below them, and

SALLY

sometimes at the black fringe of trees along the
bank, but mostly at each other. A prosaic pair, perhaps, one might have thought them ; Sally was getting stout, and she had taken to spectacles lately,
because she was near-sighted ; she wore her hair
drawn rather tightly back from her face, and twisted into a little knob; it was the quickest way to
arrange it, she said; and when every minute in your
day is full, the quickest arrangement of your hair
is a consideration. Andrew, tall and thin, had deep
lines on his forehead, that meant patient disappointment; and he had the stoop which comes from bending over cold frames and poking about roots for
borers, which made him look much older than he
was.

"Esther doesn't like Robert's wife, Andrew," Sally said ; "and she won't live with them. Grace is
going to Mercer next month to visit her ; Grace is
so good about such things !"

"Well, Sally," Andrew said, in a comforting voice,
"it would be nice if Esther felt it her duty to be
with Robert — but I can see her side of it. She
doesn't like his wife, and it wouldn't be pleasant to
live with her. And you know Esther's young yet."

"Yes," Sally agreed, with a sigh.

"Besides, she only has to finish this term," Andrew reminded her.

Sally drew in her breath, and looked away from
him. "Andrew," she said, "Esther says that she
wants to have four years at the School of Design,
instead of one ; she says it is an actual necessity.
That unless she can take the whole course"—Sally's voice began to break—"it is just a waste of
money to have taken part of it."

287

"Why, but, Sally—" he exclaimed.

"Yes, I know, I know. But I don't see what can be done. I can see that to stop in the middle is bad. Only—I never thought of it when she began."

"But, Sally," he protested, "we cannot possibly wait any longer!"

"I'm afraid we'll have to; of course I couldn't leave mother and the boys to Grace; she isn't nearly old enough. You see that, Andrew? Oh, Andrew—please help me—please!" Sally said, and put her face down on her arms on the railing, and he felt that she was crying. The poor fellow stood speechless beside her. The river whispered and washed against the wooden pier in mid-stream. Sally did not speak.

"But, Sally," he said, "why, only this afternoon I was counting up the days; and this would make it three years! Sally"—he caught his breath, almost in a sob—"you belong to me!"

At that she lifted her head, with a smile that was like sudden sunshine on a cloudy day. "Why, Andrew, that's just it! That's what makes it possible to wait; and you see for yourself I can't leave home. Mother is really an invalid now; and think how much care Johnny and David are. Grace couldn't take charge of the house. Esther wants to be an artist, and it would be cruel to take the chance away from her, wouldn't it?"

"How about the cruelty for us?" Andrew said, breathing hard.

"But Esther is eighteen now," Sally said; "she really has a right to decide for herself. Only—it's hard on you, Andrew." Sally's little round chin shook, and she looked up at him, trying not to cry.

288

SALLY

It was so hard that Andrew, though he set himself to cheer her, quietly, in his own mind, refused to accept the delay. He evolved a plan : he would ask Mrs. Smith whether, if he and Sally got married, they might come and live with her. "I'd have to bring mother," he reflected ; "she isn't well enough to live alone ; but they owe Sally that."

However, owing doesn't mean paying, as any butcher or baker or candlestick-maker can tell you ; and when it comes to relations, the payment of consideration is, alas, even more uncertain. Mrs. Smith cried, and said of course Sally must do as she thought best. If she was so anxious to get married that she had to bring strangers into the house, why, she must do it, that was all. Then she told Sally hysterically that she had always disliked Mrs. Steele ; she was a disagreeable, bad-tempered old woman, and she didn't know why, at her time of life, she should have to live in the same house with her. "If you'll wait a little while," she said, "I won't be in your way. Andrew's been content to wait ten years now ; I don't see why he should suddenly be in such a dreadful hurry. Still—do as you want, Sally ; you've always had your own way, and you always will !"

But even if Mrs. Smith had been complaisant, Andrew's plan could not have been carried out. Mrs. Steele was aghast at the very idea of such a thing. She would do anything in the world for Andrew— in reason ; but if Sally Smith didn't love him enough to leave her mother for him, she had better not marry him. In her young days a girl did not expect to take her husband home to live with her. And as for going and living in the same house with that silly Smith woman— As for giving up her own home

T   289

in Upper Chester, and going back to Old Chester (which she had always hated) — well, really! Andrew must be crazy!

"Then let me bring the Smiths here," Andrew said, boldly. At which Mrs. Steele spoke her mind with such unpleasant frankness that her son grew white with anger.

"Sally's kept you dangling round ten years," she said, "and I guess now she's afraid of being an old maid, and so she thinks she better take you, for fear she won't get another chance. I guess she—"

"*Hold your tongue!*" said Andrew Steele.

But he gave his project up.

Yes, of course, as Sally said, it was hard; but after the first shock of it, he set himself to make the best of it. When Esther should finish her course at the School of Design, and could come home, he and Sally would be married. When she was thirty and he was thirty and a half, their time would come.

Of course, Old Chester had its opinion of all this: Willy King's wife even went so far as to say that it was somebody's duty to tell the "real Smiths," flatly and frankly, that they were just sacrificing Sally to their own selfishness. There is every reason to suppose that Martha King took this duty upon herself, for it was known that after a call from her, Mrs. Smith cried steadily for two days; which lost Sally a night's sleep, and did not hasten her wedding-day at all, for Esther continued to draw ginger jars and lemons, with folds of red cloth arranged behind them, and to dream of a great future. Once she told Sally she thought she was foolish not to get married. "Mother could get along," she said.

"No, dear, she couldn't," Sally said, and that was all there was to it.

When the fall term opened, Sally again suggested that Esther should board with Robert; "mother has to help him a little, you know, Esther, and it would be easier for everybody if you would live with him."

"It wouldn't be easier for me, my dear," Esther said, laughing ; "his wife is simply impossible. She uses perfumery, and has an awful voice ! And now that there is going to be a baby—no, I thank you !"

Robert's baby came that winter ; and though he was doing fairly well, considering how young he was, his mother had to help him sometimes, which kept the family purse rather low. As for his wife, she came to visit her mother-in-law once, and told Sally she thought she was a perfect idiot not to marry her fellow, and get a house of her own with new furniture in it. "All these big, clumsy mahogany things have no style," said Carrie. "When the house comes to Rob, I'm going to send 'em all to auction, Sally. You can get beautiful parlor sets in Mercer now real cheap. Red and green rep, and tan terry, with backs all turned in grape-vines and things."

But Carrie, in her way, liked her husband's family, and was generous to them. She gave Grace a really pretty necklace, and was much affronted at the girl's attitude towards it.

"You're very kind, sister Carrie," Grace said ; "but I don't think jewelry is right. I think it is sinful. So I'll give it to Esther or Sally, if you don't mind ?"

"I don't mind what you do with it, I'm sure," Mrs. Robert said, with a toss of her head. "But I think you are a very queer little girl, to try and make Esther or Sally sinful."

Grace looked at her with her big, visionary blue eyes, and said, " I don't know what you mean, sister Carrie."

"Well, don't bother," Carrie said, crossly. " Here, give it back to me. I don't mind being sinful."

Grace, horrified, crept away and prayed for this lost soul passionately, and then as passionately for her own soul. Just then Grace's soul was of great importance to Grace. Her church-going became a little inconvenient at times ; but Sally, tender and reverent of her little sister's devoutness, was always glad to have the child go.

"She's a little saint," she told her mother, her kind eyes beaming behind her glasses.

"Oh yes, she's good," Mrs. Smith said, vaguely ; " but I think she ought to know more about house-work and sewing."

"But she hasn't time, really," Sally said ; " she reads aloud in the Poorhouse Infirmary every other morning, and she has her Sunday - school class to look after, and she goes to Upper Chester three times a week to distribute tracts. Besides, Gracie doesn't like house - work ; and I love to do her mending for her. But, mother, do you know since she came back from Mercer she's possessed that Dr. Lavender should have an early communion— 'Celebration,' she calls it — at six. She went to a very high church there. Imagine Dr. Lavender getting up at five o'clock ! And who would go, any-way ? Nobody but Grace, I'm sure. She told Dr. Lavendar about it, and what do you suppose he said ? ' Rags of popery ! Rags of popery !' "

SALLY

Afterwards—it was the winter before Esther finished her fourth year at the School of Design—when Grace, burning with the passion of her divine purpose, told her sister that she wanted to enter a sisterhood and that she believed herself "called," Sally looked back over the years of the child's singularly absorbed religious life, and admitted that the "calling" was from heaven.

"Mother dear," the oldest daughter urged, "you know Grace is old enough to know her own mind; and, indeed, indeed, I would not *dare* to interfere. Grace has been like this all her life. I have always felt that she was nearly an angel, anyhow!"

Mrs. Smith wept, in a weak, desultory way, and said that when she was young she never heard of a Protestant girl going into a convent to be a nun.

"It isn't a convent, mother dear," Sally explained; "it's a sisterhood of our Church. They've had them in England a good while, but this is the first one in this country. And Grace won't be a nun; she'll be a sister, and learn to be a nurse, so she can take care of the sick."

"She'd better be a sister to Johnny and David," sighed Mrs. Smith; "and she can nurse me, Sally. I'm sure I'm sick enough," the poor lady said. "And I don't see how she can go off and leave it all on you. It seems to me, if being a good daughter is anything, you're just as religious as Grace, every single bit."

"Oh, mother dear," protested Sally, "you know I'm not like Grace! I wish I were," she ended, with a sigh.

For Sally, who was thirty and stout and very near-sighted, never knew that she was one of the shining ones.

Yet, alas, how the shining ones, by their very shining, do make it easy for the rest of us to walk in darkness!

V

So Grace, with all the egotism of the religious temperament, set about saving her clean, narrow, good little soul. Sally had had a passing thought that, as Esther's art had held her from those household duties which she was to assume when Sally married, Grace, nearly eighteen, might offer to take them up, even though (as Sally had to acknowledge) the child was singularly incapable owing to the religious preoccupation of these later years. But, after all, Sally told herself, humbly, Grace had chosen the better part. To give her life to the service of God—how much greater that was than just the common, easy duties of love!

So Sally and Andrew waited for the end of Esther's course at the School of Design.

"I don't like it," Dr. Lavendar said, impatiently—"I don't like it at all. Andrew, I wouldn't put up with it! Go and tell Sally so, and I'll come round after supper and marry you."

Andrew laughed, and took up a trowelful of sand, and sifted it over the roots of his callas. Then he frowned, poor fellow! and sighed. "I'm afraid it can't be helped. Now just look at it: Grace is going away, and Esther is at her school. Somebody has got to run the house; Mrs. Smith isn't well enough to do it. I can't help seeing that side of it, Dr. Lavender," he ended, gloomily.

"Well," Dr. Lavendar said, impatiently, "it all

seems to me perfectly unnecessary. I can think of
a dozen ways this thing could be arranged, and you
and Sally married. First place, you needn't have
waited on Robert's account."

"That's all said and done," Andrew reminded him,
mildly; "but I'd like to hear even half a dozen ways
this could be arranged, sir?"

"Very well; I'll tell you: get married next week,
and let Sally come home every few days and look
after that poor, helpless mother of hers."

"Mrs. Smith needs her all the time," Andrew objected, with a sigh.

"Then let Grace take care of her! I don't approve
of this running out into the world to look for a duty
when you have a hundred right under your nose!"

"Well, yes; but Grace has made up her mind,"
Andrew said, sadly.

"Then let Sally make up her mind," Dr. Lavendar
retorted; "or else — well, why don't you and Sally
live at home with Mrs. Smith?"

"I can't leave mother; she's old and feeble, and
needs me."

"Take her along."

"She wouldn't like to leave her own home, sir. I
can see her side of it."

"Well, then, hire somebody to take care of her—
or else to take Sally's place with Mrs. Smith."

"We haven't money enough for that," Andrew
answered, calmly. "And I don't believe Mrs. Smith
could get along without Sally; nobody could take
her place."

"Then let Esther give up this nonsense of hers!"
Dr. Lavendar said, angrily. He did not like to be
pushed into a corner by Andrew, or anybody else.

"I tell you, Andrew," he went on, pounding the flag-stones with his umbrella, "you ought to have gone to the Smiths half a dozen years ago, and pulled the bell, and said, 'I've come for Sally'; and tucked her under your arm and walked off with her. This virtue of self-sacrifice has brought forth vice. Those other Smith children— Well, never mind that!"

"I think it has made the others selfish," Andrew agreed; "but it has been Sally's conscience," he added, tenderly.

"Sally's fiddlesticks!" Dr. Lavendar burst out. "Don't talk about conscience. Conscience without reason isn't of the Lord!"

"Oh, well, it's only four months now," Andrew said. "Esther comes home the middle of June, you know. Mind you're ready, Dr. Lavendar! It's to be on the 20th."

As for Dr. Lavendar, he went plodding home, grumbling and frowning. "It's outrageous; it's pre-posterous! I'll tell Esther what I think of it, when I see her."

But the telling Esther did little good. Perhaps because it came at a bad moment. . . .

Esther had come home as usual at the end of the week; and on Saturday morning she and Sally went up to the garret, in response to an appeal from Grace for some clothing to give away. It was a dull February day; the garret was dark and chilly, and smelled of camphor.

"Good gracious!" Sally said, panting and laughing. "Those stairs do make you out of breath!"

"You're getting fat, my dear," said Esther, standing up, slim and pretty, with an amused curl on her lip.

SALLY

"I suppose I am," Sally agreed, ruefully; "and I don't know why, for I'm sure I am always running up and down stairs, and that ought to make me thin."

"It's a good conscience," Esther declared, "and no worry. Now I've such a lot to worry me—"

But for once Sally did not press for information so that she might sympathize. She got up, and opened a drawer in a tall bureau, and folded back a sheet of silver paper. "Why, it's your wedding dress, isn't it!" Esther said, looking in. "Heavens! how old-fashioned, Sally."

"I'm going to alter it over," Sally said, touching it with loving hands; "the silk is just as good as ever."

"You can never get into it," Esther told her, carelessly; "and I'd wear gray, Sally, at your age. Don't you think it's more suitable?" Sally looked troubled—Esther was the criterion of taste in the Smith family.

"Well, I don't know," she said. "I like this, you know. I think I'd rather alter it, even if it isn't quite so nice. I'm going to work on it next week. You know it's going to be the 20th of June, Esther." She stood by the open drawer a minute, lifting a soft fold of the unfinished dress, or turning over a sleeve, and then pressing it smoothly back, smiling to herself and thinking how the days were narrowing down on the calendar. Esther winced at the sight. Sally was too heavy and too old to be sentimental, the girl told herself. Her taste was offended. It is surprising how often pure goodness does offend our taste.

"Come along, Sally," she said; "don't be spooney, my dear. Do let's get through this clothes business;

there are lots of things I want to talk to you about. Gracious, Sally, how do you manage to attend to this sort of thing? I wish Grace would look after her own charities! This camphor is horrid. It makes me nervous even to think about fussing with clothes."

Sally laughed, and shut the drawer, and went to work heartily. "You'll get used to it, my dear," she said; "but you needn't do it now. Sit down there and talk to me." So Esther sat down, and Sally unfolded, and folded again, and sprinkled camphor. And when she had finished, Esther was tired to death, she said, and Sally was hot and dusty and out of breath; so they went out and sat on the garret stairs to rest and cool off. There was a window on the landing, and they could look out across the brown February landscape to the line of hills, gray and vague in the mist.

"Why, there's Andrew over in the nursery," Sally said, screwing up her near-sighted eyes. "See him, Esther?"

"Oh, Sally, for pity's sake! don't do that way with your eyes! If you only knew how it looked. Sally, I want to talk to you about my work. I've been talking to Mrs. Tom Gordon (how she does adore that fat husband of hers!), and she said I would never really do anything if I only studied in Mercer. So I—the fact is, I've decided to go abroad for three years."

Sally turned and looked at her, open-mouthed. Then Esther, a little nervously, but with a wiry determination in her face, went on with her story: "I'm sorry, of course, if it interferes with any of your plans, but I've just got to go. I can't live unless I go on with my art. You can't understand it, because you haven't the artistic temperament; but I tell you I'd simply rather die than live the way you do in Old Chester;—with no interests, and accomplishing nothing."

Sally heard her out in silence; she leaned her cheek on her dusty hand and looked over at Andrew pruning some bushes in the plantation; it had begun to rain in a fitful, uncertain way, and she shivered a little, there on the draughty landing.

"Esther," she said, in a low voice, "I think you have some duties to mother, and the boys, and—"

"I have a duty to myself," the girl broke in, passionately. "Sally, my art is my life. Nobody has any right to ask me to give it up just to—to pack coats away in camphor. I can't do it. No; there's no use talking. I *can't*. Why did you send me to the School of Design at all, if it wasn't to fulfil—my genius? Why did you do it?"

"I—don't know," Sally said, dully.

Of course, afterwards, they discussed it at length; and by-and-by Sally was pushed into her last corner.

"I don't see how we can afford it," she said, with a worn look.

"Oh, I can manage the money part of it," Esther assured her. When Sally got down to expense, Esther saw consent ahead. But, indeed, consent was a matter of form; she had made up her mind to go, with or without it. As for the expense, she had settled all the details of that before she announced her determination; she was to pay her way by certain services which she was to render to an older and richer girl with whom she was to go. "I sha'n't ask you to help me," she told her sister, with all the cruelty of youth. After all, there is nothing quite so cruel as this beautiful, fleeting, innocent thing called Youth.

It was at this time that Dr. Lavendar got his chance to tell Esther what he thought of the situation : he met her the afternoon of that very Saturday when she had broken her purpose to Sally. "Esther, my child," he said, "I want to have a word with you."

"All right," said Esther, carelessly ; which made Dr. Lavendar look at her sharply. His young people did not use that tone with him. But Esther used it ; and when he had said his say, she answered him in the same careless way, but briefly, and to the point.

"I don't see why I should give up my life just to let Sally get married."

Then Dr. Lavendar tried argument. Esther was plainly bored, but she listened with what politeness she could. Only when, in a moment of irritation, he said, bluntly, "After all, now, Esther, what good is all this art business ? I don't see that anything but your own amusement is served by making pictures. I don't see that the world is any better for your work "—only then did she flash out at him : "Well, if it comes to that, Dr. Lavendar, I don't see that the world will be any better for Sally's getting married ! She'll have a lot of children, and there are too many people in the world now—half of 'em can't get a living."

Dr. Lavendar was very much displeased, and a good deal shocked. He had never heard a young woman allude to such matters ; but when Esther added, "Anyhow, I can't do anything about it ; I'm going abroad to study," then he was angry. "Esther," he said, "I am grieved and disappointed in you! I feel it my duty to tell you so. And I shall advise Sally and your mother not to allow it."

"*Allow* it?" said Esther, opening her eyes. "Why, I'm of age, Dr. Lavendar!" and then she said good-bye, majestically.

Dr. Lavendar stood looking after her, shaking his head, too distressed for Sally to laugh at the child's airs. "Well," he said, "Sally, God bless her! is responsible for this. It's all her fault!" He told Sally so. "You've got a monopoly of unselfishness, my dear," he said, with a twinkle in his eye, but half sadly. "You grow in grace; but it's at the expense of your family!"

And Sally, who looked a little older these last few days, laughed in her cheerful way, and supposed that this pathetic truth was a joke.

As for Andrew—"*And what about us?*" he said, roughly. And then he cried out, with passion, "My darling!"—a word so unusual that Sally blushed to her forehead, and hid her face against his breast.

It was characteristic of the relationship between these two that, in all the pleadings and protests of the poor deferred lover, Sally never made the offer of convention and custom to release him. She never thought of such a thing; and Andrew would not have understood it if she had. There are certain ties from which there is no release: motherhood is one; marriage is sometimes one; and that particular sort of love which, rooted in human passion, yet bears friendship as its blossom, is another. There was nothing for Andrew to do, Sally thought, but wait. And Andrew, protesting, waited.

VI

Afterwards, when Sally looked back upon it, this period of waiting seemed to be happiness.

The boys were doing well; Mrs. Smith seemed really a little stronger; and there was an absence of jars and worries and heartaches, which really constituted happiness, Sally thought. But she did not know it until a real and terrible unhappiness knocked at her door, and showed her this peaceful truth.

Robert. He was the unhappiness. Sally never quite understood it, and his mother never believed it—but it was something about money. Robert was so "misunderstood," he said, that he was obliged to leave his country. It was that or jail. So, suddenly, secretly, in the night, he disappeared.

Carrie came and told them, blazing with anger at the fugitive, who had left her penniless. "I suppose I've got to go to work," she said—"me! after being used to take my comfort. For my folks won't do a thing, they're so mad at him. Anyway, they can't; they're as poor as Job's turkey. But I'll tell you one thing, I won't carry all those children on my back; I'll tell you that, Mrs. Smith! I'll take care of baby, but I can't do for the rest. I—*can't!*" Then she burst out crying. "I'll work and support baby and I; but you'll take the rest of 'em, won't you Sally?" she said, miserably.

"Yes, Carrie," Sally told her, briefly.

She could not speak. She could only go to Andrew.

"If it were only death," she used to think; "if Robert had only died, and these children had come to us!"

SALLY

But Robert did not die ; on the contrary, a winter in Italy greatly improved his health. He wrote regularly to his sister, acknowledging her remittances, and blessing her for her goodness to his children. He apparently forgot his wrong-doing, though once or twice, in his letters, he referred in a good-humored way to his "mistake," which, he said, "no one regretted more than he." "He has repented," Mrs. Smith used to say, angrily, to Sally; "I don't know what more you want! You're so hard on him." Sally used to answer Robert's letters, sadly and patiently, and with no reproaches ;—that was Sally's way. And she devoted herself to his children. These three little people, so tragically bereaved, meant unceasing care and love. Mrs. Smith, too, became more helpless than ever. Mrs. Steele, whose antagonism for the poor foolish lady had become a fixed idea, was herself an invalid now, and very dependent upon Andrew, who became almost as good a nurse in those days as Sally. So, with these claims upon them, the middle-aged lovers could only wait—they called it *waiting ;* but nobody ever thought of their marrying. They were permanently lovers.

To be sure, they said to each other, that when Esther came home— But just after Robert's downfall Esther married a stout, stupid, good-hearted Englishman, as poor as a mouse, and unable to look at a picture without growing sleepy. She put down her brushes on the birth of her first child, and she wrote Sally, in the fulness and happiness of her heart, that "home was woman's sphere." And Old Chester said she was quite right.

Robert's children had been with their grandmother three years, when Dr. Lavendar made up his mind that this had lasted long enough, and rose in his wrath. That was how it came about that he made his journey out into the world.

It was a long time since Dr. Lavendar had ventured farther than Mercer; and he made as many and as solemn preparations as though he were going to the ends of the earth. He "put his house in order," he said; he burned some old letters; he added a codicil to his will; and he arranged for his grizzled little dog, Danny. Then he fared forth into the world.

He did not tell any one in Old Chester his object, so no one had apprised "Sister Mary Eunice" that she was to see him. She had been told that a clergyman wished to see her in the parlor of the hospital, and she came down-stairs with her soft, swift, sliding step, her brown robes clinging about her feet, and her ebony and silver cross dangling from her waist. Her face was the pure, austere, devout face of the little girl who used to kneel at Dr. Lavendar's communion-rail, and come to every possible service, and wish there were three times as many more.

"Why, Grace!" he said, getting up to greet her, and holding out his hands, but staring at her through his spectacles with astonished eyes.

"Dear Father Lavendar!" she murmured.

Dr. Lavendar sat down, with a distinct sense of shock. Sister Mary Eunice sat down too, with her eyes dropped, and her hands folded in her lap. She told him how glad she was to see him, and how much she wanted to hear all about dear Old Chester, and her mother, and Sally, and the boys. "You've just seen them; it's good to see any one who has really seen them." She raised her eyes with a swift look, and dropped them again. "I get letters, of course, but it isn't like seeing them."

"No," Dr. Lavendar said, "it isn't, Gracie, my dear. Well, your mother's fairly well. I saw her on Monday. Sally, bless her heart, is just the same dear, good girl. And John and David are nice boys. When are you coming home, Grace?"

She was to have two weeks' vacation in the summer, she told him, with that flashing glance followed by a downward look, which she had lately acquired, but she thought perhaps she would go into retreat for that fortnight.

"Grace," said Dr. Lavendar, twitching his eyebrows at her, "when is Sally going to get married?"

"I don't know, I'm sure," she answered, a little startled.

Then he made his appeal. He was very much moved as he told her the story of Sally and Andrew, and the long, patient, lasting love.

"They've waited all these years. Grace, isn't your duty plain?"

It was so far from plain that he had to put it into bolder words:

"Give up this artificial life, my child; come back and do your duty in that station of life where it pleased God to call you. Give Sally her chance."

It was so astonishing, so preposterous to his hearer that there was an instant when she almost laughed. Leave the hospital? Leave her sick, and poor, and sinning folk? Leave her vocation, and go back to darn Robert's children's stockings, and let Sally get married? It struck her as absolutely ludicrous.

"Why!" she protested. "But, Dr. Lavendar,

U   305

you don't realize—just think of the work to be done here—"

"There's a-plenty of work in Old Chester. My girl, listen to me : you think this work serves God ; and so it does. But there is no better service of God than the simple doing of the duty He gives you in your family life. Gracie, don't try so hard to save your soul ; he that would save his life shall lose it. Do you remember who said that? Come home and do your duty. You can wear these things in Old Chester, if you want to," he added, with eager simplicity.

At that a spark came into the eye of Sister Mary Eunice which was just a little of this world. However, she restrained any sharp expression of opinion ; she explained to him, in gentle detail, how impossible it was for her to think of what he proposed ; indeed, she was very gentle with poor, stupid, Protestant Dr. Lavendar, who sat frowning at the crucifix on the whitewashed wall opposite him, and rapping the bare floor now and then with his impatient umbrella.

When he went away she had only tender feelings for him, for, after all, she had received her first spiritual instruction (such as it was) from the simple old man ; even his sharp words did not make her angry :

"Go and seek for light, Grace ; read your Bible and get over this gimcrackery. Don't think so much about petticoats, but follow your Saviour, who went down to Nazareth with his father and mother, *and was subject unto them* until he was thirty years old. Good-bye ! I'm disappointed in you. What have I been teaching all these years to produce a child like this?"

SALLY

He went away angry, and grieved, and wondering; but most of all determined: Sally and Andrew should be married,—somehow!—if he had to use force to get 'em to stand up and listen to the marriage service! Coming down from Mercer, he sat on the box-seat with the stage-driver, and Jonas said, afterwards, that he "hardly opened his head for the whole twenty-one miles." He stabbed at the footboard with his umbrella, and frowned, and thrust out his lower lip, and looked, Jonas said, as cross as two sticks.

"It's got to stop," he said to himself. "It's wicked, and I'll tell 'em so!" Then he pounded so hard with his umbrella that the off horse twitched his ears nervously, and Jonas looked round at him openmouthed.

He made plan after plan; but each one was discarded because he saw it would encounter invincible selfishness, or invincible self-sacrifice, "and I don't know which is worse!" said Dr. Lavendar, snorting. As they passed through Upper Chester, in the pleasant afternoon light, he was deeply discouraged. "I can't see any way out of it," he thought; "that boy Andrew can't leave his mother—I admit that; and he hasn't money enough to hire somebody to look after her; I admit *that*. He ought to take her, body and bones, and make her go and live with the Smiths—but how they would quarrel—those two women! Then there's Sally's side. Mrs. Smith would threaten to die if Sally left her, and Sally hasn't the courage, poor girl, to say 'Very well, ma'am'; and go,—and discover that her mother would live to be as old as Methuselah! The only thing I can do is to make an appeal to Mrs. Steele, though it will do

about as much good as talking to a stone! Andrew
has spoiled her. Well, well; children are responsible for their parents to the Lord; but I suppose
that never struck St. Paul." The long shadows
stretched across the new-mown fields where the hay-
cocks had been piled up for the night; the air was
sweet, and there were bird-calls all about them; the
setting sun struck suddenly on the windows of Mrs.
Steele's little house, and Dr. Lavendar frowned
again, and said to himself: "Well; I'll give that
woman a piece of my mind; I wish I'd done it ten
years ago! It's probably too late now, but it will
be a relief to me, anyhow."

It was too late. When Van Horn came out to
help the old clergyman down from his perch on the
box-seat as the stage drew up at the tavern door,
there was an important look on his face. "Glad
you're back, sir," he said. "Well, things has happened since you went away. Mrs. Steele passed
away, sir, last night."

Dr. Lavendar, clambering stiffly down over the
wheel, paused midway; then he stood staring at
the landlord; then sat down on one of the big
splint chairs on the porch. "The sword of the
Lord, and of Gideon!" he said.

Van Horne sighed respectfully at this religious
exclamation, and said: "Yes, indeed, sir; we all go.
It was a fit."

As for Dr. Lavendar, he went home and told his
Mary to give him his supper as quickly as possible.

"I am going back to Upper Chester," he said;
"Mrs. Steele is dead."

Mary protested shrilly. "You'll wear yourself out

—you just home from a journey! She's gone; there isn't nothing you can do—''

"Isn't there?" said Dr. Lavendar, chuckling. "Give me my supper!"

So he went, jogging along in the summer dusk in his old sulky. The house was dark and silent when he reached it at ten o'clock; but as he came up the garden-path he heard low voices on the porch, and then Andrew rose in the shadows under the Virginia-creeper that hung thick about the pillars and over the lintel, and came and met him. "This is very kind of you, Dr. Lavendar," he said, in that subdued way which means the house of death. "Sally's here," he added.

"I supposed so," the old man said, and took Sally's hand in silence.

"It was very sudden," Andrew said; and then they all sat down, and Andrew told the story. "It was very sudden," he said again, sighing, when he had given the last detail.

"Yes," said Dr. Lavendar; "yes."

Then they were silent.

"She is better off, Andrew," Sally said, gently. "It is a blessed thing for her—isn't it, Dr. Lavendar?"

"Oh yes, yes," Andrew said. And Dr. Lavendar nodded.

"Well, Sally," he said; "well, Andrew—" Then he paused. "My dear friends, I have come here to-night not only to comfort a house of mourning, but to say to you, as your friend and minister, that I hope you will let me marry you at once."

"Oh—Dr. Lavendar," Sally said, shrinking—"we must not speak of that *now*."

"Sarah, there is no impropriety in speaking of the enduring affection which has existed between you and Andrew. In this house, where death has come, I say to you, let there be no more of this misguided delay—a delay that has wrought harm, Sarah."

Andrew suddenly stood up and put his hand out to his old friend, "God bless you, sir!" he said.

"The funeral is to be to-morrow," said Dr. Lavendar; "very well. On Monday morning, Sarah, at nine o'clock, I will call at your house and perform the marriage ceremony."

"Oh, Andrew—" Sally said, faintly.

As for Andrew, he burst out passionately: "All these years—all these years! Oh, Sally, how long it has been! Sally, not another day's delay; I will come and live at your house, dear; but not another day's delay."

When Dr. Lavendar went home that night, his old face was twinkling with pleasure; he sang softly scraps of hymns, or talked to his little blind horse; and once he said to himself, chuckling, "If I'd followed my impulse, I'd have married them then and there, and made no bones of it!"

However, when people have waited so many years, Monday is not very far off.

THE UNEXPECTEDNESS OF MR. HORACE
SHIELDS

THE UNEXPECTEDNESS OF MR. HORACE SHIELDS

I

Dr. William King had married his wife because of her excellent common-sense.

It was an evidence of his own common-sense, that he was not moved by mere prettiness, or sweetness, or whatever. Mrs. William was, as it chanced, good-looking; but Willy said that was the last thing he had thought of; he said she was a sensible woman, with no whims. She would keep his house; and his ledger, for that matter; and bring up his children; and see that his buttons were sewed on — and not bother him. Willy had seen bothering wives. His profession brought him in constant contact with them — nervous, sentimental, hysterical, nagging, egotistical wives. The doctor used to say he wondered how men had the courage to get married at all, considering; and he was convinced that this state of things was the result of marrying for sentiment; he had married for sense.

"Sentiment," said Dr. King, "is a phase of youth and growth; we've got to go through with it; but to make a phase permanent is the act of a fool."

"Well, now, William," objected Dr. Lavendar,

"look at Oscar. You can't say it's a phase of youth?"

"Oh, Oscar caught it late," the doctor said. "I have had a case of measles where the patient was sixty-two. As for Dorothea, she's young enough to be foolish; Martha says she looks under the bed every night for a man! She says she doesn't even buy her own clothes. Imagine me deciding on Martha's shoestrings! Well, Martha wouldn't have it. Nobody would resent that sort of thing more than Martha," said Willy, complacently.

Martha managed her own shoestrings in those first days; and by-and-by, such was her common-sense, she managed the doctor's also. Though Willy did not talk so much about it when that time came.

Still, he must have appreciated the way in which she expended his small income; for she fed and clothed her plump, blond William as though he had twice as much to live on. When Mrs. King made an unusually good bargain with the meat-man, or hag-gled with Mr. Horace Shields until he sold her a bottle of ink for two cents less than the general pub-lic paid, she used to say, exultingly, that it was well for Willy, considering that he would not send bills to half of his patients, that he had a wife who would look after things.

"I don't know what would have become of you, Willy, if you'd married a different kind of woman," Martha would say, good-naturedly. "You would have been in the poorhouse by this time!"

Although she did not know it, the good Martha really opened up a very interesting question which most women would do well to ask themselves in re-gard to their husbands: What would my Tom, or

Dick, or Harry, have been without *me?* Not so silent, if he had chosen a girl who did not gush; not so selfish, if he had had a wife less addicted to unselfishness; not so ill-tempered, if he had married some one less anxious and nagging. The fact is, these simple men creatures are as wax in our hands; our tempers and our tongues decide their eternal salvation—though they never know it. They all mean pretty well in the beginning, but they fall into the hands of their wives, and look at the result!

But Martha King had no time to waste in such speculations. She was secretary of the Woman's Auxiliary; and it was known in Old Chester that she had once sent a letter to the *Spirit of Missions* calling attention to the mistakes of this admirable organization. She had a Sunday-school class; and she did all the cutting out for the Sewing Society. She was an indefatigable parish worker; "invaluable in practical matters," Dr. Lavendar said, heartily. What he said when she took it upon herself to tell him that he had done wrong not to give Anna King back to her own mother nobody knew except Martha, and she never told; but her face got red when the matter was referred to at Sewing Society. Still, I remember in this connection that when Mr. Jim Shields expressed his opinion of Mrs. King to Dr. Lavendar, the old minister smoothed him down, and bade him remember that Martha had a good heart. "Good, but not graceful," Mr. Jim growled. And Dr. Lavendar chuckled.

Added to her moral excellences, Mrs. King was a remarkable house-keeper; her economies were the admiration of Old Chester;—economical house-keeping was not an Old Chester characteristic; we were too near Mason and Dixon's line for that. She was orderly to a mathematical degree, and so immaculately neat that she had been known to say that if she should see a particle of dust behind a picture-frame at twelve o'clock at night, she would rise from her bed and remove it ! The reply made to this declaration was : "If you could see a particle of dust behind a picture-frame at twelve o'clock at night, you had better rise; — and consult an oculist at once."

Any woman will know that the doctor said this : it is the reply of a husband.

But, really and truly, Mrs. King was a capable, conscientious, sensible woman ; and Old Chester was not unreasonable in expecting the same characteristics in her younger sister, Lucy ; but their only resemblance was that they neither of them had the slightest sense of humor. In every other way they could not have been more radically different if they had been relations by marriage.

Perhaps this was because they were almost strangers, Lucy having lived in the East with her father ever since she was ten years old. He came back, poor old man, at the last, to die in Mercer. And a month afterwards Old Chester was told briefly that Mrs. King's sister, Lucy, was coming to live with her.

"I don't believe in it," Mrs. King said. "Willy's sister didn't come to live with him when poor old Mrs. King died ; and I don't know why my sister should live with me. But Willy will have it. I only hope, for her own self-respect, Lucy will find something to do, so that she won't be a burden on him. I shall tell her so, flatly and frankly. I consider it my duty."

316

MR. HORACE SHIELDS

So Lucy came, with "Dick," her canary-bird, and her little caba full of worsted-work. She was only twenty-three, the idol of the old father, whose relation to her had been maternal and loverlike and brotherly, all at once. One does not just see why, for though she was a good girl, she was not especially attractive; very shy, not pretty exactly, though she had soft deer's eyes; certainly not sensible; crushed, poor child, when she came to live with the Kings, by her father's loss.

Willy looked at her once or twice the first day at breakfast, and wondered how two sisters could be so different.

"No, I don't like sewing," she said, listlessly. "No, I don't care for books." And then, later: "No, I don't know anything about cooking. I don't like house-keeping. But I like worsted-work pretty well."

"I think," said Martha, decidedly, "that father did very wrong not to let you learn to do something useful. Worsted-work is nothing but a waste of time. I think he—"

"Don't!" the other cried out. "Don't speak to me about my father!"

"Well, he was my father too," Mrs. King remonstrated. "One speaks the truth of people, Lucy, whether they are relations or not. Because he was my father doesn't make him perfect," said Martha, gravely.

But Lucy got up and went out of the room, trembling as she walked.

"You hurt her feelings," said the doctor.

"But, my dear, it's true. She ought to have been taught things; but father spoiled her from the time she was born. She was the youngest, you know; and he just lay down and let her walk over him. Which was wrong; you can't deny that?"

"I want my dinner at 1.30," said Willy King. "I've got to see Mr. Jim Shields again, and I want to go before dinner."

"You went before breakfast," said Mrs. King. "There's nothing you can do; and as you make no charge, it seems rather foolish—"

"Do you think your sister would like to go round with me in the sleigh this morning?" the doctor said, stopping, with his hand on the door-knob, and looking back into the dining-room. "It isn't cold, and the sleighing is good."

But Lucy, when her sister took the message up to her, only said, listlessly, "I don't mind."

"It will do you good," her brother-in-law called up-stairs; "come along!"

And Martha added, kindly, "Here's a cushion, Lucy, to put behind you."

"I don't need it, thank you, sister Martha," Lucy said.

"Oh, you will be much more comfortable," Mrs. King said, decidedly; and pushed the pillow behind her little sister, and tucked the robe firmly around her feet; and then they started—the quiet, apathetic, unhappy child (who had removed the cushion as soon as she was out of her sister's sight), leaning back in the sleigh behind the doctor's big shoulder, and looking off over the snow shining under a soft blue sky, but saying nothing. Once she uttered a little cry when the runner on the doctor's side went up on a drift and the sleigh heeled like a boat; and once she caught his arm, because the horse danced at the sound of the butcher's horn tooting at a customer's door.

"Scared?" said Willy, looking at her kindly. "You mustn't mind Jinny; she is a lamb. She only prances to show she feels happy."

"I'm so afraid of horses," Lucy answered, breathlessly.

After that her brother-in-law made Jinny walk down all the hills; then he told her which of his patients he was going to visit, and once or twice added interesting details of their diseases, which made Lucy turn away her head and wince, and say, under her breath, "Oh please, brother William! I can't bear to hear those things."

And the doctor whistled, and said to himself, "Sisters!"

That day the longest call was upon Mr. Jim Shields; it was so long that Willy came running out of the house after a while, bareheaded, and bade his little sister-in-law get out of the sleigh and go into the shop in the basement to wait for him.

"I hope you don't mind, Lucy," he said; "I just meant to look in on him; but he is having a dreadful—" Lucy drew up one shoulder and bit her lip. "He doesn't feel very well; so I must wait awhile. You go right into the shop; there's nobody there; Mr. Horace is up-stairs with his brother."

He helped her out, and hurried back into the house, where, in his anxiety and pity, he forgot Lucy, sitting alone in the little shop down-stairs.

There was a fire in the triangular grate in the corner, and the sunshine came in through the window in the door, behind which a little bell had tinkled as they entered. "Books, Etc. H. Shields," was the sign outside; but, to be exact, Mr. Horace's shop was mostly "Etc." Lucy, looking about, saw that the slates on the third shelf were not in an orderly pile; she glanced nervously around, and then slipped behind the counter and straightened them; then she dusted the books in the small show-case with her handkerchief, and blew the powdered chalk from the shelf where the blackboard materials were kept. Just then the bell struck out a jangling note, and the door opened; a boy wanted two envelopes. Lucy looked at him in consternation; but when the child pointed to the green pasteboard box where the stationery was kept, and even opened the till for her so that she might change his dime, she found herself quite at ease; she even hoped some more customers would come, it was so interesting to sell things. But no one came, and Lucy watched the square of sunshine move across the floor, and heard a cinder drop sometimes from the grate, or a spurt of flame bubble out between the bars. It was an hour before her brother-in-law thought of her, and came, with many apologies, to take her home.

He had quite forgotten Lucy. Like everybody else in Old Chester, the doctor's mind was full of the Twins — Old Chester always referred to the Shields brothers in this way. Being twins, the two old gentlemen were, for all practical purposes, the same age; but, as far back as I can remember, the younger had been "Old Mr. Horace" to his neighbors, while the first-born was Jim Shields to the end of the chapter—and a brave end it was too! In his early manhood he had been a high-hearted, irresponsible, generous young fool; a bit of a bully, very likely, in the way of overriding other people's views,

and insisting upon his own with a joyous dogmatism
that never irritated. And in middle life, when what
he called his "cussed body" got the better of him
and pinned him down into a wheeled chair, he was
still generous, and courageous, and merry; and he
bullied his brother and his doctor and Old Chester,
and indeed Death himself—bullied him, jeered at
him, swore at him, and lived through nearly thirty
years of dying without a wince.

James had fallen ill when he was thirty-five. He
was sailing around the world as supercargo for a
large East India trading-house; when, suddenly, he
came home. He had "had notice," he said, briefly.
"An old sawbones in London explained it to me,"
he said, "told me I mustn't try to keep going any
longer. Fact is, I've got to rust;—or bust," he
ended, cheerfully.

It was a year before Old Chester knew that that
"rusting" meant an invalid's chair, and slow, re-
lentless, invincible dying; but James and Horace
knew it, and they looked into the enemy's eyes together. Horace was a little man, with a rosy face;
he was resolute, but it was in his own fashion; he
had his quiet way of carrying out plans for Jim's
comfort, no matter how his twin roared at him, and
swore he would or he wouldn't; but he never had
his brother's vigor in expressing himself. Indeed,
once only, when, trembling with alarm, he called
Willy King a fool, was he known to have spoken
forcibly.

The two brothers lived in a brick house on Main
Street; two flights of stone steps, their hand-rails
ending in brass knobs, curved up to its front door,
which had a fan-light and a big iron knocker. Be-

hind this door was the hall, the walls covered with varnished paper which represented blocks of veined and mottled yellow marble; the staircase wound round this hall, and under it were two steel engravings—"The Maid of Saragossa" and "Bolton Abbey"—both brown and stained with mildew. The parlor was on the left as one entered; it was a big, bare room, with a high ceiling; there were green Venetian blinds in the windows, and a pale paper on the walls—landscapes in light brown, of castles and lakes; on the wooden mantel, like flat trees laden with prisms, were three candelabra, each with its ormolu milkmaid simpering under the boughs; and there were some shells, and a carved teakwood junk, and a whale's tooth—relics of Mr. Jim's adventurous days. Here, all day long, Jim Shields sat and watched life slip between his helpless fingers. Death seemed to play with him as a child plays with a fly—pulling off a wing, or a leg, or another wing, and the head last.

But nothing goes on forever. James had been dying for nearly thirty years, and one day he died.

"But," Horace had gasped when, that sunny December morning, while little Lucy was waiting in the shop, Willy King told him how it was going to be—"but it's so sudden!" And then he remembered that, after all, Willy was but a boy. What did he know about James? James was taken sick when Willy was fifteen years old. "You're a fool, Willy!" he said, trembling. "I'm going to send to Mercer for a man; this isn't a time for boys!" "I wish you would, sir," Willy said, earnestly; "and why don't you have Wilder from Upper Chester? He's first-rate."

Afterwards, as he drove Lucy home, the doctor said that if it was the slightest comfort to Mr. Horace, he wished he would call in all the doctors in the township. "Not that there is a single thing to do," said Willy, slapping his rein down on Jinny's shining flank; "Mr. Jim has come to the end. And poor old Mr. Horace will break his heart."

His little sister-in-law looked over at the runner cutting into unbroken snow at the edge of the road. "I'm sorry," she said, in a low voice.

II

Little Lucy was sorry, but her sorrow did not keep her from shrinking away up-stairs when Martha began to ask the doctor the particulars of the morning: "Another spasm at twelve? Well, I suppose his feet have begun to swell? I hope he won't last much longer, poor man. I felt just so about father; I didn't want him to linger, and—" but just here Lucy slipped out of the room, and her sister looked after her open-mouthed. As for the doctor, he plodded industriously through his very good dinner, and told her every detail; and when he had finished the dinner and the disease, he added, absently, "She is very sensitive, isn't she?"

"Who?" said Martha.

"Why, your sister."

"Oh, Lucy? She is very silly, I'm afraid. I don't believe in calling foolishness sensitiveness! And you told old Mr. Horace?"

"Yes, I told him, poor old fellow!"

"Well, he ought to be glad to have Mr. Jim free

from suffering," the doctor's wife said, kindly. "I should have told him so, flatly and frankly. What did he say?"

"He said I was a fool." Willy answered, smiling. "He's going to have further advice."

"I hope he has the money to pay for it," Martha said; "he won't find that all doctors are like you, Willy. One would think, to look at some of your bills, that you were independently rich, instead of just a poor country doctor. And now here's Lucy come to be a burden on you—"

"She isn't a burden at all," William King said. "She doesn't eat enough to keep a sparrow alive, and I guess even Mr. Horace's account will provide for that." Then he looked out of the window: "it isn't as if we had children of our own we had to save for," he said.

Mrs. King was silent.

As for Willy, he went back and spent the afternoon with the twins. The end was very near; for the "man" that Mr. Horace had sent for confirmed the "boy"; and by-and-by Jim confirmed them both.

"I can't help it, Horry," the dying man said, moving his big, lionlike, gray head restlessly—"I've—got to—let go."

Mr. Horace set his jaws together and drew a determined breath. "Of course you have—of course you have. Now don't worry. I'll get along. Come now, cheer up!"

"But you'll be so damned lonely," whimpered the other. He was blind, and could not see his little brother wipe his eyes, and blink, and swallow to get his voice steady.

"Well, yes, of course; somewhat. But I can get along first-rate; and I'll get more time for reading."

"Reading!" said the other, with a snort. "Much reading you'll do! No, you'll be—just damned lonely," he said again, with a groan.

"Don't think of it," said Mr. Horace, his voice trembling. "I—I won't mind it in the least, my dear fellow. Oh, *James!*" he ended, weakly. He looked up at Willy King, but the doctor was making a pretence of dropping some medicine into a glass, so as to hide his own blurring eyes. As for Dr. Lavendar, who was there too, he took the groping, dying hand, and said,

"Jim, we'll all stand by him—" and then he took out his big red silk handkerchief, and his breath caught in a sob. For, like everybody else, he loved Jim Shields. To be sure, he winced at certain words which honest old Mr. Jim used with surprising freedom; but apparently he never took them much to heart. "Jim—Jim, don't be profane," he would remonstrate, with a horrified look. And Jim, sweating with pain, would gasp out:

"The devil take it! I forgot the cloth. I apologize; but I wasn't profane. Profanity is unnecessary swearing, and if this isn't necessary, I'll be—"

"James! James! James!" . . . .

But now when Jim Shields lay dying, his wicked tongue, his impudent courage were an expression of his religion; and the old minister had eyes to see this. So he only patted the blind, groping hand, and said:

"Jim, we'll do all we can for Horace. Never you fear!"

"Who's afraid?" said Mr. Jim, thickly. "But I—can't hold on—much—longer. Damned if I can."

"Don't try—don't try," Horace entreated, in anguish. Then came a long, dull effort, and the heavy, muffled tongue said one pathetic word,

"Lonely?"

"No," old Mr. Horace said again—"no; I won't be lonely. Mind now, Jim, I won't be lonely. Do you hear? Jim, I won't. Jim—*do you hear?*"

So, bravely, old Horace Shields told his lie to make dying less deadly for his brother.

Then he went on living as well as he could, meeting first the visible loneliness, if one may call it so—the silent house, the empty chair, the fuller purse. The occupation of service was ended; the anxiety was over; the habits of life were torn to pieces. Ah, me! How much of the torment of grief comes from this violent change of the habits of life! For Mr. Horace there were no more duties: he need not roll a wheeled chair on the sunny side of the street; he need not taste the beef-tea to see if it had enough pepper; he need not bring out the chess-board; he need not do a hundred other small services; his habit of affection was over, and the habit of grief had not yet come to him. He went blundering and staggering through the overwhelming leisure of material loneliness. As for the spiritual loneliness — but enough of that! Those of us who have reached middle life do not need the telling; and the younger folk would not understand it if they were told. They are dancing to the piping of Life, and one of these days they'll pay the piper; then they will understand.

THE BURIAL OF JIM SHIELDS

But everybody was very good to poor old Mr. Horace in his affliction. Mrs. Dale sent him wine jelly in a rabbit mould. Mrs. Drayton presented him with a "booklet" bound in white and gold, and named *Tears Wiped Away;* but she sighed a little when she wrapped it up, and said to Mrs. Wright that poor James Shields's language was not that to fit a man for dying; however, she *hoped* the Lord would overlook it: in fact, she had asked Him to do so. Miss Wellwood—she was just then about to become Mrs. Barkley, so it was especially kind in her to think of other people's sorrows—carried him a handful of ambrosia, which, having been first dipped in water, and then rolled in flour, formed a white and shaking decoration, suitable, Miss Maria thought, for a house of mourning.

Dr. Lavendar used to come and sit with him in the evening, and smoke silently; noticing, as silently, that Jim's chair and footstool had not been removed, and that the chess-board had remained just as it had been left at the last game—that pathetic effort of grief to find permanence. Sam Wright sent Mr. Horace a case of wine; Willy King was very attentive; and Martha wrote him a kind, sensible letter, telling him that if he would remember that Mr. Jim was at rest he would be reconciled, she was sure. And then she added that she had heard that he would not have Mr. Jim's room changed, but that she did hope he would not make such a mistake. "It is easier to change things now than it will be later," she said, very truly, "so I do hope you will just have the parlor renovated. Take my word, it will be easier for you in the end."

Mr. Horace, when he had read this very good

advice, poked her letter down into the fire, and then looked around the room, fiercely, as though challenging what everybody will agree was common-sense.

A good many letters of sympathy came, but Mr. Horace did not read them. He put them away in his desk in the shop. Nor did his kindly, sorry old friends venture to talk about James. "He can't bear that, it appears," Dr. Lavendar said, sadly, and smoked in pitying silence.

It was all silence to Mr. Horace—a silence without interest. He went into the store every morning, and looked listlessly about ; there was the mail to be opened—when there was any mail, and occasional customers to be waited on. There was the trade paper to be read, and sometimes circulars. Jim used to make the circulars into spills to light his pipe, because, he said, everything ought to be of some use in the world, even lies. But the interest of the shop, the story of the day's doings to be told to Jim, was gone. After supper there was nothing for it but to sit alone in the parlor, with the faded landscapes on the wall, and the twinkle of lamplight in the prisms of the candelabra, and the chess-board open on the table. Nothing for it but to sit there and think of James with every muscle of the body and the soul held back from its customed movement of service and of care—so tense and so weary that when sleep relaxed his vigilance for a moment these faithful servants of years of affection moved automatically, and he would put his hand on the chess-board, or wake with a start, calling out : "James! What is it? James—"

MR. HORACE SHIELDS

III

"I tried to tell old Mr. Horace how I sympathize with him," said Mrs. King, "and he just said, 'Oh yes; yes, yes. Do you think we are going to have rain?' Some one ought to tell him, flatly and frankly, to try and accustom himself to speak of Mr. Jim; it would be a great deal better for him."

Lucy was silent, sitting with her hands in her lap, looking out of the window into the rainy garden. Her worsted-work had been given up soon after she came to live with her sister, for Martha had pointed out to her that it was very foolish to make things nobody needed; "the Jay girls do enough of that," said Mrs. King, with a good-natured laugh. So Lucy's hands were idle, and her sister made an impatient gesture. "How can you sit there, Lucy, and do nothing?"

"I'm going to read," Lucy said.

"What is your book?" her sister inquired, kindly; and Lucy displayed a paper-cover, which made Martha shake her head and smile and sigh.

"A novel! Lucy, don't you do *any* improving reading?"

"I don't like improving reading," Lucy said, nervously.

Martha put her work down. "Now, Lucy, look here; I don't believe you mean what you say, but if you do mean it, you ought to be ashamed to say it."

"I'll sew, if you want me to," said Lucy, turning white and red.

"I don't want you to sew for me," the doctor's wife said. "I can do my own work. But I must

329

say I don't see how you can be willing to be idle.
You do nothing but take care of that poor canary-
bird — (the most untidy thing I ever had in my
house!) Upon my word, Lucy, if I had a dozen
daughters, I'd bring every one of them up to do
something, so they shouldn't be dependent!"

"I'd like to do something," Lucy answered, faintly,
"but I don't know anything."

"Well, that's just what I say," her sister said.
"But I suppose there's no use talking!" Yet, after
the manner of ladies who say there is no use talking, the doctor's wife continued to talk. She had
talked pretty much all winter. Little Lucy had
shrunk and shivered, and gone up-stairs to cry all
by herself, but nothing had come of it. She was so
silent and apathetic, so incapable of repartee, that
it must be said in excuse for Martha, that she had
no conception how her words stung. Apparently
they made no impression whatever; which lured her
on into greater and greater frankness—that virtue
in whose name so many unpleasantnesses are committed! Once the doctor said, nervously, he did
wish she would let up on that child; and his wife,
a little hurt, said that she was only speaking for
Lucy's good. "If I had ten girls of my own," she
said, "I would bring them up to have proper ideas
of work."

"I think ten girls with proper ideas would be
dreadful to live with," said the doctor, conjugally.
And then he went up-stairs and knocked on Lucy's
door, and produced a little package.

"A present—for me?" Lucy said, and pulled open
the parcel, and found a little pin lying on a bed of
pink cotton.

"Oh, brother William !" she said, and gave him her hand; and then, on an impulse, put up her face and kissed him.

As for Willy King, he blushed to his ears. Then she bade him wait while she put the pin into the black ribbon bow at her throat. "Does it look pretty?" she said, anxiously. The doctor put his head on one side, and said that it did.

Lucy looked in the glass, and took the pin out and stuck it in at a different angle. "Isn't that better?" she said; and Willy turned her round to the light, and said, critically, he believed it was.

He went down-stairs smiling to himself. "I gave Lucy a pin," he told his wife. "She was as pleased as a little kitten."

"A pin!" said Martha. "Why, Willy King! as if you didn't have expense enough in buying her shoes and stockings! And I must say, considering how hard it is to make both ends meet, it was extravagant, my dear."

"It was only five dollars," her husband defended himself.

"Wilson's bill for fixing the drain is five dollars," Mrs. King observed, significantly. "Justice before generosity, my dear."

William King made no reply, but he knew she was right; which did not make him any more affectionate. For men love their wives not because of their virtues, but in spite of them.

As for Martha, she was really troubled. "We can't afford to make presents," she said to herself; she was putting a new binding on her dress, and her fingers were dusty, and her mind in the ruffled condition peculiar to this occupation. When Lucy came and showed her the little pin, it took real grace on poor Martha's part not to express her opinion.

Instead, she glanced at her over her glasses, and said, kindly : "You look a little pale, Lucy. If you feel chilly you had better take some quinine."

"I hurt my ankle when I went out to walk," Lucy explained, her sister's interest rousing her a little. "I tripped on the board walk on the common ; it had a hole in it."

"That's very dangerous—I mean the hole," Martha said ; "your ankle will be all right as soon as you have rested it. Put your foot up on a chair."

"I don't think I want to," Lucy said.

"Oh, you'll be a great deal more comfortable !" Martha said, with kindly decision ; and got up herself, and brought a chair and a pillow, and lifted the strained ankle gently. "There, that's better !" she said. Lucy sighed. "But about the hole in the board walk : some one might hurt themselves seriously. You had better write a note to Sam Wright about it ; he is the burgess, you know."

"Oh, I couldn't !" Lucy said, horrified.

Martha put her work down and looked at her. "Lucy, have you *no* sense of responsibility ? Don't you care to make things better ?"

"I wouldn't write to him for anything in the world !" said Lucy.

Martha shook her head. "That's not the way to look at life, Lucy. But I'm afraid it's part of your nature. I'm afraid it's the same characteristic which makes you willing to be idle when all the rest of the world is at work."

And Lucy, turning white and red, said not a single word.

MR. HORACE SHIELDS

Mrs. King sighed and went on with her binding ; arguing with Lucy was like trying to sew with no knot in your thread. Martha was seriously troubled about her sister ; not so much at the girl's absolute inefficiency as at the lack in character which it indicated. All winter she had been trying, honestly and prayerfully, to correct it, with about as much success as one who tries, with big, well - meaning, human fingers to smooth out a butterfly's crumpled wing, or to free some silken, shining petal which has caught and twisted in its imprisoning calyx.

Well, well ! if good people would only be content to know that the rest of us cannot reach their level, how much irritation they would spare themselves !— and we, too, in little ways, would be happier. Though that, of course, does not matter.

The fact was, poor Lucy's virtues were not economic or civic ; they were, perhaps, nothing more than a little kindly heart, pure thoughts, and a pretty, eager smile ; but they were her own. Martha conscientiously tried to bestow hers upon the child ; and Lucy grew more and more silent.

" I make absolutely no impression !" poor Martha said, sighing ; and Willy replied, under his breath, " Thank heaven !"

However, she did make an impression at last.

It was at night, and Martha, going up to bed, saw a light under Lucy's door. " How foolish of her to sit up so late !" she thought—for it was late. Martha had waited up to see that the doctor had something hot to eat and drink when he came in at midnight from a late call (thus was Willy justified of common-sense in a wife). And here was Lucy's lamp burning at nearly one.

Martha, in a warm and ugly gray flannel dressing-gown, knocked at the door, and entered, her candle in her hand, and her work-basket under one arm. "Why, you're rather late, aren't you, Lucy?" she said, disapprovingly.

Lucy was sitting over a little fire which had retreated into one corner of the grate; she shivered as she looked up. "I'm just going to bed," she said.

"It's foolish to sit up when you don't have to," Martha said, decidedly.

"I got worried about brother William," Lucy confessed; "I wanted to make sure he was at home—there's such a storm to-night."

"Worried!" cried her sister, laughing in spite of herself. "Why, he's at home, safe and sound, eating some supper down-stairs. My dear, worry is the most foolish thing in the world. I never worry. Now do go to bed. Here, I'll slake your fire for you."

She took up the poker, stirring the discouraged-looking fire vigorously; then she lifted the coal-scuttle in her strong hands and flung the slake on; there was a small burst of flame, and the smell of coal dust and gas.

"Oh, it's so unpleasant!" said Lucy, drawing back.

"There are a great many unpleasant things in this world, Lucy," said Martha, shortly. "Come, now, go to bed! It isn't as if you had any duty which kept you up."

"Yes; I will," Lucy said, listlessly.

"Dear me, Lucy, I don't know what you would do if you had any duties. I sometimes think it's fortunate for you that your brother-in-law is so good-natured. Most men, especially if they were poor

country doctors like Willy, would rather resent it to
have to support their wives' sisters, who haven't a
single care or duty in the world except to look after
a canary-bird. (I don't see how you can keep that
bird, it's so untidy !)"

"I don't know what to do," Lucy said, getting up
and looking at her with frightened eyes— "and —
and—I'll try not to eat so much, sister Martha."

Martha winced at that. "Oh, don't be foolish,
my dear ! It isn't the eating, or anything like that.
It's the *principle :* I would earn my way. But don't
be foolish and talk about not eating!" Mrs. King
had the sensation of having stepped down further
than she expected—a sort of moral jar.

"I would do anything I could," said little Lucy,
beginning suddenly to cry convulsively. "I don't
like to be a burden on brother William ; but I never
learned to do anything, and—"

"Yes, that's just what I said ; father never had
you taught anything. You might give music lessons,
if he had ever made you practise thoroughly ; but he
was just satisfied to have you play tunes to him after
supper. I don't blame you, but I do blame father.
I—"

"Stop blaming father ! Oh, my father ! my
father !"

Lucy ran, panting, to the other side of the room,
and caught up a little photograph of her father and
held it against her breast.

Martha looked at her in consternation and serious
disapproval. "How can you be so foolish, Lucy ?"
she said. "Well, there's no use talking ; only, I
must say, flatly and frankly—"

"Martha, I won't hear my father criticised. I wish

335

I was dead with him. Oh, father !" the poor child broke out. And then there was a fit of crying, and she threw herself on the bed, face down, and would not speak when her sister tried to comfort her.

" There, now, come !" Mrs. King said ; and patted her shoulder, which showed no yielding ;— there is nothing which can be so obstinate as the shoulder of a crying woman.

Mrs. King was really uneasy when she left her. She even went so far as to tell the doctor that she thought he had better look after Lucy.

" I think she's inclined to be hysterical," she said. " She is a foolish girl, I'm afraid, but I think she's really nervous, too. What do you suppose, Willy ? she was sitting up over a miserable little fire, *worrying*, if you please, because you were late ! I have no patience with women who worry. Either the thing will happen, or it won't ; and sitting up in the cold, until one o'clock in the morning, won't accomplish anything one way or the other."

" Worrying ? about me !" said the doctor, stopping with a suspender in one out-stretched hand ; " well !"

IV

But the worm had turned. In her hopeless, uninterested way, Lucy had made up her mind : she would not be a burden any longer. She would go to Mercer and try to get pupils, and give music lessons. She was not resentful, she was not bitter, still less was she in intelligent accord with her sister ; she was only started, so to speak, like a stone that has been pushed past a certain point of resistance.

A week after this talk she told Martha that she was going to Mercer. "I am going to visit Miss Sarah Murray; she invited me to visit her some time this winter. And I'll take Dick."

Mrs. King put down her sewing. "I shouldn't think you would want to make visits, Lucy, with father dead only six months. I should think you would rather stay quietly here with me, considering that we are both in affliction."

Lucy made no reply.

"But of course you are perfectly free to do as you please," her sister went on.

"I think I'd better go," Lucy said.

There was something in her voice that made Mrs. King uneasy. "I don't see why you say that; of course, if you want to go—why, go! But I must say it looks as though you were not contented, and it sort of reflects on your brother-in-law."

"Oh! no, no!" Lucy said, in an agitated way; "he has been so kind to me!"

Somehow, Martha King winced at that, though she did not know why.

The doctor, when he heard the news, frowned; and then he half sighed. "Oh, well, she's young," he said.

But he chucked his little sister-in-law under the chin when he came down to breakfast, and told her that if she stayed away too long he would come and bring her home. "And look here, Lucy, you must have a new cape or bonnet or something. What do you say to a pink bonnet?"

Willy smiled all over his face, but his jaw fell when Martha said, "Now, Willy! how can she wear pink when she is in black?"

"Oh—oh yes," the doctor said, awkwardly. And then, for no reason in particular, he sighed;—perhaps the child would be happier in Mercer. "Well," he said, "you can have an escort, if you go on Wednesday, Lucy;—Mr. Horace Shields. I'll ask him to look after you. He's going East to give his spring order."

"So I heard at Sewing Society," Martha said. "Well, I think he is a very foolish old man."

Mrs. King was not alone in this belief. Old Chester was greatly disturbed by this project of Mr. Horace's; he had always ordered his goods by mail, and to take a journey for the purpose was obviously unnecessary.

"I don't like restlessness," said Mrs. Dale, with a stern look.

"Sam sent him some wine," said Mrs. Wright, "and I am sure we were all very kind to him; so why should he go away from home?"

"Besides," said Mrs. Drayton, "who can make up to him for his loss so well as his friends? We all liked poor Mr. James—though he did certainly use improper language at times. I once heard him use a profane word myself. I should not be willing to repeat it. It was—not the worst one, but the one with 'r' in it, you know."

The ladies shook their heads, except Mrs. Barkley, who said, harshly, that, for her part, she didn't wonder at Jim Shields; she believed she would have said something stronger than "dear me" herself. But Martha King said, seriously, that she hoped Mrs. Drayton had told him, flatly and frankly, how wrong it was to lose one's self-control and swear.

"Well, no, I didn't," Mrs. Drayton confessed.

338

"It's so painful to me to speak severely to any one."

"Because it is painful is no reason for not doing one's duty," Martha returned, decidedly.

"Well, as for his going away," said Mrs. Drayton, "probably he hasn't been so overwhelmed by grief as we thought. I judged him by myself. If *I* had lost a loved one, I couldn't go travelling about. But I'm sure I hope he'll enjoy himself, poor man !"

And all the Sewing Society said it was sure it hoped so, too.

It was a rainy morning in March that Mr. Horace went away. The stage was waiting for him at the door of the tavern when he came hurrying down the street—he had been delayed by giving directions to Mrs. Todd, who was to keep the shop open during his absence—and there was the doctor holding an umbrella over a slim girl in a black frock, who was carrying a bird-cage in one nervous little hand.

"This is Lucy, Mr. Horace," Willy King said. "We will be so much obliged if you will look after her on the way."

"To be sure I will—to be sure I will," said Mr. Horace ; and the little girl put her hand in his without a word.

She was the only other passenger ; and when Willy had tucked the robe around her, and smuggled a bag of candy into her muff, the door, with its painted landscape, was slammed to, and the stage, pitching and creaking on its springs, started up the hill, passing the church and then the graveyard—at which Mr. Horace looked through the streaming rain on the coach window. His fellow-traveller, however, turned her face away.

There was something in the shrinking movement that touched Mr. Horace. He remembered that Willy had told him the child had had some sorrow—if one can say sorrow in connection with youth ; so he made an effort to come out of his absorption, and talk to her, and cheer her.

She had very little to say, only answering him in gentle monosyllables, until by some chance he referred to her father.

"I met him several years ago, ma'am ; and my brother James had some acquaintance with him."

Lucy's eyes suddenly filled.

Mr. Horace looked at her, with instant sympathy in his ruddy old face. So youth may grieve, after all ?

"My dear, I have recently suffered a loss myself," he said, gently.

"Oh yes," said Lucy ; "I know. I was very sorry, sir."

"Ah — well," said Mr. Horace, with a sigh—"he was sick a long time. I ought not to begrudge him his release. Yes, he had been invalid for many years. But he was the bravest of the brave. My brother was a sailor in his youth. He had many interesting adventures. He has told me stories of his adventures by the hour. But when he came to be an invalid, after such an active life, he never flinched. The bravest of the brave !"

"My father was brave," said Lucy.

"My brother had been in most foreign lands," Mr. Horace went on. "He was shipwrecked twice before he was thirty. I recollect, as well as if it was yesterday, how he came home after that first time he was wrecked. We had given him up. My moth-

"MR. HORACE LOOKED AT HER WITH INSTANT SYMPATHY"

er was up-stairs cutting out those little — ah, garments that children wear. She was cutting out a
pair to go in a missionary barrel. Well, James just
walked into the room, as casually as if he hadn't
been out of the house. My mother (I recollect perfectly) she threw up her hands—she had the scissors
on her thumb and finger — and she said, 'Why,
James, where on earth did you come from?' And
my brother he said : 'From the waters under the
earth ; from India's coral strands,' he said. (You
know the hymn ?) 'But I haven't any coral, or any
clothes — except what you see,' he said. 'I hope
you'll give me those things'; meaning the — the
small garment ; and he stood six feet two !"

Lucy smiled vaguely.

"It was a joke," Mr. Horace explained.

"Oh yes, I see. My father was a good deal like
that, saying funny things. They're pleasant to live
with, such people."

"They are, indeed—they are, indeed," Mr. Horace
agreed, sighing. "My brother's humor was invincible, perfectly invincible. Why, I recollect perfectly—"

The story he remembered was not brilliant humor,
but Lucy was as polite as if it were, and capped it
with something her father had said ; and then Mr.
Horace followed quickly with another "I remember." Perhaps they neither of them really heard
what the other said, but they found infinite relief in
speaking. Why Mr. Horace could not have "recol-
lected perfectly" to Dr. Lavendar, or why little
Lucy could not have talked, if not to her sister, at
least to her kindly brother-in-law, is one of those in-
explicable things that belong to grief. It was easier
for each because the other was a stranger.

When the stage pulled into Mercer, the wheels tired in mud, and the apron over the trunks streaming with rain, the two travellers were talking very freely. Indeed, Lucy had gone so far as to say that she was going to give music lessons.

"I'm going to visit Miss Sarah Murray first. When I get some pupils, I'll board somewhere," she added, vaguely.

"My brother Jim knew the Misses Murray," said Mr. Horace. "I have heard him remark that Miss Sarah, the eldest, was a very genteel and accomplished female. My brother Jim expressed it more as a sailor might," Mr. Horace amended, with a smile, "but his words were to that effect." And when he helped his fellow-passenger and the canary-bird out of the stage he said, with pleasant, old-fashioned politeness, that if the Misses Murray were agreeable, he would call the next day and pay his respects to them and to Miss Lucy.

"I'd like you to come, sir," Lucy said. "I'd like to show you a letter our minister wrote about father."

And Mr. Horace remembered that he had some letters, too. It came into his mind that perhaps some day he would read them; perhaps he would show some of them to this young lady, who, he was sure, would have admired Jim. "Jim was a great favorite with the ladies," he thought to himself, sighing and smiling.

V

"I recollect, just as if it were yesterday, when my brother James brought home from one of his voyages a little savage—a heathen, in fact. My mother

was exceedingly alarmed about his spiritual state;
but Woolly (that was what my brother James called
him) was converted immediately. My brother said
it was because my mother gave him a cake whenever
he named our Saviour. And I sometimes feared
there was truth in this remark."

Lucy laughed, and Mr. Horace looked pleased,
and patted her hand kindly. Miss Sarah and Miss
Emily Murray, who were sitting on either side of
the fire, smiled, and Miss Sarah observed that mis-
sionaries often used such methods as food and glass
beads to attract poor savages.

"My brother said that just before he landed he
suddenly realized that Woolly had to have clothes;
you know, being a savage and a heathen, he had no
garments of any kind. In fact, he was—ah—if I
may say so—quite—quite, as you may say, undressed.
My brother knew that, such being the case, Woolly
would be conspicuous when the ship should come
into port and the poor savage land at the wharf.
So what did my brother James do but make Woolly
lie down, with his arms extended, on a piece of cloth
spread on the deck; then he took a lump of chalk
and outlined him, as it were; then he doubled the
cloth and cut this out like those paper dolls which
are made for infants out of newspapers; and he
sewed Woolly into these two pieces. Dear me! I
wish you could have seen him! How my mother
did laugh! 'I wouldn't give a fig for your sewing,
James,' says she. 'But my sewing gives a fig-leaf
to Woolly,' says my brother. James had such a
ready tongue."

"The suit must have fitted very badly," Lucy
said, seriously.

"Yes," Mr. Horace admitted, "but it was warm, you know ; and—ah—customary."

"Oh yes, of course," said Lucy.

It was with tales like this that old Horace Shields tried to cheer his little companion when he came to see her at the Misses Murray's. He had decided not to continue his journey East to purchase stock, but order by mail from Mercer, where, he thought, he would remain for a few days and see if he could not comfort this poor child who seemed, somehow, to be on his hands. But he stayed nearly three weeks. He came to call almost every day, and the estimable Miss Murrays welcomed him warmly, and told him that they were much grieved at the depression of their young friend. "And indeed," said kind old Miss Sarah, "I fear I must add that I do not approve of the apparent indifference dear Lucy displays towards her sister. Lucy says that Martha does not like her canary-bird;—which is really a foolish reason for wishing to reside in Mercer. It almost looks like temper. I think, however, your conversation cheers her, and when she is less depressed she may come to a more proper mind in regard to her family."

Mr. Horace certainly did cheer the nervous, worried girl; and sometimes his own burden seemed lightened in his effort to lighten hers. In telling her his stories about his brother, he led her to talk about her father, and then about her own affairs; and the third time he called, when they chanced to be alone, she told him, palpitating and determined, that she would "never, never, *never* go back and live with her sister, because she would not be a burden on brother Willy."

"But, my dear young lady," he remonstrated, "you cannot live alone here in Mercer, you know."

"Oh yes," said poor little Lucy, "I know. But I won't go back to sister Martha."

"But what will you do, my dear Miss Lucy ?" Mr. Horace said, anxiously.

"Oh, I don't know !" cried poor Lucy ; and her big deer-like eyes had a hunted look in them that went to the old gentleman's heart. He made a point of seeing the Misses Murray by themselves, and they all talked the matter over with anxious seriousness.

"It is impossible for her to get pupils." Miss Sarah said ; "she is not the sort of young woman who can push and make her own way."

"I am not sure that she is not more pleasing on that account," Miss Emily said, with decision.

Mr. Horace nodded his head, and said his brother James had always disliked excessively capable ladies. "My brother James said he wouldn't want to sit down at table three times a day with a horse-marine," he said, chuckling ; "not but what he had great respect for intelligence," he added, politely.

And the Misses Murray said, oh yes, indeed ; they quite understood. And then they begged Mr. Horace, who was returning to Old Chester in a few days, to correspond with them on the subject, so that they might advise the child wisely.

Mr. Horace promised to do so ; and during the tiresome stage journey home he put his mind upon Lucy's troubles. He wondered what Jim would say about it all. Jim had his opinion of Mrs. Willy ; Mr. Horace chuckled as he thought of it. "Estimable woman," said Mr. Horace to himself, "very estimable ; but not agreeable. Poor Miss Lucy !"

345

He thought of her with an impulsive pity which brought out the youth of his ruddy old face—that fine youth of the spirit which cannot be touched by the body's age. Her grief for her father was but a child's grief, he thought, a half-smile on his lips; it was not the iron entering into the soul, but it was pathetic. He thought how she had shown him some letters of condolence that had been sent her, and that made him think, suddenly, of the letters that had come to him. It occurred to him, with a warm feeling of satisfaction, that when he got home he would unlock the drawer in the shop and take out that pile of letters, and perhaps he might send one or two to Miss Lucy. He thought of them eagerly as he walked up from the tavern to his own door; they were like a welcome waiting for him in the desolate old house.

Old Chester was full of tranquil evening light. Behind the low, dark line of the hills the daffodil sky was brightening into gold; there had been a shower in the afternoon, and the damp air was sweet with the smell of young grass and buds. There were little pools of water shining in hollows of the worn flag-stone pavement; and the brass stair rails and knobs of the comfortable old brick houses glittered, suddenly, all the way down Main Street. Mr. Horace found himself smiling as he walked; then he stopped with a start because Martha King spoke to him; she called from the other side of the street, and then came hurrying across.

"I'm glad to see you back, Mr. Horace," she said, and asked one or two questions about Lucy and the Misses Murray. "We've missed the shop, Mr. Horace," she ended, in a decided voice. There are persons whose hawklike virtue seems always ready to swoop down upon you, and Mr. Horace began to cower a little, like a flurried partridge. "I am sorry to say," the good Martha continued, "that Mrs. Todd has been remiss about keeping the shop open. I do hope you will speak to her about it, flatly and frankly. I think it is a duty we owe each other not to slight wrong - doing in servants. She has not kept regular hours at all," Mrs. King said, "and it has been a great annoyance. Won't you come in and take tea with us, Mr. Horace?"

"No, ma'am, I thank you," he said, and hurried into his house. "Poor Miss Lucy!" he said to himself; "poor Miss Lucy!"

She was in his thoughts when, sitting all alone in the shop, with his lamp on the desk beside him, he took out the letters which had been put away all these months. After all, these old friends loved James. "And well they might!" he told himself, proudly. He opened one letter after another, and read the friendly, appreciative words, nodding and sighing, and saying to himself, "Yes, indeed! Yes, he was brave; he was patient. Who knows that as well as I do?" The comfort of it came warmly to his heart, and the applause braced and cheered him until, for very happiness and pride, two little hot tears trickled down his cheeks and splashed on the pile of letters.

But when he went up-stairs into the silent house, into the dreadful emptiness of that room where James had lived for nearly thirty years—the old despair of desolation seized him again. It was that which, by-and-by, made him say he would go back to Mercer for a few days, and see what the Misses Murray had done for Miss Lucy. He wanted to get away from the house—anywhere! He thought to himself that he would take the letters to read to Miss Lucy; she had been so interested in Jim that she ought to know that his praise had not been merely brotherly regard. "And I am really anxious to know what the poor young lady is going to do," he said to himself, when, to the astonishment of Old Chester, he again took the stage for Mercer.

"Twice in two months!" said Old Chester; but Mrs. Todd, who, in spite of Mrs. King's warning, was again to keep the shop open for his few days of absence, said it was a real good thing, and would do the poor old gentleman good.

VI

Little Lucy had not secured a single pupil during the weeks she had been in Mercer. She was well aware she could not prolong her visit to the kind Misses Murray indefinitely, but what was she going to do? Poor child! how many times a day did she ask herself this question! The very afternoon of Mr. Horace's return she had gone out and walked hopelessly about until dusk in Mercer's dirty, busy streets, to think it over. The wind whirled up the street and caught her black skirts in a twist, and flung the dust into her face and into her eyes. The lights began to twinkle along the bridge that spanned the river, and then wavered down into its black depths in golden zigzags. Against the sullen sky the furnaces flared with great tongues of flame and showers of sparks. The evening traffic of the town, noisy,

dirty, hideous; the hurrying crowds in the streets;
the rumble of the teams; the jostling of workmen
—all gave her a sense of her utter helplessness, so
that the tears began to start, and she had to wipe
them away furtively. What was going to become
of her? The child, walking alone in the spring
dusk, looked down at the river, and thought that
the water was very black and very cold. I don't
suppose she formulated any purpose in her own
mind; she only thought, shivering, "The water is
very cold."

Mr. Horace met her there on the bridge, and there
was something about her that made the old gentleman's heart come up in his throat. He took her
hand and put it through his arm, and said, cheerfully,
"Come with me, my dear Miss Lucy, and let us walk
home together."

As for Lucy, she only said, feebly, "*I won't go back
to sister Martha.*"

"You sha'n't, my dear," said Mr. Horace, comfortingly, "you sha'n't, indeed."

That evening he talked the situation over with
Miss Sarah Murray; but she only shook her head
and said she hoped the child would soon look at the
matter more reasonably. "I would gladly keep her
here indefinitely," Miss Sarah said, in a troubled way,
"but our income is exceedingly limited—"

"Oh, certainly not, certainly not," Mr. Horace
broke in. He had come to feel responsible for Lucy,
somehow; he could not have her dependent upon
Miss Murray.

He got up and said good-night with a very correct
bow, his feet in the first position for dancing, his left
hand under his coat-tails.

Old Miss Sarah responded in kind, and they parted with high opinions of each other.

But Mr. Horace had not reached the street corner before he heard, "Mr. Shields! Mr. Shields!" and there was Lucy running after him, bareheaded.

"I've thought of something," she said, breathlessly, as she stood beside him, panting, under the gas-lamp on the corner. "Can't I come and take care of the shop, Mr. Shields? Can't I live with you and take care of the shop?"

Mr. Horace, in his eagerness to hurry her back to the house, hardly knew what he answered: "Yes, yes, my dear young lady. Anything that you wish. Come now, come! you must get in-doors. What will Miss Murray say?"

"I am to come and live with you?" Lucy insisted, her eyes wide and frightened. "You won't make me go back to sister Martha?"

"No, my dear; no, no!" he said. It seemed to Mr. Horace as though Miss Sarah was an hour in answering his agitated knock and opening the door. "Miss Lucy just stepped out to speak to me," he said, in reply to her astonished look.

"Oh, Miss Sarah, I am going to live with Mr. Shields!" said Lucy.

Mr. Shields came very early the next morning to Miss Murray's house, and was received in the parlor by Miss Sarah. Lucy was not present. Miss Sarah sat in a straight-backed chair, with her delicate old hands crossed in her lap. There was some color in her cheek, and a determined look behind her spectacles.

"I trust," said Mr. Horace, "that Miss Lucy is

none the worse for stepping out last night, ma'am ? I was much concerned about her when I left her."

"She is none the worse in body ; but I am deeply grieved at her attitude of mind," said Miss Sarah.

"You mean her unwillingness to live with her sister ?" said Mr. Horace, anxiously.

Old Miss Sarah shook her head. "She is quite determined not to return to her relatives."

"You don't say so !"

"She needs to be taken care of just as much as if she were a baby," said Miss Sarah. "But of course this plan of hers in regard to—to residing with you, is impossible. Even if it were not a question of burdening you (she has an idea that she would earn her board, if I may so express it), it would be impossible. I have pointed this out to her."

"And what does she say ?" demanded Mr. Horace.

"She merely weeps," Miss Sarah said ; "she has given it up at my request, of course ; but she weeps, and says she will not go back to Martha."

Mr. Horace hunted for his handkerchief, and blew his nose violently. "Dear, dear !" he said, "you don't say so ? Well, well ! I wish my brother James were here. He would know what to propose. Poor child ! poor child !"

Mr. Horace got up and stared out of the window ; then he blew his nose again.

Miss Sarah looked at the back of his head, but was silent. Suddenly he turned, and came and stood beside her.

"Miss Murray, you are a female of advanced years and of every proper sentiment ; all I have seen of you leads me to feel a deep esteem for you." Miss Sarah bowed. "Therefore I ask you, *is* it impossible ?

I could give the child a good home while I live. I have recently lost my brother, ma'am, and the little income devoted to his use could be transferred to Miss Lucy. I find myself much attached to her, and would be pleased to have her in my home. It would be less lonely for me," he said, his voice tremulous; "and my age, ma'am, is sixty-five. Surely it is not impossible?"

Miss Sarah, who was nearly eighty, grew red, but she was firm. "My dear sir, you are still young"— Mr. Horace blinked suddenly, and sat up straight— "our friend is twenty-three, and her looks are pleasing. Need I add that this is a wicked world? I have lived much longer than you, sir, and I am aware that it is both wicked and censorious. Can you say that Old Chester is exempt from gossip, Mr. Shields?"

"No, ma'am, I can't," he admitted, with an unhappy look.

"You see it is impossible," Miss Sarah ended, kindly.

Mr. Horace sighed.

Miss Murray looked at him and coughed; then she drew in her breath as one who prepares to strike. "If you were sufficiently advanced in years, my dear sir, so that—matrimony was out of the question, it would be different." Mr. Horace gasped. "But under the circumstances," continued Miss Sarah, sighing, "I see nothing before our young friend (since she is determined not to return to her sister) but to work in some factory." Miss Murray's house was in the old-fashioned part of Mercer, and there was a factory just across the street; she waved her hand towards it, genteelly, as she spoke.

The room was quite still except for a coal dropping

from the grate. Mr. Horace heard a footstep overhead, and knew it was Lucy walking restlessly about
in her pitiful, unreasoning misery. Involuntarily he
followed Miss Murray's gesture, and glanced across
the street. Two draggled-looking girls were just
entering the bleak doorway opposite. "Little Miss
Lucy do that? No!—impossible!"

"I am sixty-five; I shall not, probably, live very
much longer," he thought. "Suppose it were five
years, even; she would still be a young woman."

Poor little girl! poor little frightened, helpless
child! "And I would be less lonely," he said to
himself, suddenly. "Jim would call me an old fool,
but it would please him to have me less lonely." Mr.
Horace drew a long breath.

"Miss Murray," he said, "would I be taking advantage of our friend's youth and inexperience if I—if I
—if I suggested—matrimony?"

Miss Sarah did not seem startled; indeed she even
smiled.

"I think," she said, "it would be an admirable
arrangement."

Mr. Horace looked at her; she looked at him.
Then they began to talk in whispers, like two con-
spirators. "But would she—" began Mr. Horace.

"I'm sure of it!"

"But she is so young—"

"She will outlive you."

"I would not wish to take advantage—"

"You are only doing a kindness."

"Her relatives—"

"Her relatives have driven her to it!" cried Miss
Sarah. Which was really rather hard on Martha and
on Lucy's kind and affectionate brother-in-law.

z   353

"Well, we'll protect her," said Mr. Horace, angrily. And then he suddenly looked blank, and said: "Would you—ah—be willing to—to suggest it to her? I feel a sense of embarrassment."

"That is quite unnecessary," Miss Murray declared; "for you are doing a great favor, and if I know Lucy, her gratitude will not be lacking. But I will gladly tell her of your kindness."

"Oh, pray don't say gratitude," Mr. Horace protested, growing red; "don't say kindness. Let her regard it as a favor to me, which it is. I assure you it is."

Miss Murray rose, smiling; and Mr. Horace went away with a new and extraordinary sensation. There was something in his thoughts that came between him and his grief; a sense of excitement, of chivalry, of hope—even of hope! He found himself making plans as he walked along the street; he saw Lucy in his mind's eye at his lonely supper-table; he fancied her sitting beside him in the dreadful evenings listening to his stories of Jim—it seemed to Mr. Horace as though his fund of anecdotes of Mr. James was inexhaustible; he imagined her reading Jim's books, and laughing in her light girlish voice as Jim used to laugh in his rollicking bass. His heart grew warm and light in his breast as he walked and thought; and then suddenly it sunk: perhaps she would not consent.

VII

But Lucy consented—eagerly, feverishly. "Oh, Miss Sarah, how kind he is!" she said.

"Very true, Lucy, very true," said Miss Sarah,

solemnly. "I hope you will always remember it. Very few gentlemen, Lucy, of Mr. Shields's age would think of such a thing. I hope you will realize that to ask a young, inexperienced, foolish (yes, Lucy, I fear I must say foolish) girl to—ah—to bear his name, is indeed a compliment."

"I will take care of the shop," said Lucy, her eyes beginning to shine, and the droop of face and figure fading as she spoke. "Oh, he is so kind! And I will never go *near* Martha !"

"Fy, fy! my dear," said Miss Sarah; "a little reflection will show you that such a remark is neither ladylike nor pious."

Mr. Horace came for his answer at two o'clock; he had settled down into feeling quite sure that it was impossible, and that he and Miss Sarah must think of something else, and when Lucy met him, smiling and half crying, and saying, "You are so kind to me, Mr. Shields; and indeed, indeed I will do all I can to deserve it," he was almost dazed with astonishment. He protested that she would be doing him a great favor.

"I am so much older, my dear," he said.

But Lucy broke in, smiling, "You are good to me, just as father was."

"I will be good to you, my dear; I will indeed, to the best of my ability," he said, earnestly.

He smiled at her and patted her hand; and then he said, "I will communicate with your relatives, my dear Miss Lucy."

"Oh no," Lucy said, shrinking, "don't tell them !"

But Miss Murray shook her head; "Mr. Shields must, of course, refer to your family for permission."

Lucy looked frightened. "Martha won't allow it," she said, faintly. "Oh, don't tell Martha!"

"My dear, I could not allow you to elope," Miss Sarah, remonstrated.

And Mr. Shields said, "No, no, that wouldn't do!"

Then the two elders talked it over, Lucy listening and shivering, and saying sometimes, "Oh, Martha will say I'll be a burden to you, Mr. Shields."

"I am prepared," Mr. Horace said to Miss Murray, "to have them say I am far too old; and even that I am taking advantage of our young friend. But I am sustained," said Mr. Horace, "by the knowledge of the integrity of my motives. Miss Lucy is of age, and if she chooses my home it is not the affair of William's wife, or even of William, for whom I have a sincere regard. But I am inclined to think, ma'am, that it will perhaps be wise to—to bring this matter to a head—if I may so express it, before they have a chance to interfere. I will communicate with William and his wife; but before they can remonstrate we will take steps, we will take steps! What do you think of that, ma'am?"

"Admirable!" said Miss Murray. "Admirable!"

"However," said Mr. Horace, blinking his eyes suddenly, as though something cold had been thrown in his face, "it will be very unexpected in Old Chester!"

It was unexpected. Old Chester, too, gasped and blinked as though it had a cold douch.

Willy King was angry; but Martha, very sensibly, said that it was foolish to be angry. "But I am mortified," she said, "and I don't understand it."

MR. HORACE SHIELDS

Old Chester, when it heard the news, nearly went out of its mind with agitation and disapproval—"and sorrow," Mrs. Drayton said, "that the dead were soon forgotten!" Mrs. Dale said that Mr. Horace had taken advantage of that poor, poor child's youth. Mrs. Wright, on the contrary, felt that it was really disgusting to see a girl so mercenary as to marry an old man for a home. Mrs. Ezra Barkley said, gently, that he had been so lonely, poor Mr. Horace! no doubt he just couldn't stand the desolation of his life.

"But that doesn't explain the other fool," her sister-in-law interrupted, with a snort.

"Do you know what Dr. Lavendar said when he heard it?" Rose Knight asked, suddenly. "He said, 'Hooray for Horace!'"

"Dr. Lavendar is getting very old," said Mrs. Dale, sternly.

After the first excitement of it was over, it came to Martha King's ears that Lucy had married to escape living with her. (Those things always leak out; some friend, with a frankness as conscientious probably as Martha's own, "thought Lucy's sister should be told").

When poor Martha heard why Lucy had committed this extraordinary folly, she turned white, smitten into silence. "I tried to do my duty," she said, painfully, and made no reproaches. But she suffered. "I did everything I could for her best good," she said to herself, as she sat alone working; then she wiped her eyes furtively on the unbleached cotton sheet she was hemming for the missionary barrel. "Lucy doesn't love me," she thought, sadly; "nobody does but William. But I've always tried to do my duty." Once, blunderingly, looking down at her fingers trembling in her lap, she said something like this to Dr. Lavendar.

"Martha, my dear," he said, gravely, "*love more, and do less.* Do you remember Isaiah (and he was a pretty energetic old fellow, too) says, ' their strength is to sit still'? Our Heavenly Father is just as anxious to improve things as we are ; but if you'll notice, He lets us make our blunders and learn our lessons. And He works by love oftener than by the thunders of Sinai. But come, come ! We all love you, and Lucy will know that she does, too, one of these days."

But how happily it did turn out ! Mr. Horace lived more than the five years he had allowed himself ; and no wonder, with the affection his little girl gave him, and the need there was to take care of her, and keep her happy ; a man really can't die, no matter how good his intentions are, when he is needed. And, besides that, Lucy's eager, childlike sympathy was like some pure and healing touch. Gradually he took up old interests, and liked to meet old friends. His grief for his brother passed down through the ruined habits of living into the depths of life, and after a while settled into a habit of its own. Then the old interests closed in upon him—just as a ruffled pool smooths and closes over the crash that has shattered its even silver ; though all the while the weight is buried in its heart.

It was a sunny, placid, happy old house in those days, though nobody could say it was sensible. Dick's cage hung in a south window, and the little yellow creature splashed about in his china bath, and scattered millet seeds, and shouted his little songs all day long. Lucy used to come and sit in the shop while she shelled the peas for dinner, or did her bit of worsted-work. And she kept things dusted ; perhaps not quite as Martha would have done ; the backs of the pictures may have left something to be desired. But so long as nobody knew it, what difference did it make? This lack of principle must make the conscientious grieve; but Lucy and old Mr. Horace were just as happy as though their principles were good. They talked a great deal of Mr. Jim. In the evenings they sat up-stairs in the big, bare parlor—a little less bare now, because Lucy made gay worsted covers for all the chairs ; and Mr. Horace tried to teach her how to play chess. To be sure, the fool's or scholar's mate might end the game every night, but it gave him a chance to tell her of Jim's prowess. He gave her Jim's books to read, and though she did not know enough to laugh at the right places in Mr. Jim's beloved *Shandy*, she felt a breathless interest in the *Three Musketeers ;* and old Mr. Horace annotated it with Jim's comments.

They used to read over those letters of sympathy, too, which suggested so many stories of the big, generous, rollicking old man who had died young, that little by little, as Mr. Horace told this, or remembered that, or laughed at the other, James came back into his life. But there was never any misery in the thought of him ; only acceptance, and patience, and an understanding which mere death could never shake or break. James was dead ; but what was death between him and James?

So they went on being happy. And on winter

evenings, or when the summer dusk shut down, and Lucy sat playing foolish tunes on a little old jingling piano, it was surprising how often a certain admirer of common-sense came poking in to smoke with Mr. Horace, and listen to Lucy's chatter, or maybe take a hand at cribbage.

In fact, Martha King said that never since they had been married had William had so many night-calls.

THE END